THE ESSENTIAL
MANAGEMENT TOOLBOX

THE ESSENTIAL
MANAGEMENT
TOOLBOX

Tools, Models and Notes for Managers and Consultants

Simon A. Burtonshaw-Gunn

John Wiley & Sons, Ltd

Copyright © 2008   John Wiley & Sons Ltd, The Atrium, Southern Gate, Chichester,
West Sussex PO19 8SQ, England

Telephone (+44) 1243 779777

Email (for orders and customer service enquiries): cs-books@wiley.co.uk
Visit our Home Page on www.wiley.com

All Rights Reserved. No part of this publication may be reproduced, stored in a
retrieval system or transmitted in any form or by any means, electronic, mechanical,
photocopying, recording, scanning or otherwise, except under the terms of the
Copyright, Designs and Patents Act 1988 or under the terms of a licence issued by
the Copyright Licensing Agency Ltd, 90 Tottenham Court Road, London W1T 4LP,
UK, without the permission in writing of the Publisher. Requests to the Publisher
should be addressed to the Permissions Department, John Wiley & Sons Ltd, The
Atrium, Southern Gate, Chichester, West Sussex PO19 8SQ, England, or emailed to
permreq@wiley.co.uk, or faxed to (+44) 1243 770620.

Designations used by companies to distinguish their products are often claimed as
trademarks. All brand names and product names used in this book are trade names,
service marks, trademarks or registered trademarks of their respective owners. The
Publisher is not associated with any product or vendor mentioned in this book.

This publication is designed to provide accurate and authoritative information in
regard to the subject matter covered. It is sold on the understanding that the Publisher
is not engaged in rendering professional services. If professional advice or other expert
assistance is required, the services of a competent professional should be sought.

Other Wiley Editorial Offices

John Wiley & Sons Inc., 111 River Street, Hoboken, NJ 07030, USA

Jossey-Bass, 989 Market Street, San Francisco, CA 94103-1741, USA

Wiley-VCH Verlag GmbH, Boschstr. 12, D-69469 Weinheim, Germany

John Wiley & Sons Australia Ltd, 42 McDougall Street, Milton, Queensland 4064,
Australia

John Wiley & Sons (Asia) Pte Ltd, 2 Clementi Loop #02-01, Jin Xing Distripark,
Singapore 129809

John Wiley & Sons Canada Ltd, 6045 Freemont Blvd, Mississauga, ONT, L5R 4J3,
Canada

Wiley also publishes its books in a variety of electronic formats. Some content that
appears in print may not be available in electronic books.

British Library Cataloguing in Publication Data

Library of Congress Cataloging-in-Publication Data

Burtonshaw-Gunn, Simon A.
  The essential management toolbox : tools, models and notes for managers and
consultants / Simon A. Burtonshaw-Gunn.
       p. cm.
  Includes bibliographical references and index.
  ISBN 978-0-470-51837-3 (cloth : alk. paper)
  1. Management.   I. Title.
  HD31.B85246 2008
  658 – dc22

                                                                        2007050374

A catalogue record for this book is available from the British Library

ISBN 978-0-470-51837-3 (HB)

Typeset in 11.5/15pt Bembo by SNP Best-set Typesetter Ltd., Hong Kong
Printed and bound in Great Britain by TJ International Ltd, Padstow, Cornwall, UK

1082157
£24.99

To 'The B-Gs' – Carole, Alex and Edward

CENTRE	Newark
CHECKED	82
ZONE	Mauve
ZONE MARK / SUFFIX	658 BUR
LOAN PERIOD	1 month

CENTRE	
CHECKED	
ZONE	
PERIOD	

CONTENTS

FOREWORD

*T*his book from Simon Burtonshaw-Gunn will be of great use to management consultancy practitioners at all levels. It covers a wide range of consultancy tools and techniques that are well displayed, well described and well referenced. The reader will find the tools and techniques helpfully divided into 20 recognizable skill sectors within management consultancy fields and specialisms. There is no reference source available currently that concisely lists and briefly describes management consultancy tools and techniques across such a wide range of sectors. The contents are written up by the author with the accuracy and brevity of the unique blend of an experienced practitioner and a seasoned educator. This is also reflected in the author's unerring choice of safe, reliable, robust and instantly recognizable models, principles and practices. The method of depiction of the content, mainly in diagrammatic form, aids the process of quick reference and ease of understanding. The tools and techniques can be utilized across the whole range of organizational sectors and both the private and public sectors.

The tools described will be useful to the inexperienced management consultant to explain the working of tried and tested interventions and relating them back to solid and trusted reference books. The value of this is for the beginner to have a quick reference source and then, if necessary, undertake further and deeper research into the methodology from the identified source. There are clear benefits in this to contribute towards the professional and personal development of the management consultancy practitioner.

For the more experienced management consultant there is always an advantage in having a 'quick reference' source of tools and techniques to remind them of the specifics of a principle or to enable a common understanding to be established in a consultancy team or with a client.

Thus, I can envisage that this book, with the simple idea of being a repository of the 'bare bones' of management consultancy tools and techniques, will be of great value to all management consultants (and managers) in the field.

Alan Beckley

Alan Beckley is a company director of several management consultancy companies that hold ISO 9001 accreditation and IBC Recognized Practice status; he is an operational management consultant. He is also the External Verifier for management consultancy qualifications provided by the Chartered Management Institute (CMI) and an Assessor for the Institute of Business Consulting (IBC) for the Certified Management Consultant (CMC) award. He has been the managing editor of the IBC's *Professional Consultancy* web-based quarterly management consultancy magazine for several years.

INTRODUCTION

With a technological background the use of engineer's tables and formulae has for me been a common occurrence to help both in my student days and as a practising professional. In progressing a career in management it seems that a similar reference book is absent despite a relentlessly growing list of management and business publications. Even a brief scan of the bookshelves will reveal that there is a wide spectrum from specialist publications to generalist 'Bluff your way in . . .', 'Dummies guide to . . .' and others claiming to provide MBA knowledge from a day's reading.

In the same way as providing engineers with a formula that relies on a level of prior knowledge and competence, the purpose of this book is not to short-cut any formal learning and understanding of the use of established and practical management tools and techniques but to provide an easy access to various management approaches through a collection of models and occasional brief prompting notes. The intention of this book is to provide a set of tools and models from tried and tested sources which can be used by scholars, practising managers, experienced consultants or newcomers to the profession to use in a practical way.

Just like the typical craftsman's toolkit rarely are more than a few tools used on a single project; nevertheless, the advantage of a full set of tools at least provides the opportunity to select the correct, efficient and safe tool – even if this is no guarantee of the proficiency of the user! While there will always be specialist tools for an expert – rarely needed by the majority of users – the generalist tools provided in this book cover a range of generic management themes. There is a widely held view that many management consultancy tools feature the use of a two by two matrix – and while this book does seem to support this view, these should be considered to be the equivalent of a set of spanners as each one may have the same appearance but will differ in its application. Where possible I have made reference to the origin of the models and tools in this book to guide the reader to where further information and detailed 'operating instructions' may be gained. Full details of the material used are provided in the References section.

So often the various topics of management are interwoven: for example, some of the tools described in strategic management are also of use in marketing, business planning, HRM and international business. In many ways the massive topic of 'management' itself can be thought of as a giant jigsaw of many interlocking pieces and as such the tools described in each alphabetically arranged section of this book can often be directly used or adapted for use in other management areas.

Many of the tools shown here are from works published over the last 30 years which coincide with the move to specialization and the jigsaw analogy of the field of management with the development of specialist topic areas. Indeed this trend for greater specialization continues as managers have to understand newer developments such as e-commerce and advances in business to business (B2B) and business to customer (B2C) relationships.

ACKNOWLEDGEMENTS

Following the concept of the 'engineers' formula handbook' described in the Introduction I am not claiming to present anything new but from my own experience have tried to compile a useful book for a number of users. Naturally this would not have been possible without the fine efforts from all those management authors, research publications and course notes, etc. which I have collected over the years. As such I am greatly indebted to all whose work appears in the book, and also to my own teachers and mentors who have aided my own journey through many management topics.

As time progresses and new tools, models and techniques become used there is opportunity for us all in the 'management community' to develop this further, indeed if you have any comments on the models so far identified or wish to add more for a future edition then I would be very happy to hear from you. My contact details are: toolbox2008@hotmail.co.uk

I am very grateful to the following publishers, individuals and copyright holders who gave their permission to allow previously published work to be used in this book. Every effort has been made to ascertain copyright and seek permission; however, any omissions will be corrected in any future edition.

- Academy of Management Review
- Christopher Ahoy, Iowa State University, USA
- American Association of Marketing
- American Psychological Association
- Michael Armstrong
- Ashgate Publishing
- Professor Henry Assael, Leonard N. Stern School of Business, New York, USA
- Association of Project Management Group Ltd
- Dr Mike Baxter
- Berrett-Koehler Publishers Inc.
- Blackwell
- Boston Consulting Group Inc.
- Butterworth-Heinemann
- Chartered Management Institute, UK
- Chartered Institute of Management Accountants
- Professor Colin Coulson-Thomas
- Professor Michael Czinkota, McDonough School of Business, Georgetown University, USA
- Department for Work and Pensions, UK
- Edwards-Deming Institute, MIT
- Elsevier
- European Foundation of Quality Management
- Nick Eve, Elements Ltd
- FT Prentice-Hall
- Gower Press
- HarperCollins
- Jean Harris

- Harvard Business Review
- Julie Hay
- Institute for Sport, Parks and Leisure
- Institute of Management Consultants
- Kogan Page
- Liverpool Academic Press
- Dennis Lock
- Professor Simon Majaro
- McGraw-Hill
- New York Productivity Press
- Open University Press
- Oxford University Press
- Palgrave Macmillan
- Pearson Education Inc.
- Pearson Education Limited
- Penguin
- Peter Honey Associates
- Kate Piersanti
- Pitman Publishing
- Praeger
- Prentice-Hall
- Project Management Institute Inc., USA
- Psychological Bulletin
- Kit Sadgrove
- Dr Malik Salameh
- Simon & Schuster Inc., New York
- Dr Stuart Slater
- SPCK Publishing
- Springer Science and Business Media
- Taylor & Francis
- Thompson Learning
- University of Virginia Darden School Foundation
- University of Salford
- John Wiley & Sons

I would also like to record my sincere thanks to those that have supported my efforts in reviewing my draft manuscripts and providing such encouragement. Finally, but not least, my thanks go to Francesca, Jo, Emily, Sam and Natalie and all at John Wiley & Sons for their support and help in bringing this project into reality.

CHAPTER 1

BUSINESS PLANNING

*T*his chapter covers the task of business planning which is applicable to all businesses whether a sole trader or a multinational conglomerate. The production of a business plan is needed to describe the business, its objectives, its strategies, the market it is in and its financial forecasts. It is often used as a tool for measuring the performance of the organization against that intended over a short- or medium-term period, typically three to five years. For many new businesses the business plan may be used as a tool to promote an interest in the business and to secure external funding and as such needs to be undertaken as a serious task. In addition to this, a business plan has several other purposes as it:

• Prompts management to logically examine the business in a structured way and consider what it currently does and what it wishes to do in the future.

- Encourages management to set future business objectives and then monitor progress against the plan.
- Identifies the resources and time needed to implement the business plan.
- Can be used to communicate the key features of the business plan to employees and provide them with an awareness of the business's direction.
- Provides links to the detailed, short-term functional strategies.

This chapter also shows the basic stages in producing a business plan and the planning cycle which also looks at past performance and what needs to be addressed as new targets and objectives. Indeed the focus on the business plan is likely to be on three areas: setting realistic goals for the business to aim for, demonstrating how its objectives will be met and finally identifying what resources in terms of people, plant and investment will be required by the organization to achieve the plan.

Although there is no set formula for the contents of a business plan, a typical layout is provided in this chapter as a good starting model for those embarking on its production. For those who do so with an external reader in mind – bank, shareholders, etc. – then adopting a common format is likely to convince the lender that the organization at least knows how to portray its business and ambitions in a professional and recognizable way. On completion of the task a checklist on the business plan feasibility is also included, this covers the key questions on the management, marketing and financial aspects of the plan which need to be addressed either directly or indirectly in the plan.

For new businesses the business plan should also describe how the company will operate from its launch until it has established itself in the market. In practice there should be a detailed narrative on the first six months as this is when costs in establishing the business are being incurred – in developing a market, recruiting staff, negotiating with suppliers, etc. – contrasted with no or low income, particularly if part of a supply chain, when customers' terms of payment are unlikely to be favourable in terms of timescale and hence the subject of cash flow needs to be described. Having invested time, effort and some cost in producing the business plan with its objectives clearly articulated, this should not be limited to senior management or shareholders but should be used in the business and updated as new environmental opportunities and threats arise. This tool will help to keep track of current performance and development plans. The final point to consider is that business planning is not a on/off isolated event; it needs to be used, reviewed and periodically repeated to ensure that the business is achieving its desired level of performance.

TRADITIONAL APPROACH TO STRATEGIC IMPLEMENTATION AND BUSINESS PLANNING

While this model presents the ideal approach, in practical terms this is a much more inter-related process; however, the benefit of the model is to illustrate that determining the Vision and Mission are important steps in strategy formulation and in setting the business plan.

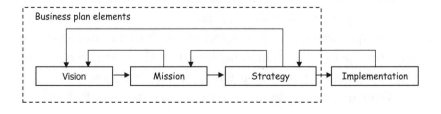

THE PLANNING CYCLE

This simple model has links into research and data gathering, analysis and options studies, strategic management in the form of setting objectives and finally in performance management often related to people performance objectives. While this is shown here in a business planning context it also has applications at an individual level as part of career appraisal and personal development and in training needs identification.

UNDERSTANDING THE PRODUCT/SERVICE

This is a typical approach which can be used to understand a product or service business with a client organization to demonstrate and promote the planning process.

The questions shown below, together with establishing a view of the future for the organization and identifying barriers or constraints, can be linked to a workshop format to maximize the amount of involvement, creative thinking and agreement to a way forward.

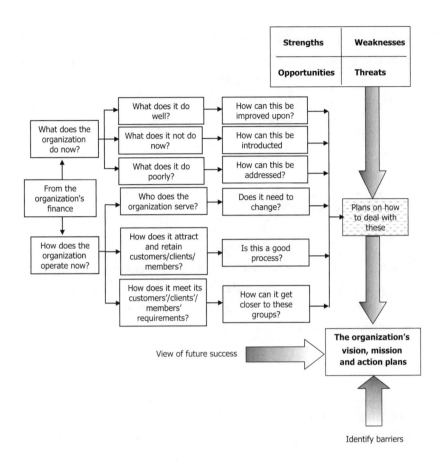

TYPICAL BUSINESS PLAN CONTENTS

While there is no set format for a business plan the majority of these follow a typical presentation format; this is mostly because companies looking for investors will want to show that the business is being professionally managed and investors will want to understand the business activities, its future aspirations and the potential that the business wishes to address. Thus a typical layout of a what may be regarded as an extended business plan is shown below:

Executive summary

Business concept	Company market potential	Management team
Distinct competencies	Required funding and its use	Exit strategy

Company description

Mission statement	Summary of activity to date	Current stage of development
Competencies	Product/service description	Benefits to customer
Objectives	Keys to success	Location and facilities
Differences from current offerings		

Industry analysis

Entry barriers	Supply and distribution	Technological factors
Economic influences	Regulatory issues	

Market analysis

Overall market	Market size and growth	Market trends
Market segments	Targeted segments	Customer characteristics
Customer needs	Purchasing decision process	Product positioning

Competition

Competitor profiles	Competitor products	Competitor market share
Competitor services	Competitive evaluation of product	Competitive advantage
Competitive weaknesses	Future competitors	

Marketing and sales

Products offered	Pricing	Distribution
Promotion	Advertising and publicity	Trade shows
Partnerships	Discounts and incentives	Sales force
Sales forecasts		

Operations

Product development	Development team	Development costs
Development risks	Manufacturing (if applicable)	Production processes
Production equipment	Quality assurance	Administration
Key suppliers	Product/service delivery	Human resource plan
Facilities	Customer service and support	

Management and organization

Management team	Open positions	Board of directors
Key personnel	Organizational chart	

Capitalization and structure

Legal structure of company	Present equity positions	Deal structure
Exit strategy		

Development and milestones

Financing commitments	Product development milestones	Prototype testing
Launch	Signing of significant contracts	Additional funding
Expansion	Details break–even performance	Other major milestones

Risks and contingencies

Increased competition	Loss of a key employee	Regulatory changes
Suppliers' failure	Change in business conditions	

Financial projections

Average inventory	Sales forecasts	Balance sheet
Income statement	Cash flow statement	Break even analysis
Key ratio projections	Financial resources	Financial strategy

Summary and conclusions

Appendices

Management résumés	Competitive analysis	Sales projections
Plus any other supporting documents		

PRODUCING THE BUSINESS PLAN

Producing a business plan must cover four basic stages of business development:

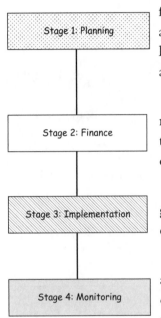

The management's best estimate of future operations is set out in a logical and organized way. This should crystallize ideas and identify any problems and areas for further analysis.

To determine when money is required and whether it needs to take the form of loan capital or other forms of funding.

This provides the management with guidelines for running the business efficiently.

To allow the management to assess and control the company's progress by comparison with financial projections in the plan.

CHECK ON BUSINESS PLAN FEASIBILITY

Having completed the production of a business plan, its success in business depends on three crucial elements:

- The management of the business
- Its approach to marketing
- The money that the business needs and will generate

These three elements are detailed below and testing them against these questions will provide the organization with a level of confidence before it faces any external investor, bank or stakeholder.

Management

- Does the management team have the motivation and skills to deliver the products/services you envisage?
- Does the management team have the skills to look after the administration side of the business, including all of the money matters?
- Has the organization the ability to sell the services to the potential clients identified?
- Are you prepared to modify the business plan in the light of what people want?
- Is the company confident that it is able to manage skills and time to full effect?
- Does it need any new people to make this plan work?
- Does it need 'different' people to make the plan work?
- Can the plan work and the business carry on if current key people leave the company for another job, retire, win lottery, etc.?

Marketing

- What is so special about the services that the company intends to provide?
- How do you know that anyone will want to buy them?
- How often will they buy from you?
- How much will you charge for the services and are people/companies prepared to pay those prices?
- Are you sure that you can provide these services at these prices, make a profit and manage the cash flow?
- Why should anyone buy from the company rather than others in the market?

- Is this the right time to start providing the services that you have in mind?
- Will you be able to develop them as the market develops?
- Have you considered how you will advertise or promote the company's services and how much will this cost? (See also Money)
- Where will you advertise or promote?
- Do you know who the competitors are and what services/products they are selling?
- Have you spoken to any potential customers about the company's services that you provide or intend to provide?

Money

- Will the business make a profit?
- Will you be able to pay each bill as it arrives?
- What financial resources will you need to be successful?
- Are you confident that you can pay back any loans over a reasonable period, and pay the interest?
- Have you researched, listed and costed the expenditure items that you will incur?
- When will income start to flow?
- Which part of the market provides the revenue? Is this secure or high risk?
- What are customers prepared to pay for the company's services?
- What revenue can we expect from new markets?
- What revenue can we get from repeat business?
- What is the cost of acquiring new business, in bidding, making contacts, marketing, presentations, etc.?

FACTORS INFLUENCING COMPETITIVE SUCCESS

Business performance is determined not just by income from the company's services and products but also by how it manages its relationship with a number of factors. The model below shows these factors, some of which are outside of the control of the organization. For those tasked or advising on the production of an organization's business plan, consideration of the model will help to ensure that the major factors have been addressed and planned.

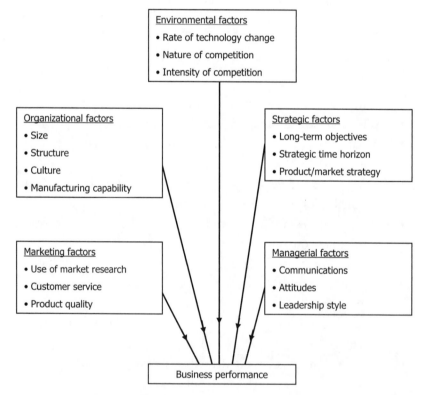

From Edgar P. Hibbert, *International Business – strategy and operations*, 1997, Macmillan Business. Reproduced with permission of Palgrave Macmillian.

CHAPTER 2

CHANGE MANAGEMENT

All organizations are destined either to perish through business failure from being left behind by the competition or to accept that undertaking change is a natural part of business life in order to keep in line with customer requirements, the need for improvements or customer or fashion demands. While this chapter provides a number of models around managing change, it is stressed that any change management plan is destined to fail unless supported by a main sponsor, often the senior management of the organization. The organization's stakeholders have to accept that such change is seen as being appropriate for the specific organization and its customer base will respond positively to the change. There are a number of reasons for change, through either incremental drift of lagging behind others or the need for a more large-scale change initiative through evolution or revolution.

Even on the basis of senior management support, the change process is likely to be time consuming and management will have to consider the type of change strategy best suited to pursue the organization's new direction. There are a number of factors that should be considered when choosing how to implement the necessary changes as each approach will be appropriate in different circumstances. Indeed, those that are inconsistent with the demands of the situation – the people, the cultural setting and the business environment – will undoubtedly run into problems and fail to support the long-term required changes.

This chapter provides some approaches to planning organizational change and gaining commitment, and also includes a number of models around managing resistance. With few exceptions people's reaction to change will follow the change curve, itself influenced by issues around security, status and self-esteem. Clearly, implementing change needs to be planned, executed, reported and reviewed.

The process of change implementation needs to be aligned and appropriate to the organization and an example of a three-phase approach is described below.

Phase 1: Organizational pre-positioning – the first phase focuses on the preparations for change through communications with staff and stakeholders, it concentrates on preparation for the introduction of changes to the organization's structure and the delivery of general change management awareness training to staff. This important phase is aimed at preparing the organization for change, gaining commitment from those involved and managing the associated risks.

Phase 2: Change management plan implementation – this phase concentrates on the implementation of the changes in accordance with the agreed plans and the business objectives. The four key change components described in this chapter are undertaken by the change management team. During this phase typically any new senior management appointments will be initiated and the new organization structure implemented.

Phase 3: Ongoing support and consolidation phase – here the focus will be on continual support and improvements as the changes become embedded within the organization and regarded as the 'way to do business'. This third phase leads to the longer-term and more difficult cultural change as shown in the 'change pyramid'. This phase is important for the changes to be successful within the transformed organization and for employees to understand their new roles and their contribution to the success of the organization.

PATTERNS OF STRATEGIC CHANGE

While there are periods of continuity where established strategy remains unchanged, typical organizations inevitably change as strategies are gradually formed. Some organizations without a clear direction undergo a period of flux where change also takes place. Planned major change can also take place but is often an infrequent action and part of a larger change management initiative.

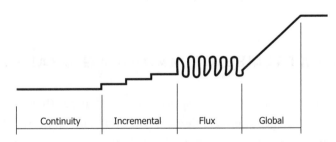

From Gerry Johnson and Kevan Scholes, *Exploring Corporate Strategy*, 2002, 6th edition, text and cases. Reproduced with permission of Pearson Publishing.

STRATEGIC DRIFT

Even where organizations are engaged in their own change derived from incremental improvements this can often be behind that demanded by the changes in the business environment resulting in further action being needed to gain closer realignment. The model shows that the business environment changes although the organization's strategy fails to develop in line with it. In reality it is often difficult to ensure that the organization remains aligned with external influences as each subtle change can be undetected on its own; however, many organizations will recognize the reality shown in the model.

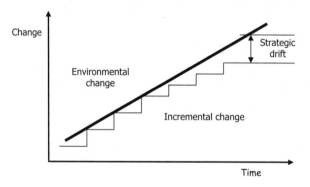

From Dr Tim Hannagan, *Management Concepts and Practices*, 2005. Reproduced with permission of Pearson Education.

TWO EXTREMES OF MANAGING CHANGE

While there are a number of approaches to change, there are two extremes of major step change (revolution) and a more gentle, incremental change (evolution). This is not to suggest that one of these types is good and the other poor – it depends on a range of circumstances and the client organization's drivers for change.

REVOLUTION	EVOLUTION
BPR – Business process re-engineering	Continuous improvement Kaizen
Start from scratch	Build on what has gone before
Very rapid	Slowly and steady
Innovative	Maintenance and improvement

THE CHANGE CURVE
(OR LOSS TRANSITION CURVE)

This model originates from studies by the American psychiatrist Dr Elizabeth Kübler-Ross, first published in 1969, on bereavement and five stages of grief. This work has been shown to have wider applications in understanding how individuals deal with change within organizations. Although the bereavement model stages are denial, anger, bargaining, depression and acceptance, these have been adapted to the workplace situation. In this regard it is used to show the energy consumed in the change process over a period of time, although this time period is unique to each change event: it may cover a day or many months. Only after acceptance of the change can individuals move forward with the change being then regarded as an opportunity. This model is developed further below.

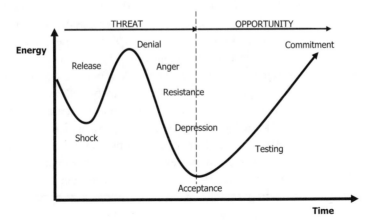

MANAGEMENT OF CHANGE WITHIN AN ORGANIZATION

This model has been developed taking the reactions to change concept, as shown above, to understand organizational change and the impact on individuals. While the graph follows a similar trend the stages have been retitled. The table below corresponds to the graph and indicates how managers may be able to identify the change stage for individuals and how they need to react to it.

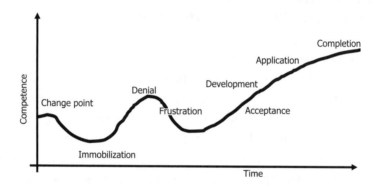

STAGE	CLUES	NEEDS
Immobilization	Withdrawn, marks time	Time to get used to new situation
Denial	Acts as if nothing changed, wastes time	Patience, clear authority, permission to explore
Frustration	Doesn't know how to make needed change	Tolerance, permission to think on own
Acceptance	Selects options, lets go of past attitudes	Acceptance, permission to be self in situation
Development	Acquires new skills, knowledge	Support permission to grow and succeed
Application	Applies new learning, develops own views	Encourage permission to take responsibility
Completion	Competent	Give self permissions

MANAGEMENT OF CHANGE – CHANGES IN SELF-ESTEEM DURING TRANSITION

This final graph and table show the changes in self-esteem that individuals often follow:

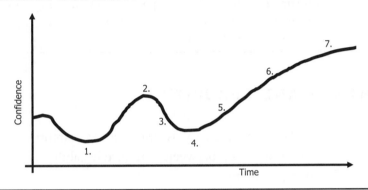

STAGE	CHARACTERISTICS
1.	**Numbness** – Shock, immobilization and a sense of being overwhelmed. The less positive towards and unfamiliar you are with the situation, the more pronounced the symptoms.
2.	**Minimization/Denial** – Here the change is minimized, even trivialized or perhaps denied. The systems may be building up defences for the full impact of changes to come.
3.	**Self-doubt or depression** – An awareness of the need to change, self-doubt arises out of powerlessness and lack of control, typified by swings of energy, anger, hopelessness, resistance to change and frustration of not being able to cope.
4.	**Accepting reality/letting go** – This is a stage where the past is released as the obvious need to move on is accepted for what it is. Can also be relief and the beginning of reshaping.
5.	**Testing** – Here the person starts testing for new ways to behave and manage in the new situation. Often pre-formed and stereotyped patterns are used and modified. Irritation with progress is common behaviour at this stage.

STAGE	CHARACTERISTICS
6.	**Searching for meaning** – At this point there is a gradual shift towards understanding, looking at meaning as to how and why things are different. A period of reflection.
7.	**Internalization** – The final phase of internalizing all the meanings and incorporating them into a changed behaviour, routines or lifestyle.

CHANGE AND SECURITY

As well as self-esteem, security is also tied to stability in the workplace; the relationship between change and stability is shown in the following diagram:

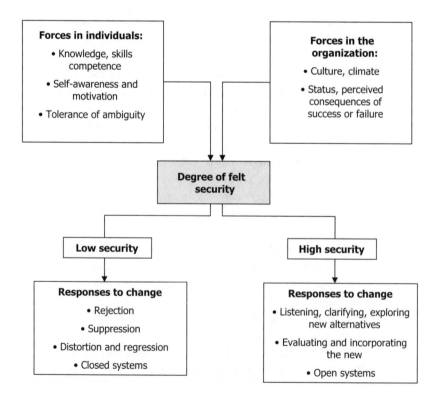

Forces, both within individuals and within organizations, contribute to the degree of felt security and can promote feelings of either insecurity or high security. In turn these feelings of security can lead to contrasting responses to planned organizational change. It is important to recognize that the forces which contribute to the culture and the attitudes of the individuals within the organization are key to establishing a high degree of security which will support a positive response to organizational change.

CHANGE PYRAMID

Within the model is the range of changes which an organization may wish to adopt. The model also suggests that the easier changes at the bottom of the pyramid have the least level of discomfort for employees. These lower level changes also require the least amount of time and cost; similarly the higher levels necessitate substantial time and investment.

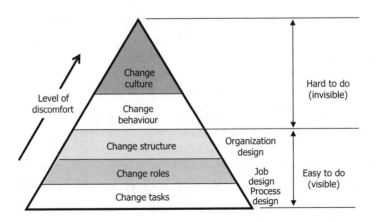

VECTORS OF CHANGE MANAGEMENT

SKILLS MANAGERS NEED FOR HANDLING CHANGE

Research suggests that there are three inter-related skills categories which managers need to possess to promote effective change. These are:

Transforming skills where managers need to be able to create a supportive risk-taking environment, and have self-awareness and self-confidence. Managers need to possess the ability to share the benefits that the change will bring and take the journey needed to undertake this through visualization techniques.

Mental skills will require managers to think holistically and help others to see the big picture. These managers will be able to work with rules of thumb based on action learning.

Finally managers in a change environment will be required to have the 'softer' skills of **empathy and understanding of feelings**. Often this will be witnessed though the use of symbols, analogies and metaphors to relate to the change process and will need the ability to tolerate stress and resist confronting every issue. This demands use of both left- and right-side brain techniques.

FOUR CHANGE OPTIONS FOR INDIVIDUALS

While there are a number of models to assist individuals in the change process it should be noted that the only available choices are shown below:

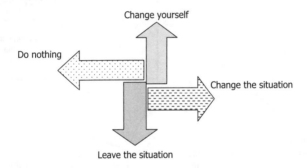

There are no other options but these four!

RESISTANCE TO CHANGE – LESSONS FROM HISTORY

Resisting change is not new, as the writings of the Italian courtier Niccolo Machiavelli reveal in his book *The Prince*, which was first published in 1532. This quote is often used at the start of many change management programmes to demonstrate an acknowledgement to resistance to change and the difficulties which may be encountered.

> *"There is nothing more difficult to take in hand, more perilous to conduct, or more uncertain in its success, than to take the lead in the introduction of a new order of things."*

PLANNING ORGANIZATIONAL CHANGE

Similar to a quality management 'Plan-Do-Review' cycle the four phase change life cycle approach evaluates as well as implements the change. The planning phase is linked to two other models: one for the four types of organizational change and one showing that planning an approach of resistance to change is part of this overall process.

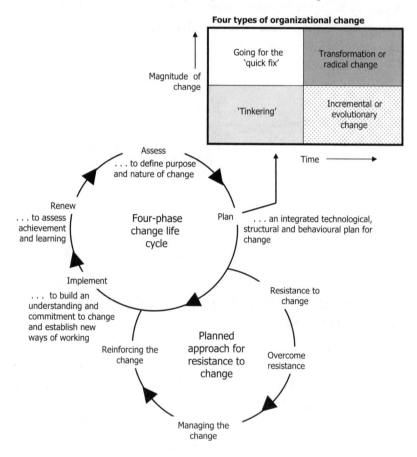

Considering addressing any resistance to change plays an important part of the planning process and needs to be under-taken before embarking on the implementation phase. (See other notes in this chapter)

MANAGING RESISTANCE TO CHANGE

Resistance to change
- Purpose of change not clear
- Persons affected by change are not involved in planning
- Change is based on personal reasons
- Habit patterns of the work group are ignored
- There is poor communication regarding change
- There is a fear of failure
- Excessive work pressure is involved
- The 'cost' is too high or 'reward' inadequate
- Anxiety over job security is not relieved
- 'Vested' interest of individual or sub-unit is involved
- Satisfaction with no status quo
- Change is too rapid
- Past experience of change is negative
- Honest difference of opinion

Reinforcing the change
- Constantly identify benefits
- Force-field analysis
- Invite questions and answer them
- Explain why
- Educate and train
- Set standards
- Avoid surprises
- Reinforce staff sense of security
- Model flexibility
- Keep communications two way
- Admit difficulty
- Seek input
- Inform and involve informal leaders

Overcome resistance
- Encourage participation
- Start with the top officials
- Show that change will reduce rather than increase burdens
- Connect proposals with traditional values
- Bring out novel or existing aspects
- Give assurance the autonomy will not be threatened
- Include participants in the diagnostic efforts
- Aim for consensus decision
- Build in feedback mechanisms
- Try to build mutual trust
- Keep a path open for reappraisal and revision

Managing the change
- Involve individuals in the planning
- Provide accurate and complete information
- Give individuals a chance to air their objections
- Beware of breaking up work groups, disrupting schedules, cancelling vacations, splitting up lunch partners and violating the norm of the group
- Make only essential change
- Develop a trust environment

CONSIDERATION OF CHANGE STRATEGIES

Before considering change – what type of change, how to do it, identifying who is to be involved or who is affected by any change, two points need to be made. First, it is absolutely crucial to gain the most senior level support and commitment as any change management plan is destined to fail unless supported by a main sponsor, often the senior management of the organization, the organization's stakeholders and in some cases its customer base too. Second, acceptance is needed within the organization that such recommended change is seen as being appropriate for the specific organization. On this basis acceptance by the management of the business plan objective and its change recommendations will then allow them to consider the type of change strategy best suited to pursue a new direction or initiate changes necessary to facilitate increased organizational performance.

There are a number of factors that should be considered by management in choosing how to implement the necessary changes, as each approach will be appropriate in different circumstances. Indeed those that are inconsistent with the demands of the situation – the people, the cultural setting and the business environment – will undoubtedly run into problems and fail to support the long-term required changes.

In agreeing an appropriate strategy or combination of strategies for change, the organization's management will need to take into account the following factors:

- The degree of the opposition expected.
- The power base of the change initiator.
- The need for information, communication and commitment when planning and carrying out the change.
- The nature of the current organization's culture and its likely response to change.

After considering the above factors there are five broad optional approaches which can be deployed in change implementation.

Expert strategy:
manage change as problem solving

Educative strategy:
winning hearts and minds

Negotiating strategy:
bargaining about change

Directive strategy:
management's right to
introduce change

Participative strategy:
get all involved in making the
change

**Implementation of
selected change
strategy**

Directive strategy

Here the management can use its authority to impose the changes required and will be able to carry them out speedily. However, the disadvantage of this approach is that it is likely to increase resistance or even undermine change implementation.

Expert strategy

This approach is usually applied when a 'technical' problem requires solving, such as the introduction of a new IT system.

Negotiating strategy

This approach involves a willingness to negotiate with individuals and teams affected by the change and to accept that adjustments and concessions may have to be made. Opting for this approach does not remove the management's responsibility for the direction and initiation of change, but acknowledges that those affected have the right to have some input in the changes proposed, or that they have some power to resist it if they are not supportive.

The advantage of this approach is that resistance to change is likely to be less; however, the implementation time may take longer. Changing work practices in return for increased pay and/or other benefits is a classic example of the negotiating strategy.

Educative strategy

This approach involves changing people's values and beliefs so that they support the change and are committed to a shared set of organizational values. Winning hearts and minds is a complex process that involves a mixture of activities, such as: communication, persuasion, education, training and selection.

The advantage of such an approach, if successful, is that people will be positively committed to the change. In general this approach typically takes much longer and requires more resources than the previous three strategies.

Participative strategy

This strategy has a number of advantages: changes are more likely to be widely acceptable over the others, it promotes the active involvement of people and is likely to increase their commitment to and enthusiasm for the change process. Additionally there will be opportunities for both managers and employees to learn from the experiences and skills of this wide participation.

While this has a number of advantages due to the participation of staff, the identified changes are likely to take longer and require additional resources to support the change.

From 'Change management and organizational performance' by Professor Simon A. Burtonshaw-Gunn and Dr Malik G. Salameh, published in *Effective Executive*, June 2007. Reproduced with permission of ICFAI University Press, Hyderabad, India.

SIX APPROACHES TO DEALING WITH RESISTANCE

Leading on from the change strategies, the management of an organization or a consultant advising on a change programme will need to have an understanding of resistance and how this may best be addressed. These six approaches provide some guidance to the reader:

Education and communication

If people have little information they will assume the worst. Briefing meetings, roadshows, letters to staff and volunteers can be used to communicate and educate staff on the proposed changes.

Participation

Consultation meetings and working parties can be used to invite comments on draft proposals. The advantage is that people feel involved and the changes are based on more valid information. This approach also has disadvantages as it may raise false expectations, takes time and can backfire.

Facilitation and support

Listen to people to understand their reasons for resistance and provide support as necessary. This may in turn lead to a negotiation stage.

Negotiation	Can be used both formally and informally when someone will clearly lose out and they have the power to resist. Part of the negotiation is to try to trade things which are low cost to you and high value to them.
Manipulation	This approach is often used by people unwittingly. If used, people tend not to trust you again.
Coercion and use of authority	This is not the best approach as it may leave people feeling rejected and worthless. However, it can be justified if speed is essential or if other business reasons dictate.

A BUSINESS TURNAROUND MODEL

This model shows a typical methodology for diagnosis planning and implementation of change. It shows a number of required inputs at each of the four main stages and how these stages are linked to one another.

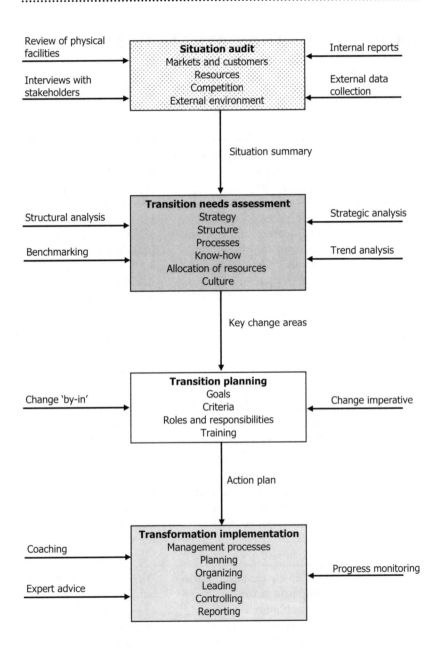

CHOICE OF CHANGE STRATEGIES

This table presents four change management strategies and their associated features:

FEATURE	SYSTEMS APPROACH INTERVENTION STRATEGY	BUSINESS PROCESS RE-ENGINEERING
Origin	Originated in systems engineering and operations research (hard methods) but has taken on board a 'softer element'.	Originated as a response to intense competitive pressure in a context where IT developments raised new questions and possibilities.
Assumptions	Assumes rational appeal but encourages consultation. Emphasizes on changing the systems to empower the people.	The need for and possibility of radical change in performance.
Scope	Will probably focus on one part (or subsystem) of the organization at a time.	Focuses on cross-functional business process.
Process	Iterative with frequent reference to project sponsor. Structured interaction using a range of standard techniques.	Unclear; probably a group of senior managers working with a consultant.
Application	Suited to change situations which measure structured, logical approach. Task/project oriented – relatively prescriptive.	Where an elaborate and poorly understood array of processes has evolved to do the business and is costly, poorly understood and cumbersome; where new IT are being envisaged.

ORGANIZATIONAL DESIGN AND DEVELOPMENT	BUSINESS TURNAROUND	FEATURE
Calls upon a range of social science disciplines to inform and enhance the change process (soft methods) but has taken a more 'bottom line' perspective.	An articulation of 'practitioner knows how' identified through systematic research.	Origin
Assumes reactions and resistance to change of part of life. Emphasis on empowering the people in order to change the system.	The need for decisive action including the replacement of senior managers.	Assumptions
Focus on whole organization (the complex inter relationships of many subsystems).	The organization as a whole (or the parts that are salvageable).	Scope
Iterative with frequent reference to chief client. A philosophy of helping not reducible to a set of techniques.	Intense; initially directive and decisive with little scope for iteration.	Process
Suited to change situations which are complex with high political content. Process oriented, highly facilitative.	Where a business with significant assets is facing an organizational and financial crisis.	Application

FEATURE	SYSTEMS APPROACH INTERVENTION STRATEGY	BUSINESS PROCESS RE-ENGINEERING
Trigger	Triggered by the need to understand and resolve many problems. Stimulus usually comes from within the organization.	Varied – perception of excessive complexity, of inflexibility, and of poor returns from existing IT.
Timescale	Relatively short decision cycles, although can take months.	Unclear – probably 6–24 months from initiation to realization.
Type of intervention	The decision process usually narrows to a preferred option: moving forward in discrete stages.	Large-scale work flow and job redesign usually in relation to new IT.
Leadership	Will usually be led by an internal project manager, and will be team based and reporting to an identified problem owner.	Varying, but probably in the IT department.
Outcomes	Apparent at the end when implemented.	Simplification of processes; reduced cost; greater speed of response; enhanced service to customers.
Evaluation	Options evaluated in quantifiable terms, and overall outcomes measured against tangible criteria.	Economy, efficiency and effectiveness of the process.

From 'A comparison on change strategies' from *Corporate Recovery* by Dr Stuart Slater (Penguin Books, 1999). Copyright Stuart Slater, 1982, 1984. Reproduced with permission.

ORGANIZATIONAL DESIGN AND DEVELOPMENT	BUSINESS TURNAROUND	FEATURE
Need to improve on organization objectives and relationships or to revise/adapt new ways of working.	Impending bankruptcy.	Trigger
Long – need to take account of evolving objectives. Will probably take years – 6–12 months for specific objective.	Most changes within 3 months with results becoming apparent.	Timescale
Less likely to test interventions – more equivalent to ongoing 'action research'. Will usually lead to a strategy involving several related initiatives.	Simultaneous action in operations, finance, marketing and HR.	Type of intervention
Usually facilitated by an external or internal consultant working closely with a chief client in the organization.	New chief executive.	Leadership
Apparent as the process unfolds in terms of improved communication and changing culture with new thinking and strategies and in due course improved performance.	Recovery of a slimmed-down enterprise or closure.	Outcomes
Outcomes will often be difficult to measure or attribute causally.	Presumably net worth of the business emerging from the turnaround.	Evaluation

ERRORS IN COPING WITH CHANGE AND CONFLICT

There are a number of 'standard' errors in managing a change process; recognition of these errors can be used to develop a plan to address these before they occur.

Error 1: Not establishing a great enough sense of urgency
Error 2: Not creating a powerful enough guiding coalition
Error 3: Lacking a Vision
Error 4: Undercommunicating the Vision by a factor of 10
Error 5: Not removing obstacles to the new Vision
Error 6: Not systematically planning for and creating short-term wins
Error 7: Declaring victory too soon
Error 8: Not anchoring changes in the organization's culture

ASSESSING READINESS TO CHANGE

Here is another model on change and security which re-emphasizes some common factors that play a role in perceived security. For those involved in initiating or implementing a change programme, knowledge of the perceived security needs to be gained to aid communications and gain support from those affected.

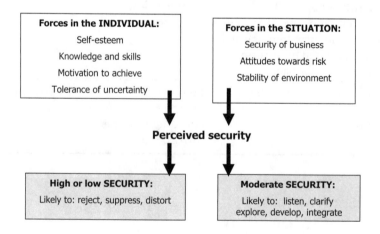

FOUR TYPES OF CHANGE 'JOURNEYS'

Fine tuning	*Definition*

Fine tuning

Definition
- Streamlining/small-scale change

Example
- Work process simplification
- Cost reductions

Outcomes to support change
- Communicate changes
- Training/retraining

Building

Definition
- 'Clean slate' journey

Example
- Greenfield start-up
- New joint venture
- New department/function

Outcomes to support change
- Communicate vision and values
- Define new roles and responsibilities and identify new skill sets
- Design/develop new organization structure and new HR philosophy
- Align organization to values, vision, etc.

Transforming

Definition
- Planned holistic organizational change for the enterprise

Example
- Entering new markets/repositioning marketing strategies
- Corporate self-renewal or redefining strategic intent
- Redefining/reviewing core competencies

Outcomes to support change

- Communicate vision and values and create ownership strategies
- Create new performance/reward structures and identify required skills
- Provide tools for management to facilitate new organization structure
- Develop training curriculum and conduct training

| Crisis | *Definition* |

- 'Reacting' to survive due to impact of internal/external forces

Example

- High turnover in organization
- Downsizing
- Decreased consumer confidence
- Change in market perception
- Decreased market share

Outcomes to support change

- Identify the stakeholders and communicate what is going on
- Redesign organization to match structure/jobs/teams
- Plan training

FOUR KEY CHANGE COMPONENTS

Regardless of the change, the following four key components of project management, enablement projects, executive leadership and business ownership must be undertaken by the dedicated change management team. The tasks in each of these groups are shown below:

Programme management: Planning for moving 'as is' organization to the desired 'to be' state.

Project management tasks for the change management team:

- Create and support effective project teams
- Monitor pace and scope of transformation
- Ensure integration of concurrent journey efforts
- Identify issues to manage risk of client investment
- Provide guidance using frameworks and methodologies

Enablement projects: Critical products developed which provide individuals and organization with knowledge, skills, tools, frameworks and support to perform their work successfully.

Tasks for the change management team:

- Design and development of organization, processes and jobs
- Design and implement communication strategy
- Align HR processes with organizational design
- Design and implement education and training programmes

Executive leadership: Sponsorship of change by key executives, illustrating to entire organization management's commitment to change effort.

Executive leadership tasks for the change management team:

- Create shared vision and leadership agenda
- Communicate vision and agenda to market change initiatives
- Facilitate executive decision making for critical steps
- Maintain and support sponsors' focus on change effort

Business ownership: Ownership and commitment to change experienced by all individuals throughout the organization.

Business ownership tasks for the change management team:

- Utilize change agents/champions at all levels
- Pilot enablement projects to increase awareness, excitement and organizational commitment
- Facilitate transfer of knowledge from journey team to business sector implementation teams
- Facilitate team decisions and provide with tools for self-management
- Manage resistance through communication and involvement

THE EVOLUTION AND REVOLUTION CURVE

Larry Greiner's model shows growth as a series of changes forced by crises. In Phase 1, called Growth Through Creativity, Greiner describes a Crisis of Leadership. At this stage, a youthful organization's founder must begin to delegate authority and accept non-founder managers. Surviving the first crisis propels the organization into Phase 2, Growth Through Direction, where the crisis is one of autonomy. Phases 3, 4 and 5, respectively, describe growth through delegation, coordination and collaboration.

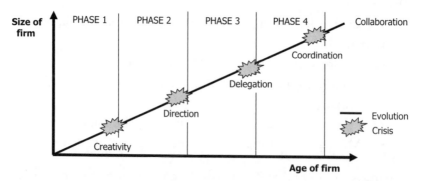

Reprinted with permission of *Harvard Business Review*. An exhibit from 'Evolution and revolution as organizations grow' by Dr Larry E. Greiner, Volume 50, Number 4 (July/August 1972). Copyright by the President and Fellows of Harvard College, all rights reserved.

KEY ACTIVITIES FOR SUCCESSFUL IMPLEMENTATION

Key management activities for managing a change process are:

- Provide help to face up to the change.
- Avoid overorganizing.
- Ensure early involvement.
- Regularly communicate with all involved.
- Work at gaining commitment.
- Turn perceptions of 'threats' into opportunities.

FORCE-FIELD ANALYSIS

The principle behind a force-field analysis is that it identifies the forces that facilitate or inhibit change within an organization. By assessing these factors it may be possible to change the equilibrium and affect a change. The concept of the force field model came from Kurt Lewin more than 50 years ago. These factors can be listed on each side of the equilibrium line to understand the driving forces and identify resisting forces which need to be removed.

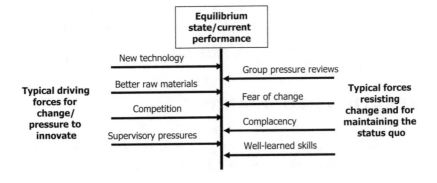

CATEGORIES OF RESISTANCE BEHAVIOUR

Reactions to change can be categorized as one of four groups: ranging from those who openly resist the change and may even try to prevent it to those who merely go along with the change but may not be committed to its success.

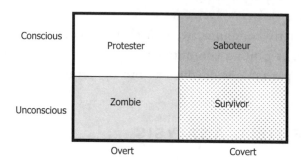

- Protesters openly make their objections known to the organization and colleagues; however, once issues are identified they can be considered and managed.
- Zombies have no strong opinion and are happy to go along with any proposed changes without offering any constructive comment.
- Saboteurs like to show that the old ways were fine and openly finds fault with any new systems or process change and seek opportunities to make the change fail.
- Survivors accept the change and make best use of any new situation for their own advantage.

REACTIONS TO CHANGE

In looking at people's reaction to dealing with change four categories of behaviour type are described below.

'Guardians'

- Need data and proof that it really will work.
- Want to know what is expected of them – how their job/responsibilities will be affected.
- Want to see all the steps between now and the future vision.
- Want to know who will be responsible for each step.
- Want things decided and clear.
- Have difficulty with uncertainties.
- Feel overwhelmed by too many possible directions.
- Focus on practical requirements and results.

'Artisans'

- Want to plunge into change immediately, see how it goes, make course adjustments along the way.
- Need to take action, little tolerance for analysis.
- Enjoy risks, respond to crises and changes of the moment.
- Are energized by the unexpected and the different.
- Are irritated by long-term change with planning and timelines.
- Like 'how to' problems not 'why' questions.
- Focus on the immediate effects.

'Idealists'

- Experience change initially as a loss – have attachments to people, places, objects
- Have great loyalty to people and the way the organization has been
- Identify with people caught up in change – especially the negatively affected

- Want those in charge to listen to their opinions
- When benefits are seen and people needs met, they are enthusiastic and energetic in helping others deal with change
- Focus on impact on people

'Rationals'

- Want to be involved in planning change and designing the logistics.
- Create plans based on the wider perspective.
- See almost all change as improvement.
- Are bored by doing things the same old way.
- If excluded from planning or don't see the logic, can become detached and take on the role of critical cynic.
- Focus on the logical systems involved.

CHAPTER 3

CUSTOMER RELATIONSHIP MANAGEMENT

*O*rganizations have to recognize, respond to and satisfy the requirements of their customers if they intend to stay in business and benefit from future growth. Once the key phrase was 'customer satisfaction', followed by a period where companies aimed to 'delight' their customers. More recently there has been a move to managing customer expectations which suggests closer contact with the customer base through proactive communications aimed at gaining a closer understanding of their present and future customers' requirements. In line with these developments has emerged customer relationship management (CRM) as a formal strategy aimed at capturing, storing and analysing customer information in order to learn more about customers' needs and behaviours and develop a stronger relationship with them. For some suppliers this has meant orientating the organization around meeting these identified customer requirements.

Customer relationship management aims at knowing, understanding and meeting customer requirements by encouraging customers to feel part of the supplier's business through a number of techniques including listening to customers through complaints procedures and meetings; learning about their requirements and their business needs; undertaking market research and concentrating on providing customer services with customer culturally aware staff. In this chapter are models to illustrate the benefits of listening to and observing customers, and communications and customer-care training. These also feature in one model which brings this together as part of an integrated CRM.

Companies use this customer knowledge not just to react to the immediate feedback but also as part of their longer-term approach to marketing, balancing the marketing 4 Ps to the customers' needs (see also Chapter 7). Indeed understanding the customers' needs and wants involves a number of areas of management covered in this book, for example: in finding out the views of the customer (Chapter 7); in many predictions from the research (Chapters 18 and 4); in considering necessary changes arising from the customer feedback (Chapter 11); and finally in addressing comments on price (Chapter 5).

Many companies believe that adopting a customer relationship management strategy is not an option as understanding customers' needs and behaviours can lead to stronger customer relationships which provides a greater level of customer satisfaction, increased revenue generation and profit contribution. The time and effort needed to make CRM work should not be underestimated although it does lend itself to the use of technology to improve communications, increase efficiencies and manage databases in recording and disseminating customer information in the supplier's business. There are also natural benefits from having a CRM system linked into the organization's marketing function. In order to obtain and retain customers there has been much research to examine the time and effort required by companies to follow the strategy of 'hunting', i.e. seeking new customers or taking business away from competitors. On the other hand 'farming' is developing the existing customer base to encourage repeat business and brand loyalty; needless to say that farming is many times more efficient than hunting although it is unlikely to be a sustainable long-term business strategy as expansion is more closely linked to extending the geographic market base.

A CUSTOMER-FOCUSED ORGANIZATION

This model illustrates that in order to create a customer-focused organization there are a number of elements that need to be addressed.

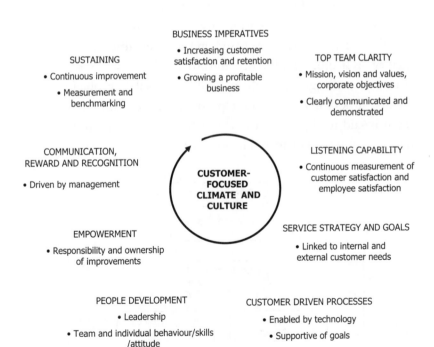

Model from Sarah Cook, *Customer Care*, 2000. Reproduced with permission of Kogan Page Limited.

CUSTOMER DESIRES

Understanding customer desires, even if these are aspirations, can help in the delivery of goods and services. These desires can be categorized as 'MoSoCoW'.

Must haves – a 100% requirement.
Should haves – a genuine requirement although not business critical.
Could haves – extra features.
Would have – nice to have if customer could afford it.

THE POWER OF EXISTING CUSTOMERS

Companies are better able to maximize both their sales overheads and resources if they can develop repeat and multiple business relationships with their existing customers. Customers' reasons for initial purchase decision are based on both **tangible** (performance, quality, reliability and cost) and **intangible** (sense of caring, courtesy, willingness to help, ability to solve problems, etc.) factors. In looking at a specific product, in the automobile industry it is said to typically cost as much as 17 times more to attract new customers than to retain its existing customer base.

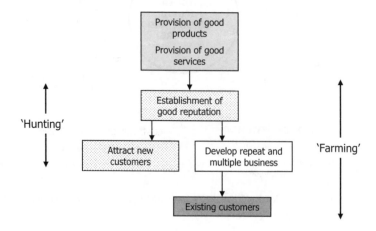

THE SERVICE/PROFIT CHAIN

The model below links employee relationship and how they are treated with employee and customer retention and profit.

OBSERVING CUSTOMER BEHAVIOUR

Accepting that it is a business imperative to look at the organization's performance, the competition and to test the customer experience being offered allows simple, everyday benchmarking to be undertaken. Stepping into the 'customer's shoes' provides an understanding of what the competition can offer, why customers choose them, lessons for the organization and helps identify any new standards that have to be set.

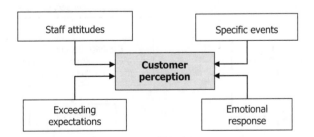

From Steve Morris and Graham Willcocks' *Connecting with your Customers*, 1996, Pearson Education Limited. Reproduced with permission.

CUSTOMER INTERACTION

This model suggests that customer information of their contact preference can be used to maximize the value of each type of interaction and still meet customer requirements.

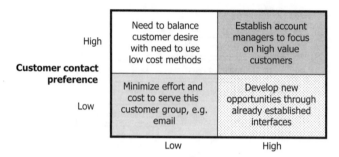

LISTENING TO CUSTOMERS

A number of organizations not only listen to their customers but also undertake a systematic benchmarking process in order to identify areas for improvement according to the best practices they can find. Benchmarking helps to identify differences in processes and performance and can result in an action plan to bring about changes.

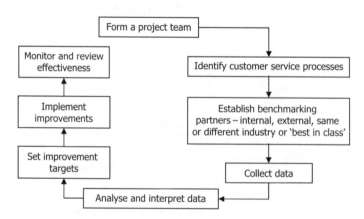

Model from Sarah Cook, *Customer Care*, 2000. Reproduced with permission of Kogan Page Limited.

There are four methods of benchmarking that can be used:

- Against direct competition,
- Against parallel industries,
- Against other parts of the same organization, and
- Against different industries or 'best in class' organizations.

CUSTOMER CARE TRAINING

National standards are set for some National Vocational Qualifications (NVQ), in the UK to show competence in particular skill areas. For customer services these standards have been developed by a customer services led body under the sponsorship of the Government's Education Department. The five main parts of this NVQ are shown below:

1. Maintain reliable customer service	• Maintain records relating to customer service. • Organize own work pattern to respond to the needs of customers. • Make use of networks.
2. Communicate with customers	• Select information for communication to customer. • Facilitate flow of information between organization and customer. • Adapt methods of communication to the customer.
3. Develop positive working relationship with customers	• Respond to the needs and feelings expressed by the customer. • Present positive personal image to customer. • Balance the needs of customers and organization.

4. Solve problems on behalf of customers	• Identify and interpret problems affecting customer. • Generate solutions on behalf of customers. • Take action to deliver solutions.
5. Initiate and evaluate change to improve service to customers	• Obtain and use feedback from customer. • Communicate patterns and trends in customer service within the organization. • Contribute to the evaluation of changes designed to improve services to customers. • Initiate changes in response to customer requirements.

COMMUNICATIONS WITH STAKEHOLDERS

At the beginning of developing a customer service strategy there is also a need for a communications strategy focused on delivering a constant message in both content and format to all stakeholders.

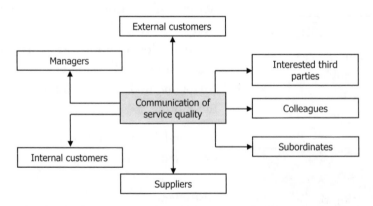

From Sarah Cook, *Customer Care*, 2000. Reproduced with permission of Kogan Page Limited.

CUSTOMER BEHAVIOUR

This 2 × 2 matrix illustrates the relationship between product or services differences and the involvement in the customer base. This also shows the affect of business competition for customers and their response. A good understanding of customer behaviours can provide marketing with a knowledge that can be used to sell the product or services.

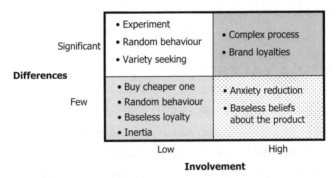

Model reproduced with kind permission of Professor Henry Assael, from *Consumer Behaviour and Marketing Action*, PWS-Kent Publishing, Boston, 1992.

INTEGRATED CUSTOMER RELATIONSHIP MANAGEMENT

Linkages between customer, marketing and quality are key factors in the development of a holistic customer relationship approach. It is suggested that the customer is evolving from a web-based technology customer case programme into a business-value enterprise as organizations consider customers as important assets that need to be developed and nurtured.

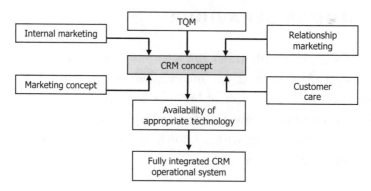

This model was published in *Marketing Made Simple* by Geoff Lancaster and Paul Reynolds, 2002, page 131. Reproduced with permission. Copyright Elsevier.

PARETO ANALYSIS

It has to be said that Pareto theory, named after an Italian economist, is a general concept which has many uses. From Pareto's studies a 80%–20% division was found as a general finding and has been used in a number of business areas ever since. For example, in stock valuation where the most expensive 20% of stock represents 80% of the total stock value. (Also known as the 80/20 rule.)

Looking at CRM it is often found that the top 20% of customer accounts equate to 80% of a company's income and correspondingly 80% of customers only contribute 20% to the business. On this basis, with such investigation, it is possible to identify the key customers and arrange products/services, etc. to meet their requirements.

CHAPTER 4

DECISION MAKING AND PROBLEM RESOLUTION

*I*ncluded in this chapter is a selection of models aimed at assisting managers and indeed organizations in decision making, which is usually linked to problem solution to aid performance enhancement. The topics of decision making and problem resolution may be tackled as a reaction to internal and external influences or, on the other hand, as a proactive approach to lean thinking and continuous improvement such as the 4M checklist and the adoption of Rudyard Kipling's 'Six honest serving-men' as an aid to systematically question operations with a view to making business improvements. There are a number of different styles of decision making from which to choose, centred around the involvement of other people in the decision-making process. The advantages and disadvantages of these are provided.

Apart from using a problem resolution process to resolve problems it can also give rise to innovative solutions and the use of creativity and its relationship with innovation. An extensive methodology in this area comes from the Russian 'TRIZ' approach to inventive problem solving which seeks to transpose a problem into other already known problems and suggests that the solutions to these can equally be transportable across industries, disciplines and products. This can give rise to innovation and help identify stages of evolution for products and services. Another useful management or consultancy tool in support of problem resolution is the Ishakawa or 'fishbone' diagram which can be very powerful when used in groups to identify common problem issues and then seek solutions to each significant problem area. Like most tools in this book the strength of this 'cause and effect fishbone model' comes from the use of visualization which promotes a shared understanding of the issues and leads to ultimate diagnosis and group proposed solutions to the problem. While the fishbone approach is generally centred around set areas; typically materials, resources, machinery, etc. another free-form method applicable at group or individual level to creative thinking is the use of mind mapping. This is a highly visual graphical technique that uses colours, pictures, numbers and networked linkages to stimulate arranging ideas and their interconnections which develops related thoughts that may lead to creative ideas.

Pressures which impact on the decision-making process come from two sources: first, from the organization, as making the 'right' decision may be regarded as key to business success, and second, from the complexity and perhaps time available to assimilate the necessary information on which to make a firm decision. Where problems are identified and their resolution leads to change which impacts on the organization as a whole or its staff – entire or in part – Chapter 2 offers some models and notes in implementing change and managing any resistance to it.

It should be noted that over the last decade or so, with a move towards a closer supplier/buyer collaborative working arrangement, many businesses have established a problem resolution process prior to any problems being identified so that when a problem does emerge both parties know what processes they will use to address it. In addition, as part of customer care training, many organizations are encouraged to 'step into the customers' shoes' to identify and solve problems on behalf of their customers. Decision making and problem resolution should be considered to be not just a process to be deployed when issues need to be addressed but also a proactive way to promote innovation and encourage creativity within the organization.

DECISION MAKING, PROBLEM SOLVING AND CONTINGENCY PLANNING

This model shows a suggested linkage between the causes of past problems and an understanding of possible future problems which can provide information on which to undertake effective decision making.

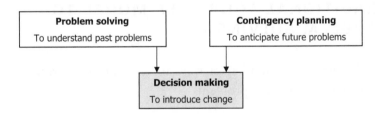

STEPS IN PROBLEM ANALYSIS AND DECISION MAKING

An iterative process is shown in this model of problem analysis and decision making. The model offers a number of possible starting positions (★) depending on the level of information known about the problem.

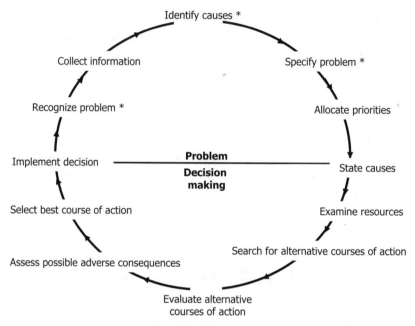

This model was published in *The Management Task* by Rob Dixon, 2002. Copyright Elsevier.

TRADITIONAL FOUR STEP MODEL TO PROBLEM SOLVING

While there are a number of ways to solve problems some solutions give rise to new problems.

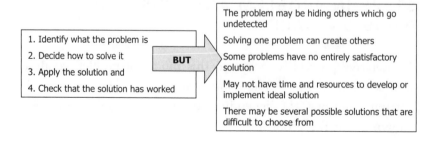

PROBLEM SOLVING PROCESS FROM INDUSTRIAL MANAGEMENT/WORK STUDY

This approach to problem solving is taken from Industrial Management/Work Study from the mid to late 1970s; however, its concept still remains valid today. Previously there was often a focus on the immediate problem resolution with less thought applied to the maintenance and longer-term implications of such decisions. Today problem solving in business now considers to a far greater extent the longer-term product through life costs of such decisions.

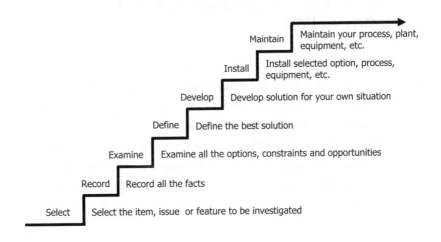

Maintain — Maintain your process, plant, equipment, etc.

Install — Install selected option, process, equipment, etc.

Develop — Develop solution for your own situation

Define — Define the best solution

Examine — Examine all the options, constraints and opportunities

Record — Record all the facts

Select — Select the item, issue or feature to be investigated

CAUSE AND EFFECT (FISHBONE) DIAGRAM

The cause and effect diagram was devised by Kaoru Ishikawa, who pioneered quality management processes in the Kawasaki shipyards. The cause and effect diagram explores all the possible or actual causes (or inputs) resulting in a single effect (or output).

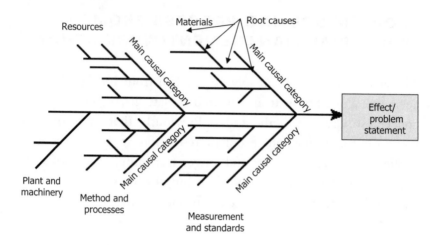

RELATIONSHIP BETWEEN INNOVATION AND CREATIVITY

This model shows the relationship between creativity and innovation where creativity may be impractical, extreme or just plain wild, while innovation on the other hand must be practical, results oriented and realistic. However, often, successful innovations emerge from the refinement of creative outlandish ideas although research suggests that on average the quantity input is more than 60 ideas before a single quality output innovation is put into practice.

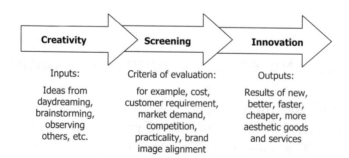

Reproduced with kind permission of Professor Simon Majaro from *Managing Ideas for Profit: the creative gap*, McGraw-Hill, 1988.

MODELS OF DECISION MAKING: TYPES OF UNCERTAINTY

This matrix shows the relationship between the lack of objectives and the lack of clarity of causal relationships and shows the style of decision making that managers then adopt.

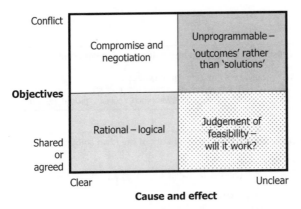

Model from Richard Turton in *Behaviour in a Business Context*, page 188, 1991. Reproduced with kind permission of Springer Science and Business Media.

DECISION-MAKING PRESSURES ON THE MANAGER

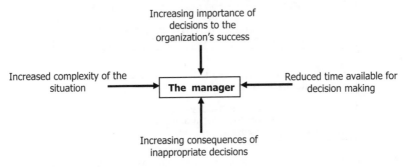

From Dr Tim Hannagan, *Management Concepts and Practices*, 2005. Reproduced with permission of Pearson Education.

DECISION MAKING – BERNHARD-WALSH MODEL

This step-by-step approach is adapted from the text of Linda Bernhard and Michelle Walsh. Its strength is its logical approach which can be used in a range of business settings and at different levels within an organization.

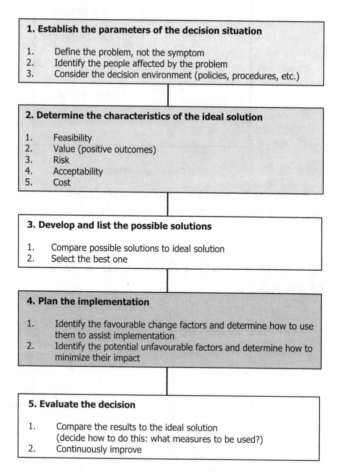

1. Establish the parameters of the decision situation

1. Define the problem, not the symptom
2. Identify the people affected by the problem
3. Consider the decision environment (policies, procedures, etc.)

2. Determine the characteristics of the ideal solution

1. Feasibility
2. Value (positive outcomes)
3. Risk
4. Acceptability
5. Cost

3. Develop and list the possible solutions

1. Compare possible solutions to ideal solution
2. Select the best one

4. Plan the implementation

1. Identify the favourable change factors and determine how to use them to assist implementation
2. Identify the potential unfavourable factors and determine how to minimize their impact

5. Evaluate the decision

1. Compare the results to the ideal solution
   (decide how to do this: what measures to be used?)
2. Continuously improve

Adapted from book *Leadership – the key to professionalization of nursing*, by Linda Anne Bernhard and Michelle Walsh, 3rd Edition, page 134. Published by Mosby, St Louis.

CONTINUOUS IMPROVEMENT METHODS – THE 4M CHECKLIST

Man (operator)

1. Does he follow standards?
2. Is his/her work efficiency acceptable?
3. Is he/she problem conscious?
4. Is he/she responsible/accountable?
5. Is he/she qualified?
6. Is he/she experienced?
7. Is he/she willing to improve?
8. Does he/she maintain good human relations?
9. Is he/she healthy?

Machine (facilities)

1. Does it meet production requirements?
2. Does it meet process capabilities?
3. Is the lubrication adequate?
4. Is the maintenance inspection adequate?
5. Is the operation stopped often due to mechanical trouble?
6. Does it meet precision requirements?
7. Does it make any unusual noises?
8. Is the layout adequate?
9. Are there enough machines/facilities?
10. Is everything in good working order?

Material

1. Are there any mistakes in volume?
2. Are there any mistakes in grade?

3. Are there any mistakes in brand name?
4. Are there impurities mixed in?
5. Is the inventory level adequate?
6. Is there any waste in the material?
7. Is the handling adequate?
8. Is the work-in-process abandoned?
9. Is the layout adequate?
10. Is the quality standard adequate?

Method (of operation)

1. Are the work standards adequate?
2. Is the work standard upgraded?
3. Is it a safe method?
4. Is it a method that ensures a good product?
5. Is it an efficient method?
6. Is the sequence of work adequate?
7. Is the setup adequate?
8. Are the temperatures and humidity adequate?
9. Are the lighting and ventilation adequate?
10. Is there adequate contact with the previous and next processes?

★ **MEASUREMENT** is often added to create the '5M checklist', see also fishbone diagram.

DECISION-MAKING STYLES

Different-decision making styles have been identified together with the associated advantages and disadvantages of each one.

Consensus

All team members get a chance to air their opinions and must ultimately agree on the outcomes.

Advantages
- Produces innovative and creative solutions, elicits commitment from all team members to implement the decision.
- Uses the resources from all team members.
- Future decision making is enhanced.
- Useful in making serious decisions where team commitment is needed.

Disadvantages
- Takes a lot of time and psychological energy.
- Needs a high level of members skills.
- Time pressure must be minimal.

Majority rule

Majority decision making is a democracy in action. The team votes the majority wins.

Advantages
- Can be used when there is no time for full consensus decision making or the decision is not as important and consensus is not necessary.
- Can be used when 100% commitment is not critical.

Disadvantages
- Usually leave an alienated minority – a time bomb for future team effectiveness.
- Important talents of minority team members may be snubbed.
- Not full commitment.
- Not full team interaction.

Minority rule

Usually takes the form of a subcommittee making recommendations to the decision-making body.

Advantages
- Can be used when everyone cannot be got together to make a decision; when time is tight or when only a few members have the expertise.
- Also when broader team commitment is not required.

Disadvantages
- Does not utilize the full talents of the team members.
- No broad commitment for decision implementation.
- Unresolved conflict may harm team effectiveness.

Averaging

The epitome of compromise. Team members haggle, bargain and negotiate to reach a middle position. Usually no one is happy except the moderates on the team.

Advantages
- Individual errors and extreme positions tend to cancel each other out.
- Better than authority rule with no discussion.
- Usually the team average is no worse than letting the experts make the decision.

Disadvantages
- Opinions of the least knowledgeable members annul the opinions of the most knowledgeable.
- Little team involvement in decision making so commitment to the decision will be weak.

Expert

Find an expert and listen to them. Then follow their recommendations.

Advantages

- Can be useful when the expertise of one member is greater than the rest.
- Useful if little is to be gained from discussion and membership action in implementing is slight.

Disadvantages

- Questions arise on who the expert is.
- No commitment to build for implementing the decision.
- Advantages of team interaction are lost.
- Knowledge and skills of other team members is lost and they may resort to sabotage if there is disagreement.

Authority rule without discussion

This usually is where there is no room for discussion, and the decisions are handed down from on high. Trust is often killed in this method particularly if the team leader tried to fool people that there views count.

Advantages

- Simple, useful for routine decisions or where little time is available.
- Works well when team members expect to be delegated to and the leader makes decisions.
- Also useful if team members lack the information to make an informed decision.

Disadvantages

- One person cannot be a good resource for all decisions.
- Team interaction is lost.
- No commitment is developed for implementation. Sabotage may result if team members are not used.

Authority rule with discussion

This is participative decision making. People have an input into the decision-making process, but it is clear that the leader will make the decision. The leader must make it clear how people's input has affected the decision.

Advantages

- Gains commitment from all team members and develops a lively discussion.
- Uses skills and knowledge of all the team.
- Has clarity over who is ultimately accountable for the decision.

Disadvantages

- Requires good communication skills on the part of team members.
- Requires a leader willing to make decisions and be accountable.

Reprinted with permission of the publisher, from *Why Teams Don't Work. What Went Wrong and How to Make it Right*, copyright © (2000) by Harvey Robbins and Michael Finley, Berrett-Koehler Publishers, Inc., San Francisco, CA. All rights reserved. www.bkconnection.com

CONTINUOUS IMPROVEMENT METHODS

Using the 'Six honest serving-men' approach from Kipling provides a framework for examining approaches to improvement by questioning current or proposed operations. As an approach it can be used as the basis for individual investigation of problems, as a framework for interviews and also as a basis and tool within a facilitated workshop environment.

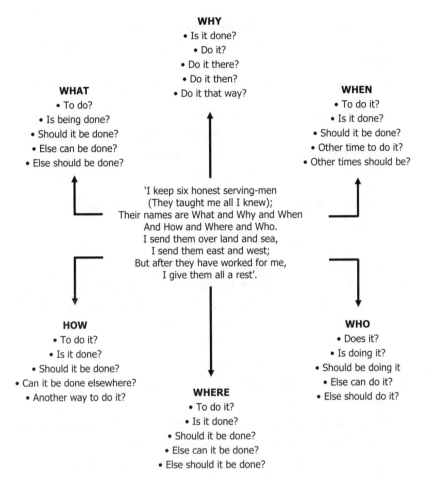

WHY
- Is it done?
- Do it?
- Do it there?
- Do it then?
- Do it that way?

WHAT
- To do?
- Is being done?
- Should it be done?
- Else can be done?
- Else should be done?

WHEN
- To do it?
- Is it done?
- Should it be done?
- Other time to do it?
- Other times should be?

'I keep six honest serving-men
(They taught me all I knew);
Their names are What and Why and When
And How and Where and Who.
I send them over land and sea,
I send them east and west;
But after they have worked for me,
I give them all a rest'.

HOW
- To do it?
- Is it done?
- Should it be done?
- Can it be done elsewhere?
- Another way to do it?

WHO
- Does it?
- Is doing it?
- Should be doing it
- Else can do it?
- Else should do it?

WHERE
- To do it?
- Is it done?
- Should it be done?
- Else can it be done?
- Else should it be done?

Text of the 'Six honest serving-men' by Rudyard Kipling, from 'The Elephant's Child' in the *Just So Stories*, published in 1904.

CONTINUOUS IMPROVEMENT METHODS

A suggested six-step approach to continuous improvement:

1. Identify the work you do . . . your product
2. Identify who your work is for . . . your customer
3. What do you need to do your work and from whom. . . . ?

4. Map the process . . . identify areas of improvement

5. Mistake proof the process . . . introduce prevention, reduce delays

6. Measure quality and cycle times . . . set improvement goals

Some companies benefit from a systematic approach to continuous improvement set out in a continuous improvement plan. The following ten key points may be useful for those charged with this task:

1. Continuous means ongoing and as such the process never stops.

2. Once a year, have an outsider review your business as they can often see what you cannot.

3. Do the simple and cheap things first and quickly. Concentrating on what is referred to as the 'low hanging fruit' builds credibility, momentum and commitment within the organization. It may also give you practice and lessons which may be useful in the future.

4. Do not try to do it all at once. Set up a plan and do it in stages.

5. Try to work on two or three top priorities. Working on more than that can diffuse effort, energy and resources.

6. Celebrate, acknowledge and reward accomplishment. This creates a positive environment for improvement.

7. Make certain that improvements involve the organization's customers with a focus on delivering increasing value.

8. Look for breakthrough improvements. Some small improvements can turn out to be major improvements. Often these breakthroughs are not known until tried. Be aware that breakthroughs will exist and always look for them.

9. Develop a continuous improvement system that works for the specific business. Do not copy others without trying first in a small way – what works for one business may not work for another.

10. Look inside your industry at the competition and seek out examples of best practice. Competitors can often show you a better way and if it works after testing then adopt, adapt and improve it!

NATURE OF KNOWLEDGE

This matrix shows that knowledge comes from either our own efforts or that of others and falls into one of two categories of explicit or tacit knowledge.

		Explicit	Tacit
Source	Self	Books we have read Reports we have written Advice given to colleagues	Green fingers Rules of thumb – intuition, heuristics Unarticulated
	Group	Disseminated knowledge	Apprenticeship Unarticulated

Knowledge

FINDING AND ANALYSING PROBLEMS IN AN INNOVATIVE SYSTEM

If an innovative system is not performing, the following steps can be applied to examine the issues and help lead to a solution.

Step 1
What is the problem and what goal are you not reaching?
Consider: fit, speed, cost

Step 2

What part of the innovative system is the source of the problem?

Could this be idea generation, funding or development.

Step 3

What management systems could be contributing to the problem?

Examine project management systems, business management systems and senior management behaviour

Step 4

How do we change the management systems that are contributing to the problem?

From James Christiansen, *Building the Innovative Organization*, 2000, Macmillan Business. Reproduced with permission of Palgrave Macmillan.

MANAGING INNOVATION

Successful innovators acquire and accumulate technical resources and managerial capabilities over time and organizations needs to regard innovation less as a lottery and more as a process which can be continuously improved. Holding such a view the authors of this model suggest that it is possible for organizations to construct a checklist and a crude blueprint for effective innovation management. Their suggested process is given below which outlines the activities which need to be addressed during each of the five stages.

Phase 1: Signal processing

Scan the environment for technological, market, regulatory and other signals.

Scan forward in time.

Collect and filter signals from background 'noise'.

Process signals into relevant information for decision making.

Phase 2: Strategy

Analyse, choose, plan and assess signals in terms of possibilities for action.

Link with overall business strategy and with core knowledge base competencies.

Assess cost and benefits of different options and then select priority options.

Agree and commit resources and plan next steps.

Phase 3: Resourcing

Procure solution(s) which realize strategic decisions.

Invest in-house through R&D activities, use existing R&D or acquire via external R&D contacts.

License or buy-in and consider technology transfer.

Phase 4: Implementation

Develop to maturity and in parallel undertake technical development and development of the relevant market. For product development this will be the external customer market.

For process development this is the internal user market. Both will require 'change management'.

Launch and commission and provide after-sales support.

Phase 5: Learning and re-innovation

Learn from the experience.

Reproduced with permission of John Wiley & Sons. Adapted from Joe Tidd, John Bessant and Keith Pavitt, *Managing Innovation*, 2001.

FACTORS THAT UNDERPIN A FIRM'S ABILITY TO RECOGNIZE THE POTENTIAL OF AN INNOVATION

There are four elements that inhibit a company's ability to recognize the potential of an innovation. First, the way it collects and processes information which may be a function of its strategies, organizational structures, and people; second, its local environment; third, its dominant management logic; and finally the type of innovation in question.

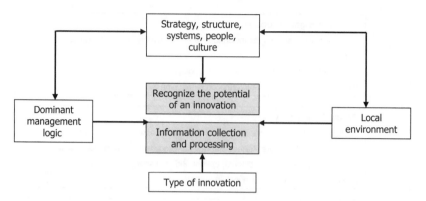

Reproduced with permission of Oxford University Press, from *Innovation Management* by Dr Allan Afuah, 2003.

ROADBLOCKS TO ADOPTING AN INNOVATION

Clearly this model shows that between the potential innovation and its successful implementation are two sets of roadblocks which need to be addressed. In this model the innovation is recognized by the company as being either economic, organizational or both and is likely to result in a required change for the company on implementation.

Reproduced with permission of Oxford University Press, from *Innovation Management* by Dr Allan Afuah, 2003.

INNOVATION MANAGEMENT MATRIX

The matrix below shows the interaction between management and the process of innovation in a company. The process of innovation has inputs which are transformed to create outputs: new products. Effective innovation management is needed to develop the creative ideas of individuals within the company together with the freedom to develop them.

		Inputs	Innovation Transformation	Outputs
Management			*Investment in innovation* ← →	
	Corporate	• Screening procedures and acceptance criteria	• Use of informal product development procedures	• Strategy: what new products are wanted
	Team	• Multi-disciplinary teams for early assessment and specification	• Team composition and organization • Responsibility and accountability for development decisions	• Hand over responsibility or • Continued involvement throughout product life cycle
	Individual	• Creative freedom • Access to decision makers	• Involvement, commitment and 'ownership'/ championing of new products	• Recognition and reward for success

Reproduced with kind permission of Dr Mike Baxter, from *Product Design: a practical guide to systematic methods of new product development*, Nelson Thornes (Publishers) Ltd, 1995.

CREATIVITY IN STRATEGY

A conceptual model of three levels of the firm and their tasks which can be enriched through creativity.

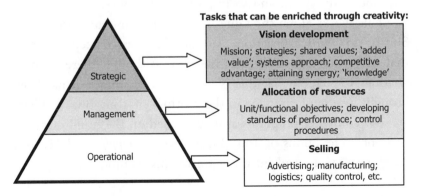

CREATIVE THINKING – 'MIND MAPPING'

This tool is effective at an individual and team level, it works by giving your brain a central focus and structure within which to record and remember information as well as develop ideas.

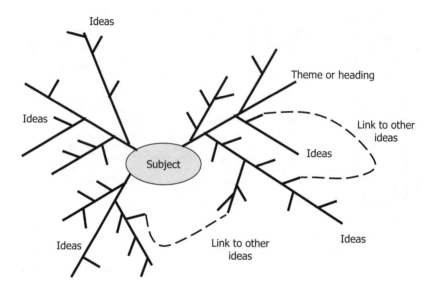

It increases the probability of creative association and integration; it can encourage humour when it is used in a team, taking you out of the norm and so improving creativity.

This works along the same lines as the cause and effect tool. Similar to word association this tool develops related thoughts that may lead to a truly creative idea. Although there is some writings to suggest that this is a very old technique it has been brought into modern usage in the writings of Tony Buzan. There are also computer programs available based on the mind mapping concept. (The books of Tony Buzan, *Mind Mapping* and *Use your Head*, provide a good introduction to this technique.)

DISCOVERY

'Discovery consists of seeing what everybody has seen and thinking what nobody has thought.'

Albert Nagyrapolt

'The real voyage of discovery consists not in seeking new landscapes but in seeing with new eyes.'

Marcel Proust, French novelist

INNOVATION

Innovation is the use of new technologies and market knowledge to offer a new product or service that customers will want.

The product is considered to be 'new' when it never existed in that market before . . . or when its costs are lower; or its attributes are improved; or it has new attributes it never had before. An innovation can have two types of impact on a company; since knowledge underpins an organization's ability to offer new products, a change in knowledge changes such ability. On the other hand innovation results in superior products (lower cost, better features, etc.) it can be classified as rendering old products non-competitive. These organizational and competitive definitions are linked to the model below.

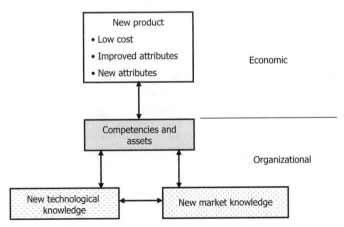

Reproduced with permission of Oxford University Press, from *Innovation Management* by Dr Allan Afuah, 2003.

IMPLEMENTING NEW IDEAS

While new thoughts may present new solutions to problems, a traditional response in many organizations is that new ideas also bring about change and often result in the following reactions . . .

- 'We've never done it like that'
- 'We're not really ready for it'
- 'We're doing all right anyway'
- 'That doesn't sound very practical'
- 'It's against company policy'
- 'It's not up to us'
- 'It won't work here'
- 'We tried it before'
- 'It cost too much'

Recognizing these barriers will at least allow for the implementation of new ideas to address these concerns and remove any such barriers. Implementing new ideas is often linked to 'change management'; see also thoughts on Nicholo Machiavelli.

TEORIYA RESHENIYA IZOBREATATELSKIKH ZADATCH – 'TRIZ'

Azerbaijani scientist Genrich Saulovitch Altshuller (1926–1998) was the originator of TRIZ (Russian for 'The Theory of Inventive Problem Solving'). Altshuller together with a team of engineers analysed over 2.5 million patents worldwide in an attempt to understand what made them innovative and successful. They discovered that:

- The same problems and solutions appear again and again often in different industries and sciences.
- Most truly innovative patents resolve a contradiction and can be used outside the field where they were developed.

- There is a finite number of basic trends which govern all technical evolution – knowledge of these trends allows us to predict the future.

The 'TRIZ' approach is to build upon the above understanding, so that it is possible to relate your problem onto the world' problems to see how others have solved this and then to examine if this solution can in turn be used on your original problem.

Ultimate ideality is when there is all benefit and no costs or harm. This is called ideal solution or ideal final result.

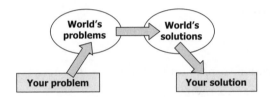

The 'TRIZ' overall philosophy is to increase 'ideality', increase benefits, solve contradictions and reduce costs and harms.

The key parts of TRIZ are:

Functionality:	What do we want (why, when and where)? If we already have a system does it work? What are the problems with it?
Resources:	Recognizing that everything is a resource to be used
Ideality:	Seeking solutions which have maximum benefits and minimum harm (cost, complexity, damage, danger, reduced range of uses)
Contradictions:	Understanding what events, features or actions get worse when you identify an improvement
Trends of evolution:	Understanding current and predicted evolution

A LIST OF WAYS TO IMPROVE SOMETHING

It is said that some of the major problems in modern living are too much noise, too much information, too many decisions, too much complexity, together with a general lack of quality and reliability. Addressing these problems in connection with your idea should produce welcome improvements to it.

- Simplify – remove complexity
- Apply to new use
- Automate
- Reduce cost
- Make easier to use, understand
- Reduce fear to own, use
- Make safer
- Give more performance, capacity
- Make faster, less waiting
- Provide more durability, reliability
- Give better appearance
- Create more acceptance by others
- Add features, functions
- Integrate functions
- Make more flexible, versatile
- Make lighter weight – or heavier
- Make smaller – or larger
- Make more powerful
- Reduce or eliminate drawbacks, bad side-effects
- Make more elegant
- Give better shape, design, style
- Provide better sensory appeal (taste, feel, look, smell, sound)
- Provide better psychological appeal (understandable, acceptable)

- Provide better emotional appeal (happy, satisfying, enjoyable, fun, etc.)
- Aim toward ideal rather than immediate goals
- Give larger capacity
- Make portable
- Make self-cleaning, easy to clean
- Make more accurate
- Make quieter

Improvements to objects can mean thinking beyond the conventional approach – 'out of the box thinking'. The classic, textbook example item is the cup. Suggested improvements have included things like:

- Multiple handles
- Anti-skid
- Anti-tip over
- Anti-spill (lids)
- Built-in heater
- Wheels
- Tea bag holder on side
- Insulated
- Self-brewing
- Self-cleaning

THE FIVE PRINCIPLES OF LEAN THINKING

In a major piece of work by J. P. Womack and D. T. Jones in the 1996 publication *Lean Thinking*, the research finding suggested that there are five principles which need to be adopted. These are:

- To specify what does and does not create **value** from the customer's perspective and not from the perspective of individual firms, functions and departments.
- To identify all steps necessary to design, order and produce the product across the whole **value stream** to highlight non-value adding waste.

- To make only those actions that create **flow** without interruption, detours, backflows, waiting or scrap.
- To make only what is **pulled** by the customer.
- And finally to strive for **perfection** by continually removing successive layers of waste as they are uncovered.

CREATIVITY ASSESSMENT GRID

This matrix shows the relationship between the level of innovation and that of creativity. For long-term sustainability, innovation based on an organization's own creativity must be considered to be far better than that developed or improved on from others.

		Low	Medium	High
Level of innovation	High	Uncreative plagiarist	Creative imitator	Winner
	Medium	Uncreative bumbler	Average	Creative innovator
	Low	Loser	Creative waster	Extravagantly creative
		Low	Medium	High

Level of creativity

Reproduced with kind permission of Professor Simon Majaro from *Managing Ideas for Profit: the creative gap*, McGraw-Hill, 1988.

CHAPTER 5

FINANCIAL MANAGEMENT

No company – where profit driven or a charitable organization – can survive or even operate day to day without money and a professional financial management approach. This topic is so important that it is difficult to find any management course where an appreciation of finance is not included; this does not mean that every manager needs to be a financial expert but should at least understand budgets, spending, the way income is generated and how the organization's costs are established.

In this chapter there are some simple economic models of supply and demand showing sales and income which have to be borne in mind when managers undertake business planning, new product development, and business development as part of a company's longer-term strategic plans. In many cases managers are often tasked with identifying cost savings either through process improvement and increased efficiency or through reduction in material and resources costs; as such this chapter includes a model which illustrates increasing demand as an alternative to cutting costs and hence a clear link to marketing approaches and organizational performance. There are a number of options open to those asked to reduce costs and one of the models provides some indication of how these relative approaches compare.

In addition to the simple economic models the chapter includes the standard financial ratios which can be used to examine the performance of an organization; again these are generally covered on many management and business courses as they are considered to be fundamental indicators of the financial health of the organization.

ACCOUNTING AND FINANCE

This model shows three distinct but related subjects:

- Financial accounting, which incorporates financial management which includes the design and management of the recording systems for cash and bank balances, receipts, payments and various assets and liabilities.
- Cost and management accounting, which is involved with satisfying the information needs of management. It is to assist management decision making, for example: planning the organization's economic performance, controlling costs and improving profitability.
- Auditing both internal and external to ensure compliance/ governance in line with company processes and external audits to verify the existence, ownership and basis of valuation of fixed assets and investments.

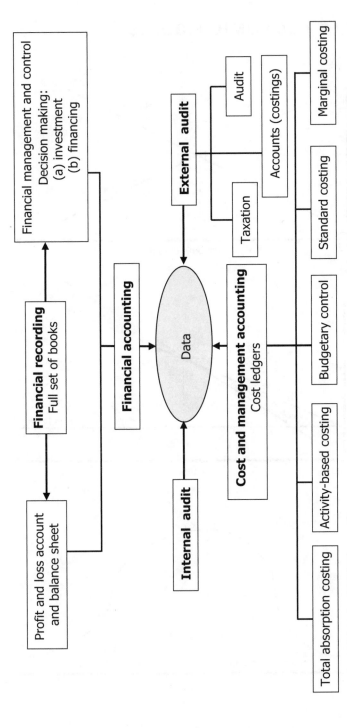

From Dr Tim Hannagan, *Management Concepts and Practices*, 2005. Reproduced with permission of Pearson Education.

SIMPLE ECONOMIC MODELS

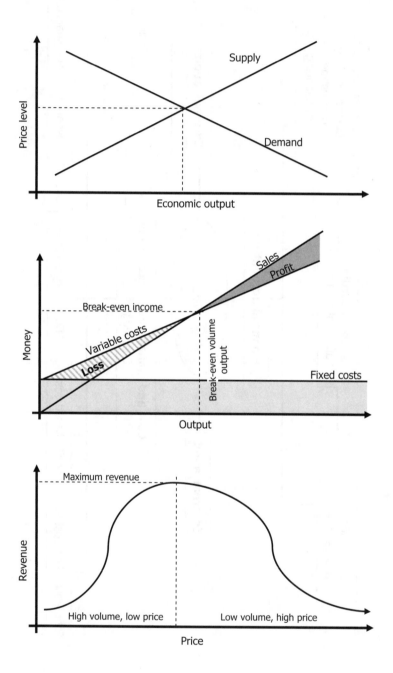

CAPITAL INVESTMENT DECISION PROCESS

This model shows how objectives are linked to decision making through data collection and assessment of financial and non-financial alternatives. While this is about capital investment decision making and comes from the UK's professional body the CIMA, it also shows the linkage to corporate strategy and to the relationship with the internal and external environment. While the internal and external assessment may be undertaken using the SWOT approach, in this model the external environment uses an extended PESTLE tool by the addition of product and factor markets and the topic of risk.

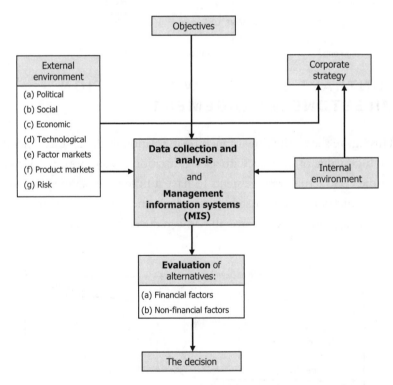

Reproduced with kind permission of the Chartered Institute of Management Accountants (CIMA) from L. Chadwick and Richard Pike, *Management and Control of Capital in Industry*, 1982.

UNDERSTANDING THE PRODUCT/ SERVICE – STRATEGIC FOCUS MODEL

Without recourse to increasing prices, long-term profitability can be achieved through two routes: simply this is either more sales or products (or services) or advances in efficiency.

CONTRACT CASH FLOW PROJECTION – MILESTONE MANAGEMENT

This figure shows the flow of income in relation to the cost expended. On high value or projects with a long duration, a common approach is for the contractual arrangements to have a milestone payment philosophy which attempts to match costs and income to reduce the provider's borrowing and hence the overall cost is reduced to the client.

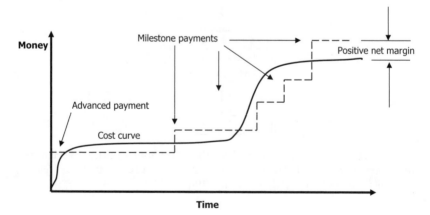

FINANCIAL RATIO ANALYSIS

There are a number of standard approaches of undertaking a financial analysis of a company and the following ratios and calculations will often feature in any assessment of its current commitments and as an indication of potential performance.

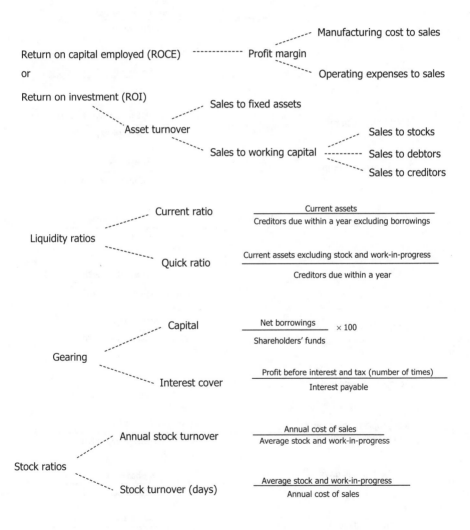

Employee ratios
- Profit per employee
- Added value per employee
- Sales per employee

Debtors and creditors

Debtors $\dfrac{\text{Debtors at year end}}{\text{Annual sales}} \times 365$

Creditors $\dfrac{\text{Creditors at year end}}{\text{Annual purchases}} \times 365$

Administration effectiveness $\dfrac{\text{Cost of administration}}{\text{Annual sales}} \times 100\%$

Market to book ratio $\dfrac{\text{Market capitalization}}{\text{Total ordinary funds}}$

Price/earnings ratio $\dfrac{\text{Market price of share}}{\text{Earnings per share}}$

Raw material days $\dfrac{\text{Raw material}}{\text{Cost of goods sold}/365}$

Trade creditor days $\dfrac{\text{Trade creditors} \times 365}{\text{Cost of goods sold}}$

Work-in-progress days $\dfrac{\text{Work-in-progress} \times 365}{\text{Cost of goods sold}}$

Accrued expenses days $\dfrac{\text{Accrued expenses} \times 365}{\text{Cost of goods sold}}$

Net property, plant and equipment turnovers $\dfrac{\text{Sales}}{\text{Property, plant, equipment}}$

Finished goods days $\dfrac{\text{Finished goods} \times 365}{\text{Cost of goods sold}}$

Receivable days $\dfrac{\text{Receivables} \times 365}{\text{Sales}}$

APPROACHES TO COST REDUCTION

Different decision-making styles have been identified together with their associated advantages and disadvantages of each one.

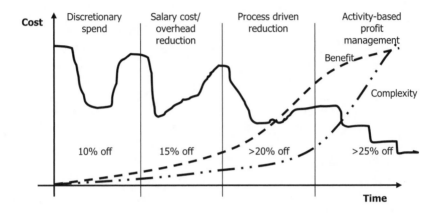

- **Discretionary spend** is not sustainable and costs creep back because authorization to spend becomes onerous and the system relaxes. However, discretionary spend is often the first action taken but is better suited to be the last action.
- **Salary cost/overhead reduction** presents a quick hit but creeps back over a period of time but not to the original level.
- **Process driven reduction** offers a gradual reduction from the introduction of new processes. Some small increase occurs over time.
- **Activity-based profit management** is based on activity-based costing; offers stepped cost reductions over time.

CHAPTER 6

INTERNATIONAL MANAGEMENT

While historically all but the very large companies were satisfied to operate in their home-based market with a growing trend to use a global supply chain, many companies have to consider becoming an international trader far earlier than in the past. Expanding a business to cover new geographical territories outside the organization's home market should not be considered as a simple operation if this is to be successfully undertaken. For those considering such a move, the four factors shown in the model from *The Colombian Journal of World Business*, i.e. market, government, competition and economic drivers, need to be understood and addressed.

The model illustrating the reasons for foreign direct investment also supports the company decision-making process on whether to expand into new markets; however, there are also risks in developing or expanding into new international markets which need to be given serious thought to gain a full understanding before an organization finds itself contractually committed and therefore taking risks it had not previously experienced or considered. As such organizations will need to have recognized and developed plans to address a whole range of risks such as those listed in this chapter. It should be noted that this list is not exhaustive and new risks are likely to emerge as part of this process. How organizations deal with these will largely be a matter for each company to address.

The role of the government in the target location also has a bearing on the attractiveness of operating there and should not be underestimated. The matrix of global strategy and industry structure provides some guidance on how an organization may react to various levels of government involvement.

THE DEVELOPMENT OF INTERNATIONAL BUSINESS

International business cannot be undertaken without knowledge of many factors external to the organization. The drivers of international business can be grouped into four main themes as shown below.

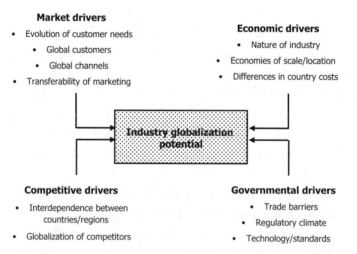

Adapted from text of 'How to take your company to the global market' by G. Yip, P. M. Loewe and M. E. Yoshino, published in *The Columbia Journal of World Business*, Winter 1988.

KEY INFLUENCES ON INITIAL INTERNATIONAL INVOLVEMENT

This model comes for a US promotion policy document by Professor Michael Czinkota and shows the key factors which need to be considered in terms of organizational culture and the requirement to understanding the details of the export market to allow informed decisions to be made. The model shows the interaction of the different forces such as latent and direct influences on the behaviour of the organization; some of these are internal to the organization and some external. Companies react to changes to the business environment by exploring overseas markets and such reactive factors apply especially to the competitive position of the organization and the state of the home market.

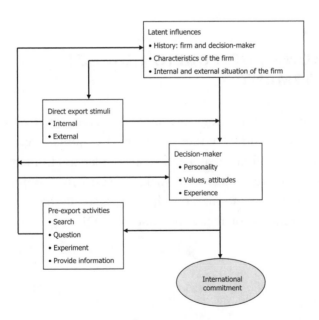

Reproduced with kind permission of Professor Michael Czinkota, first published in *Export Development Strategies: US promotion policy*, Praeger, 1982.

DIFFERENT WAYS OF BEING GLOBAL

It is suggested that developing a global strategy is complicated by the fact that there are at least five major dimensions of globalization and each of these can offer significant benefits. These proposed choices are:

- Playing big in major markets.
- Standardizing the core product.
- Concentrating value-adding activities in a few countries.
- Adopting a uniform market positioning and marketing mix.
- Integrating competitive strategy across countries.

Each of these choices is detailed in the publication *The Columbia Journal of World Business* by Professor G. Yip, P. M. Loewe and M. E. Yoshino, 1988.

REASONS FOR FOREIGN DIRECT INVESTMENT

This model illustrates four reasons for foreign direct investment in external countries rather than in the home organization's country. These four areas need to be understood, analysed and addressed before companies make investment commitments. Marketing considerations and the corporate desire for growth are major reasons for recent increases in FDI.

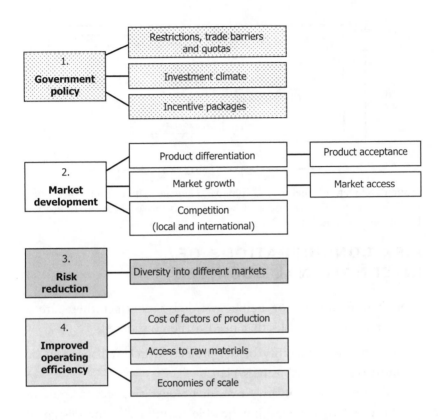

Foreign direct investment is seen by many governments in newly industrialized countries as a means of developing industrial capacity and competitiveness.

From Edgar P. Hibbert, *International Business – strategy and operations*, 1997, Macmillan Business. Reproduced with permission of Palgrave Macmillan.

INTERNATIONAL ENTRY STRATEGIES

Depending on the level of ownership and the investment requirement a number of options are available to enter new international markets.

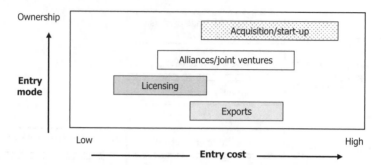

From deKluyer, Cornelius A., *Strategic Thinking: An Executive Perspetive*, © 2000, page 133. Reproduced with permission of Pearson Education Inc., Upper Saddle River, NJ.

RISK CONSIDERATIONS OF INTERNATIONAL BUSINESS

Even before bidding or being awarded a contract there are a number of business risks that need to be considered:

- The financial viability of the project, which will need to be built on a sound business plan.
- The limitations of any investment/operating consortium in the event that it may not be able to influence the design of the project as this may already have been done with the risk of incorrect or inappropriate design features.
- The risk that the business forecast income potential may be flawed or overoptimistic.
- The project location – country, area, regional development, political stability and support for foreign investment.
- Changes in environmental legislation that may impact on the project operations.
- Agreeing the right terms and conditions of contracting.
- The management of the supply chain, as there may be pressure to use local suppliers proposed by government and the investing consortium rather than those preferred.
- The risk that the project financiers will only be interested in the share of profits and not in other long-term business opportunities.

Professor S.A. Burtonshaw-Gunn, *Considerations of Pre-contract Risks in International PFI Projects*, 2005. Reproduced with kind permission of the Salford Centre for Research and Innovation, University of Salford, UK.

DEVELOPMENT OF INTERNATIONAL ADVERTISING OBJECTIVES

This model shows the factors, opportunities and restrictions which need to be considered in the development of an international advertising objective.

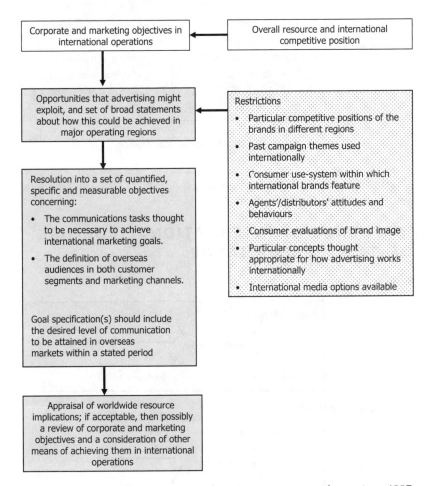

From Edgar P. Hibbert, *International Business – strategy and operations*, 1997, Macmillan Business. Reproduced with permission of Palgrave Macmillan.

GLOBAL STRATEGY AND INDUSTRY STRUCTURE

The range of relationships which cover global concentration and government intervention are shown in this matrix.

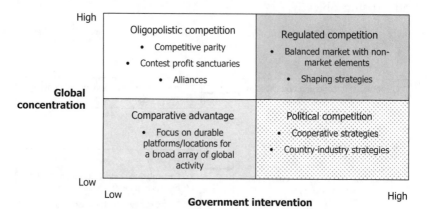

From deKluyer, Cornelis A., *Strategic Thinking: An Executive Perspetive*, © 2000, page 133. Reproduced with permission of Pearson Education Inc., Upper Saddle River, NJ.

INFLUENCE OF INTERNATIONAL CULTURE ON TASK PERFORMANCE

Western culture:

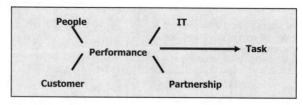

Far Eastern culture:

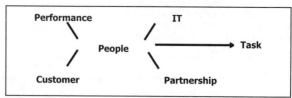

EXPORT MARKETS – DEMAND AND OPPORTUNITIES

One way of analysing the opportunities that exist in different export markets is to divide the target countries into three broad zones. Each zone offers opportunities for a wide range of products but careful analysis needs to be made of the option open to a company for entering into that county/zone. This analysis needs to be balanced against the organization's own strengths and weaknesses. On this basis can a company make informed decisions about the attractiveness of an export market? Typically, to penetrate an export market the products must have strengths in at least one technical specification, reliability, simplicity, specialist application, aesthetic features and price.

MARKET TYPE	MARKET DEMANDS/EXPORT OPPORTUNITIES
Developed world	• Higher technology • Unique features • Sophisticated distribution • Superior promotional support • Well-developed back-up and support • For consumer products, a clear difference (objective and subjective) when compared with local suppliers
Underdeveloped world	• Medium and lower technology, especially capital plant • Good support, especially technical • Limited luxury goods • Specialist consultancy services • Basic distribution (though physical distribution can be a problem) • Limited promotional support • Longer-term finance • Local manufacturing opportunities

MARKET TYPE	MARKET DEMANDS/EXPORT OPPORTUNITIES
Developing world	• Technology for licence agreements/ local manufacture/investment • Finance • Luxury goods • Medium- and high-technology imports • Good distribution • Good promotional and technical back-up

Model taken from *The Handbook of Management*, page 324, 3rd edition, Gower Publishing 1992. Reproduced with kind permission of the Editor Dennis Lock. Copyright Dennis Lock.

CHAPTER 7

MARKETING MANAGEMENT

Within this chapter are a number of marketing related models, although at the strategic level there is a natural proximity between marketing, business planning and organizational strategy development as successful marketing management leads to sales of goods or services necessary to sustain the business through income generation.

Marketing is not just about the final action of sales – it is far more than this and has implications across the whole organization. In the UK, the Chartered Institute of Marketing defines marketing management as *'the management process responsible for identifying, anticipating and satisfying customer requirements profitably'*. A similar definition comes from the American Marketing Association, which proposes this to be *'the process of planning and executing the concept, pricing, promotion and distribution of ideas, goods and services to create exchanges that satisfy individual and organizational objectives'*. A number of parts from the American definition can be seen in the 'marketing mix model' (the 4Ps) while the UK definition also shows some linkage to market research and consumer requirements management.

A number of models in this chapter show a relationship between the organization and that of its current or potential customers in terms of demand, customer influence and approaches to promotion. The most famous of these is Ansoff's product-market matrix which may be supported by other models to form a basis for business development. Linked also to the marketing of a product or service is its position on the product life cycle, which not only prompts the organization to respond with a strategy matched to its life cycle position but also relates this to the future demand from its customers and the four categories that these are likely to follow.

An extension of the 4Ps model is matching the marketing mix to meet customer needs. Within this chapter are a range of models to examine product and marketing activities seen in the widely known and used product performance matrix of the Boston Consulting Group. In addition to this is the product life cycle and how this can be used to understand both the external market and the effects on the internal business in terms of constraints and opportunities. The marketing function should not be an isolated internal management activity as it draws a heavy reliance on an understanding of the market needs from customer analysis; from an understanding of the market in terms of growth potential, sustainment and attractiveness and from marketing intelligence. These factors provide reliable information on which to base market decisions which are then reflected in the product design and development, and in the strategic level business planning task.

STEPS TO THE PRODUCTION OF A MARKETING STRATEGY

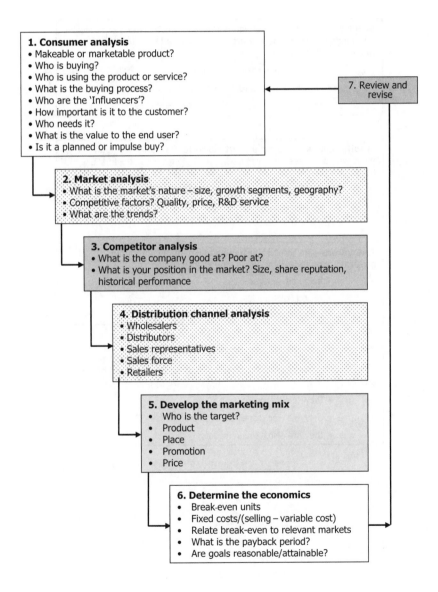

1. Consumer analysis
- Makeable or marketable product?
- Who is buying?
- Who is using the product or service?
- What is the buying process?
- Who are the 'Influencers'?
- How important is it to the customer?
- Who needs it?
- What is the value to the end user?
- Is it a planned or impulse buy?

7. Review and revise

2. Market analysis
- What is the market's nature – size, growth segments, geography?
- Competitive factors? Quality, price, R&D service
- What are the trends?

3. Competitor analysis
- What is the company good at? Poor at?
- What is your position in the market? Size, share reputation, historical performance

4. Distribution channel analysis
- Wholesalers
- Distributors
- Sales representatives
- Sales force
- Retailers

5. Develop the marketing mix
- Who is the target?
- Product
- Place
- Promotion
- Price

6. Determine the economics
- Break-even units
- Fixed costs/(selling – variable cost)
- Relate break-even to relevant markets
- What is the payback period?
- Are goals reasonable/attainable?

NATURE OF DEMAND

When examining who buys a company's products, customers are likely to fall into any one of four categories:

Sceptics – once the product enters saturation/maturity and sales level off, the group buying the product is often referred to as the 'late majority' or sceptics:

- they question the truth in claims
- they let the product become 'tried and tested'
- they buy it in the late stages of market growth

Traditionalists – here the product moves to the decline stage and those who buy it are often referred to as 'laggers', 'non-adopters' or traditionalists:

- they only buy the product when fully established
- they cling to the status quo

Innovators – are the first customers to buy newly introduced products; normally exhibit dominant values including:

- being adventurous
- taking risks
- eager to adopt and be technically informed

Adopters – upon product entering the next stage of growth (i.e. success) with dramatic sales increase; adopters are those who rush and buy the product:

- they seek respect
- they are well respected by peers
- they are also opinion leaders

STAKEHOLDER MAPPING: THE POWER/INTEREST MATRIX

Analysing the importance of the customers and stakeholders in relation to the business allows companies to know where to concentrate their efforts in managing these important relationships.

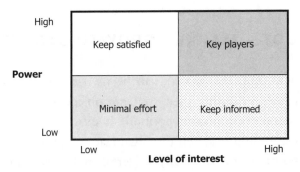

Reproduced with kind permission of Springer Science and Business Media, from A. Mendlow, *Proceedings of the Second International Conference on Information Systems*, Cambridge, MA, 1992.

MARKETING INFORMATION SYSTEM

This model illustrates all of the information in a typical marketing information system designed to collect, process and report. Marketing research is a function of the information process and is a continuous activity which involves finding and monitoring that customer needs have been interpreted correctly. Market intelligence is concerned with monitoring the market and the wider issues that affect the organization.

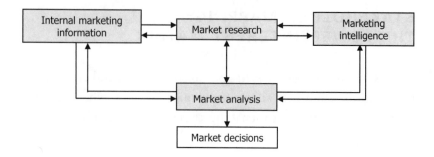

Model reproduced from *Marketing Made Simple* by Geoff Lancaster and Paul Reynolds, 2002, page 36. With permission from Elsevier.

PRODUCT – MARKET GROWTH STRATEGIES

This widely applicable matrix can be used to provide guidance for companies in setting their strategic objectives or by analysis to understand their market position. It examines choices based on the relationship between the organization's products and their market position and is usually undertaken for each product or service within the company's portfolio. Understanding this position offers some direction to future strategy; indeed this is shown in the text below.

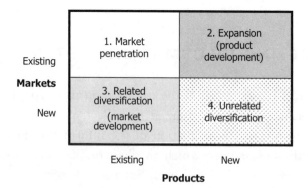

From H. Igor Ansoff, *Corporate Strategy*, 1968. Reproduced with permission of Penguin Publishing.

STRATEGY DEVELOPMENT DIRECTIONS

As a development of the above Ansoff model many later management publications offer some direction on how this may be used; typical views are shown below:

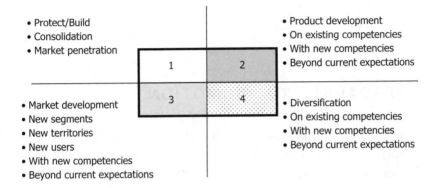

- Protect/Build
- Consolidation
- Market penetration

- Product development
- On existing competencies
- With new competencies
- Beyond current expectations

- Market development
- New segments
- New territories
- New users
- With new competencies
- Beyond current expectations

- Diversification
- On existing competencies
- With new competencies
- Beyond current expectations

PESTLE

This analysis tool can also be used to identify and address external issues which are likely to act on product/services launch and operations.

- **P**olitical
- **E**conomic
- **S**ocial
- **T**echnology
- **L**egal and
- **E**nvironmental

MARKETING COMMUNICATIONS

- **What** are we saying?
- To **whom**?

- With what **objective**?
- Through what **medium**?
  - Personal contact
  - Advertising
  - Internet
  - Exhibitions
  - Direct marketing
  - Telephone
  - Public relations

APPROACHES TO PROMOTION

There are a number of ways that promotion of a product or service may take and each has its own merits and shortfalls as shown below where the amount of investment required for each approach is shown against the task of leading to a sale.

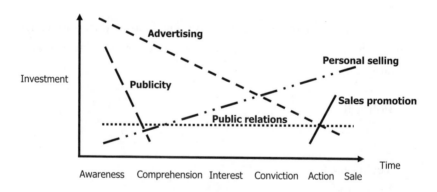

THE MARKETING STRATEGY

This model shows the linkage between corporate vision and the marketing plan with linkages to its competitive and industry position.

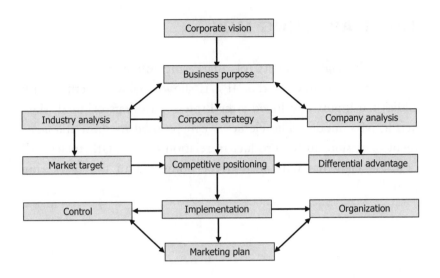

The development of a marketing plan should be based on careful analysis of the following factors:

- The present and potential size of the markets.
- The degree and type of the competitive activity.
- Prevailing price levels.
- Advertising, promotional and servicing support for products and services.
- Quality and performance comparisons with the competition.
- Assessment of the tariff and non-tariff barriers to trade.
- Assessment of relative costs, efficiency and effectiveness of supporting organizations.
- Sales volume and profit targets for both the short and long term.
- Budget forecast and financial plan for the marketing.
- An assessment of the credit and political risks involved.

THE 'MARKETING MIX'

The traditional elements of marketing often referred to as the 'marketing mix' or the '4Ps' is shown below together with additional inputs developed after Professor Kotler's original Marketing Mix model. The elements can be used to show management's decision on the product in relation to the marketplace. All of these elements will need to be addressed in the marketing plan.

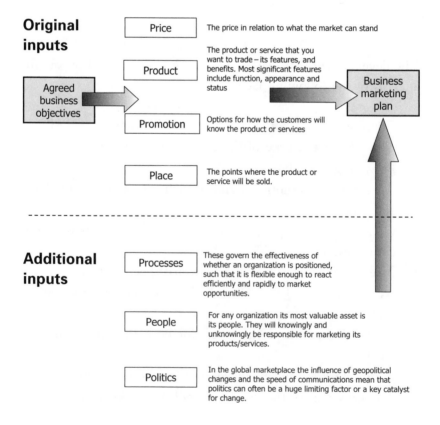

Original inputs

Agreed business objectives

| Price | The price in relation to what the market can stand |

| Product | The product or service that you want to trade – its features, and benefits. Most significant features include function, appearance and status |

| Promotion | Options for how the customers will know the product or services |

| Place | The points where the product or service will be sold. |

Business marketing plan

Additional inputs

| Processes | These govern the effectiveness of whether an organization is positioned, such that it is flexible enough to react efficiently and rapidly to market opportunities. |

| People | For any organization its most valuable asset is its people. They will knowingly and unknowingly be responsible for marketing its products/services. |

| Politics | In the global marketplace the influence of geopolitical changes and the speed of communications mean that politics can often be a huge limiting factor or a key catalyst for change. |

USING THE 'MARKETING MIX' TO MATCH CUSTOMER NEEDS

Here the 4Ps can be used to match the identified customer needs ideally gained from undertaking market research, customer focus groups, complaints, etc.

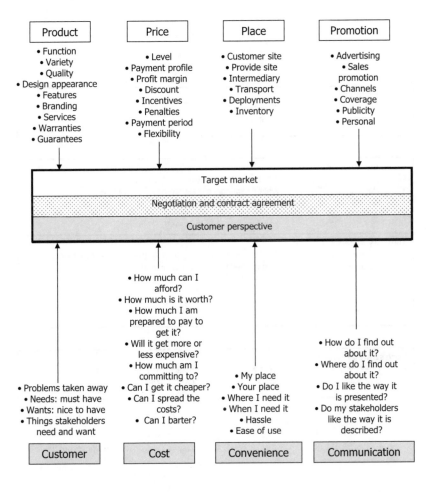

DEVELOPMENT OF THE MARKETING STRATEGY (1)

The contents of a typical marketing strategy are presented below. These cover an amount of data collection and research work necessary to make informed decisions. It has (and must have) clear links to the organization's main business plan and corporate strategy and is much wider than just product or services selling as seen below.

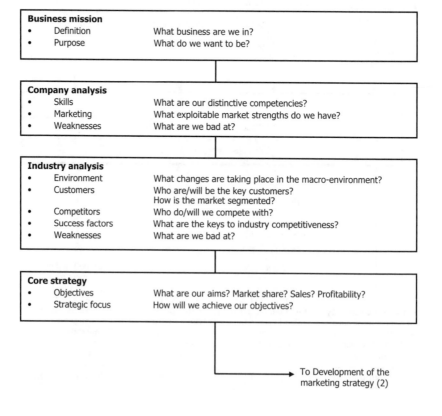

Business mission
- Definition   What business are we in?
- Purpose   What do we want to be?

Company analysis
- Skills   What are our distinctive competencies?
- Marketing   What exploitable market strengths do we have?
- Weaknesses   What are we bad at?

Industry analysis
- Environment   What changes are taking place in the macro-environment?
- Customers   Who are/will be the key customers?
  How is the market segmented?
- Competitors   Who do/will we compete with?
- Success factors   What are the keys to industry competitiveness?
- Weaknesses   What are we bad at?

Core strategy
- Objectives   What are our aims? Market share? Sales? Profitability?
- Strategic focus   How will we achieve our objectives?

To Development of the marketing strategy (2)

DEVELOPMENT OF THE MARKETING STRATEGY (2)

From Development of the
marketing strategy (1)

Market targets
- Customers   Who will we serve? Market share? Sales? Profitability?
- Competitors   Who will we compete with?

Differential advantage
- Product positioning   How will we serve the customers?
- Competitive positioning On what basis will we compete?

Marketing mix
- Products/Services   What benefit will we offer?
- Price   What level, discounts, credit mix?
- Promotions   What message, media, mix (PR, Adv, selling)?
- Place   How will we distribute our products and services?
- People   What skills mix do we need?

Organization
- Style   What corporate culture will we adopt?
- Structure How will we organize our efforts?

Control
- Evaluation   How will we judge our efforts?
- Adaptation   How will we adapt to changing circumstances?
- Contingency plan What if?

PRODUCT LIFE CYCLE

This chart illustrates the rise and fall of a typical product; for those that are of a 'fad' nature this is heavily concentrated on the introduction and growth phase followed by a rapid decline, completely omitting the maturity period of the product.

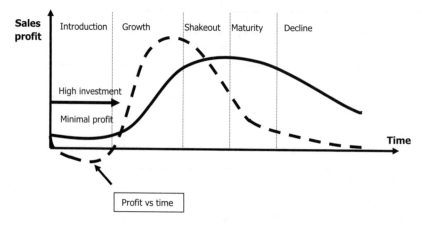

	INTRODUCTION	**GROWTH**	**SHAKEOUT**	**MATURITY**	**DECLINE**
Users/ Buyers	Few trial of early adopters	Growing adopters: trial of product or services	Growing selectivity of purchase	Saturation of users Repeat purchase reliance	Drop-off in usage
Competitive conditions	Few competitors	Entry of competitors Attempt to achieve trial Fight for share Undifferentiated products/ services	May be many Likely price cutting for volume Shakeout of weakest competitors	Fight to maintain share Difficulties in gaining/ taking share Emphasis on efficiency/low cost	Exit of some competitors Selective distribution

Reproduced with permission of Pearson Publishing, from Gerry Johnson and Kevan Scholes, *Exploring Corporate Strategy*, 2002, 6th edition text and cases.

As a development of the product life cycle an understanding of the product/service can be gained using the table below:

	INTRODUCTION	GROWTH	MATURITY	DECLINE
Sales	Low	Fast growth	Slow growth	Decline
Profits	Negligible	Peak level	Declining	Low
Cash flow	Negative	Moderate	High	Low
Customers	Innovative	Mass market	Mass market	Laggards
Competitors	Few	Growing	Many rivals	Declining

Understanding the product life cycle position may help the company respond using a strategy selected from table below:

	INTRODUCTION	GROWTH	MATURITY	DECLINE
Sales	Expand market	Market penetration	Defend share	Productivity
Marketing expansions	High	High (declining %)	Falling	Low
Marketing emphasis	Product awareness	Brand preference	Brand loyalty	Selection
Distribution	Patchy	Intensive	Intensive	Selective
Price	High	Lower	Lowest	Variable
Product	Basic	Improved	Differentiated	Rationalized

From Clive Reading, *Strategic Business Planning*, 2nd edition, 2002, pages 337 and 338. Reproduced with permission of Kogan Page Limited.

UNDERSTANDING PRICE

This model illustrates the price matched to what the market will pay, rather than a function of the product or service cost. When a high price is charged, this is referred to as a skimming policy and is used when:

- One has a monopoly.
- Sales are insensitive to price change.
- Short product life cycle exists.
- Competition is anticipated.

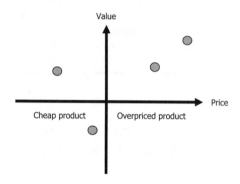

When a low price is charged, this is referred to as a penetration policy and is used when:

- Sales are price sensitive.
- Large market share is essential to compete.
- Competition is to be eliminated.

Complementary items often provide an opportunity for premium prices to be obtained

COMPETITION

Even in a company's traditional areas competition is potentially broader than may be first suggested; the main competition particularly for organizations diversifying into new areas may be very different from their normal experience. The competition may come from some or all of the following:

1. Other providers of the same product or service.
2. Providers of an alternative product or service.
3. Other ways of doing the same thing.
4. Other competitors for the customer's disposable income/funds.
5. The customer – by doing it him/herself.

ESTABLISHING A PRODUCT/MARKETING MATRIX

This is a development of the Boston Consultancy Group Product Matrix which can be used to provide a framework for prioritizing key product sectors for development across global markets.

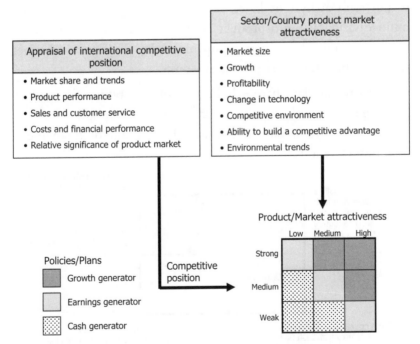

From Edger P. Hibbert, *International Business – Strategy and Operations*, 1997, Macmillan Business. Reproduced with permission of Palgrave Macmillan.

SEGMENTING CUSTOMER MARKETS

Understanding customer profiles is an important part of market research and can be used to 'target' various potential customer groups. Such segmentation can cover:

- Geographic – country region.
- Demographic – age, gender, income.
- Psychological – lifestyle, personality.
- Behavioural – usage, brand loyalty, responsiveness to price and promotion.

PRODUCT PERFORMANCE ANALYSIS

The Boston Consultancy Group's Growth/Share Matrix approach to portfolio analysis is based on observations in the 1970s that multi-divisional, multi-product companies have a strong advantage over non-diversified companies: the ability to channel resources into the most productive units.

- Relative market share – indication of the ability of a product to generate cash, relative to the largest competitor.
- Market growth rate – indicates the amount of financing a product requires.

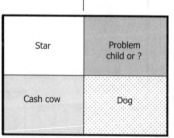

Star – usually a product with high cash generation, but likely to require further investment

Problem child or **question mark** – usually newly launched product or one in difficulty such as low market share in a growing market; generates low cash and requires high cash injection

Cash cow – usually a product which generates high cash flow from a dominant market position in a declining or static market. This is likely to require careful maintenance and low cash input

Dog – products have low market share and little or limited market sector growth, low cash generation and are termed to be in decline

Product portfolio analysis reveals an organization's state of product performance and gaps in the creation of its strategic plans

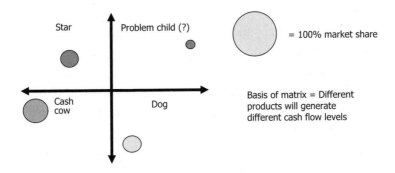

The BCG Growth/Share Matrix from the Product Portfolio Matrix reproduced with kind permission of the Boston Consulting Group Inc. © Copyright 1970. All rights reserved.

INTERNATIONAL MARKET STRATEGY

Central to strategic thinking when considering international markets is a model put forward by Warren Keegan in 1969 which examines the mix of products and communication. This results in identifying five strategies for international marketing. (This model is also clearly linked to Chapters 6 and 15).

		Products		
		No change	**Adapted**	**New product**
Marketing communications	**No change**	Straight extension	Product adaptation	–
	Adapt	Communications adaptation	Dual adaptation	Product invention

Keegan's five strategies for international marketing are:

- Straight extension – The product or service and the type of communication message is the same for each market whether home or overseas.
- Communications adaptation – The promotional theme is modified and the product or service remains unchanged.
- Product adaptation – The product or service is different for the home and overseas markets whereas the promotion is the same for both.
- Dual adaptation – The communication message and the product are altered for each market.
- Product invention – The above strategies are appropriate where product needs and market conditions are similar to the home market but in some countries this may not be the case resulting in new product development to meet the new customer needs typically in terms of functionality and product affordability.

Reproduced by permission of the American Marketing Association, from 'Multinational product planning: strategic alternatives' by Warren J. Keegan, published in the *Journal of Marketing*, No. 33, 1969.

MARKET ANALYSIS PROCESS – OVERVIEW

With product success many companies have to move from a product driven strategy because technical improvements in producing new products have improved their competitors' ability to easily duplicate a product. These competitors then offer this to the market at a cheaper selling price.

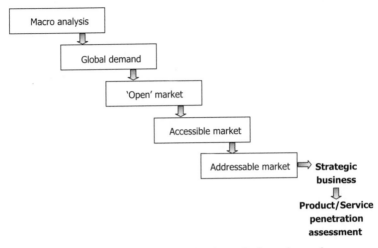

- Market driven – market need identified and product created to satisfy need/gap in market.
- Product driven – organization makes products and then tries to sell them.
- Technology push – technological development allows new product to be created to fulfil a need.

BUSINESS INTELLIGENCE FROM MARKET RESEARCH

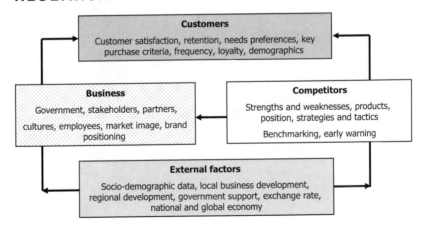

CHAPTER 8

ORGANIZATIONAL DEVELOPMENT

*I*t would not be an exaggeration to say that there is no other topic in management that impacts on the whole of the business operation than that of the topic of Organizational Development: from business planning, production, improvement processes, quality systems, and marketing through to customer relationships management, and from a personnel viewpoint covering both individual performance and team working. This should not be merely considered to be the production of a company's organogram – it is far more than this. Organizational Development (OD) involves understanding the culture of the company, identifying its strengths and opportunities and trying to minimize its weakness and real (or perceived) threats throughout the whole company. OD often goes hand in hand with change management and as such both this chapter and Chapters 2 and 20 may be of assistance to the reader.

As a management discipline OD evolved into a topic some 60 years ago although it has some important historical milestones prior to this, the most famous being the experiments undertaken between 1924 and 1932 by Harvard Professors Elton Mayo and Fritz Roethlisberger and their teams at the Hawthorne works, owned by the Western Electric Company and located outside of Chicago, USA. The experiments looked at the reaction of the workforce to imposed changes to their working conditions, for example varying lighting levels, rest breaks, etc., and revealed interesting links to productivity rates by those in the experiment and also those who were not part of the experimental groups. While this experiment may be considered to be dated, it should be noted that an experiment on this scale and for this duration has never been repeated and the results have influenced organizational design ever since. For this reason alone there is a clear link between OD and change management when looking to maintain and improve individual and hence the organization's performance.

Having said above that OD grew to become a subject in its own right, this chapter provides a number of models relating to various management areas and how they may be brought together either as subjects, activities or management levels. There is a close relationship with the HR function and how people are managed, rewarded and developed with a heavy reliance in understanding the role and importance of culture at both an organizational and individual level.

While linking the role of HR to OD the model of performance management illustrates the relationship between mission, strategy, culture, performance and people through succession planning, recruitment, rewards and performance target setting. The separate models by Hannagan and Dawson shown in this chapter offer some thoughts on the cultural make-up of an organization as a whole and the matching of culture to the company's style is likely to follow one of Charles Handy's identified four groups. The final model in this chapter covers knowledge management, which again has a cultural significance and the requirements for the development of the 'right' organization in terms of trust, sharing, behaviour, and senior level support for it to successfully provide organizational benefit.

THE BASIC MANAGEMENT ORGANIZATION

This first model shows the traditional hierarchical structure still used in a number of organizations depending on type of business, culture, etc.

Senior management such as board, directors, chief executive, senior functional managers. Tasked with strategy and policy design and development

Middle management, typically production managers, sales managers, section managers involved in planning, innovation and implementation of strategy

Junior management involved in organizing, supervising, controlling operations activities

Operations, including production, sales and service employees

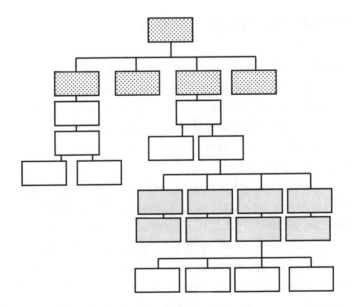

In this second model a matrix structure is shown with a typical project-based organization.

Here the projects are resourced from staff in sales, production and research and development.

It offers a flexible approach to allow effort to be placed on priority projects although sharing staff across the organization requires good management control. It also offers staff greater opportunities to acquire more experience across a range of projects.

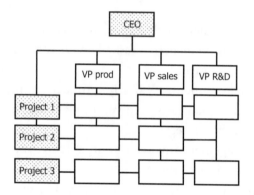

SYSTEMS THEORY

The model below comes from the work of Professor James Clawson on systems theory who proposes that this likens organizations to living organisms. In the same way as animals have digestive, reproductive, nervous systems, etc. which enable them to live, organizations can be considered to have subsystems that enable them to function.

The managerial subsystem is responsible for goals, plans and controls; this can be regarded as a brain in the model below. The adaptive subsystem acts as the company's eyes looking outward to monitor the environment and to make sure that the products and services are appropriate in a changing environment. The boundary spanning in subsystem equates to the mouth, controlling the intake of 'organizational food'; in a company this function is likely to include recruiting people, buying raw materials and raising money. Within the model the production subsystem is similar to the digestive processes in converting raw materials, enhancing the organization's performance and leading to the boundary spanning out subsystem which equates to the bowels, which can equates to personnel leaving the organization who have not met the required standard. During the life of an animal or organization the maintenance subsystem tries to keep the other subsystems working efficiently.

Systems theory provides another way of analysing an organization to assess its health or make a change to its 'lifestyle'.

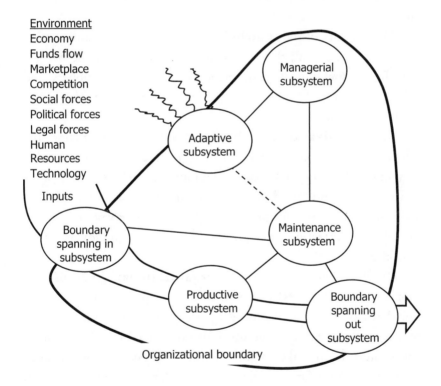

From *Systems Theory and Organizational Analysis* by Professor James Clawson, published 1983. Copyright 1993 The University of Virginia Darden School Foundation, Charlottesville, Virginia, USA. Reproduced with kind permission.

ELEMENTS OF AN ORGANIZATION

This model supports the view that while there are a number of elements which comprise an organization, its author advises that this is not the only model but it does encompass all of the main elements of organizational design and can be used as part of the considerations and planning around implementing a change management programme.

The **mission and strategy** is an important element of the organization as it provides a clear declaration of intent and serves as a reference point to establishing any required changes.

The support of the **stakeholders** is important for any change plan to be successful; this should not be restricted to the owners but should include all staff, principal customers, suppliers and others who provide support to the business in its day-to-day or long-term business activities.

An **organization's culture** is one of the major influences which makes each business different – typically this is witnessed in its rules on behaviour; its beliefs about what is important and good for the organization; its management style and levels of authority; and finally the corporate image of the organization as portrayed to an employer or a customer.

Development of the 'right' **organizational structure** in support of the business plan can lead to improvements in functional responsibility and business performance. The introduction of a new organization structure will often need careful planning and should not be taken lightly as this will take senior management time and effort to help staff to understand their new roles and processes.

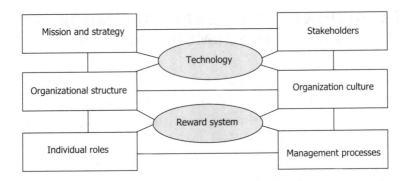

The world is continually changing through process improvements and the introduction of new **technology**; from a customer expectations viewpoint both of these increase the pressure on the business to perform efficiently. Any technology changes identified in the business plan must be seen to contribute to the main objectives, its stated mission and longer-term vision statement.

All organizations are made up of **individual** people whose **roles** interact, as such the design of their roles is important and will be a key aspect in the organizational development of a company as it changes to embrace a new business focus. Such learning and development will focus on enhancing personnel operations to achieve higher standards of competence and performance.

Depending on the company structure, some of the important **management processes** usually take place across the functional hierarchy such as planning and budgeting, systems development, customer related activities and management/staff development.

Reward systems are an important part of any organization's attractiveness and ability to encourage people to become and remain as employees; to secure a level of commitment and effort; to encourage the necessary behaviour to support the organization performance targets, and finally to support flexibility, creativity and innovation.

Model by Kelvin Hard in *Strategies for Human Resource Management*, M. Armstrong (ed.), Kogan Page Limited, 1992. Reproduced with kind permission of Michael Armstrong. Text by Prof. S. A. Burtonshaw-Gunn and Dr M. G. Salameh, from *Change Management and Organisational Performance*, ICFAI University Press, 2007.

TRADITIONAL (AND EXPANDED MODEL OF) IDENTIFIED MANAGEMENT FUNCTIONS

Five management competencies were identified in the work of Henri Fayol (1841–1925) and considered to be the foundation stones of modern management; these cover planning, organizing, commanding, coordinating and controlling and are shown in the original model below. These are further developed where the five management competencies are now linked to the organization's functional areas where managers in each of the functions will need to perform their tasks by utilizing the original competencies.

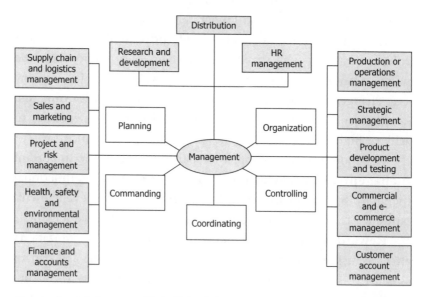

Original model was published in *The Management Task* by Rob Dixon 2002. Copyright Elsevier. Development by S. A. Burtonshaw-Gunn.

LINKAGE BETWEEN HR AND ORGANIZATIONAL DEVELOPMENT

Influences from both the internal and external environment impact on both business strategy and HR in the form of culture, people, systems and organizational structure.

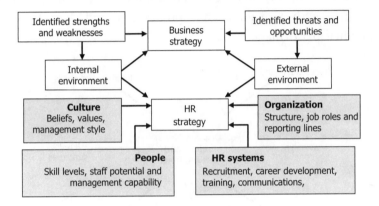

UNDERSTANDING ORGANIZATIONAL ACTORS

Constant external influences impact on the organization as seen in this environmental map.

INFLUENCES ON ORGANIZATIONAL CULTURE

Within this model can be seen the range of influences that impact on organizational culture, its values and assumptions, and the 'way we do things around here'. Understanding this is an important feature in organizational development particularly when combined with a major change programme and the impact of individual performance.

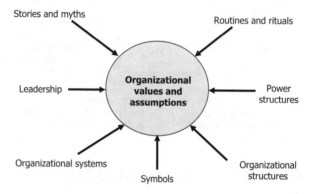

From Tony Dawson, *Principles and Practice of Modern Management*. Reproduced with kind permission of Liverpool Academic Press, 2000.

The work of Charles Handy (*Understanding Organizations*, 1976, Penguin) built on the unwritten or shared rules that become entrenched in organizations and led to the identification of four groups of behaviour:

- **Power culture** – where the key to the whole organization sits in the middle like a spider's web, typically dominated by a charismatic figure or founder; here personality is more important than formal structures.
- **Task culture** – heavy focus on job or project completion. Assumes that the organization's purpose is of paramount importance.

- **Person culture** – Puts individuals and their interests first and views the organization as a means to an end. It is seen as a resource on which individuals can draw to enhance their own talents, abilities or concerns.
- **Role culture** – the central focus is impersonality where the organization is seen as a set of inter-related roles; individuals are role occupants and communications tend to be formalized into systems and processes.

ELEMENTS OF CULTURE

Understanding organizational culture is neither easy nor quickly achieved; however, there are a number of models that help to provide some understanding of culture. While some would merely say 'it's the way we do business around here' more academic research shows this to be a collection of traditions, values, policies, beliefs, and attitudes. Elements of organizational culture are also evident at the individual level.

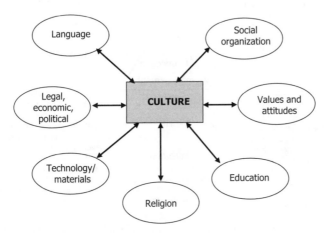

From Dr Tim Hannagan, *Management Concepts and Practices*, 2005. Reproduced with permission of Pearson Education.

KNOWLEDGE MANAGEMENT

The term knowledge management is now in widespread use and over the years companies have been using techniques to capture and share knowledge across their operations. For many of these techniques this has followed a two-fold approach of, first, organizing existing information and data and, second, facilitating the creation and development of new knowledge.

Information, knowledge, and wisdom can be seen to be fundamentally interlinked as components together with three key cultural/behavioural factors: senior management support, common culture and trust. For knowledge management to provide maximum business benefits all of these elements need to be embraced and valued.

Senior management support
Management support means thinking of knowledge as a resource as part of its intellectual capital. Senior management support is fundamental to creating a culture of learning, innovating, sharing and achieving.

Information
Covers the 'what, who, when and where' and relates to description, definition, or perspective, this might consist of facts, opinions, ideas, theories, principles, and models or frameworks together with subject matter information and expertise.

Knowledge
Covers the 'how' and comprises strategy, practice, method, and approaches and is linked to a person's state of being with respect to some body of information. These states include ignorance, awareness, familiarity, understanding, facility, expert, etc.

Knowledge management

Common culture
Precondition to effective knowledge transfer includes the absolute need for a common language, common values and a common culture where individuals share the same understanding of concepts such as time, delegation, and accountability.

Wisdom
Concentrates on the 'why' and embodies principle, insight, moral, or archetype.

Trust
Trust exists on an individual level through close working relationships with colleagues and is able to exist on an organization level by the adoption of a culture that rewards knowledge sharing and penalizes hoarding. People must get credit for sharing and this must start at the top to develop trust.

From Professor S. A. Burtonshaw-Gunn, *Knowledge Management: a tool for gaining competitive advantage through intellectual capital development*. Reproduction with permission of Professional Consulting, 2006.

THE PERFORMANCE MANAGEMENT PROCESS

In looking at performance management this model links strategy, cultural values and business objectives into the performance systems of measurement against critical success factors and performance indicators.

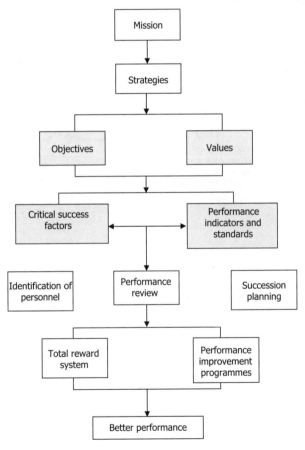

Reproduced with kind permission of Michael Armstrong, from Lawrie Philpott and Louise Shepherd in *Strategies for Human Resource Management*, Michael Armstrong (ed.), 1992, Kogan Page Limited.

HUMAN RESOURCES STRATEGY – 'COPS'

The checklist below is useful in assessing the COPS features of an organization; this information can be used in the development of various action plans as part of the overall HRM strategy.

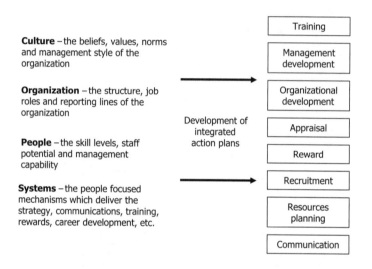

Culture – the beliefs, values, norms and management style of the organization

Organization – the structure, job roles and reporting lines of the organization

People – the skill levels, staff potential and management capability

Systems – the people focused mechanisms which deliver the strategy, communications, training, rewards, career development, etc.

Development of integrated action plans

Training

Management development

Organizational development

Appraisal

Reward

Recruitment

Resources planning

Communication

CHAPTER 9

PEOPLE-FOCUSED PERFORMANCE MANAGEMENT

*C*ompanies measuring their business performance results often divide these into strategic, financial, operational, behavioural and ethical groups and these will typically impact on operational management (business planning, objective setting, performance assessment, etc.) and those in HR management (training and career development, succession planning, reward systems, etc.). Over the past few years many companies have become more results driven through the publication of their performance results and in some circumstances their relative position with competitors is seen in published league tables. In addition there has been an increasing interest in the introduction of performance indicators which focus on company results through assessment and monitoring aimed at assisting decision making and ultimately contribute to the organization's long-term success. Naturally there has developed a range of initiatives to support the topic of performance management and where these focus on people they have often focused on matching staff competencies and capabilities to their work. In looking at the HR management theme this chapter supports this with models which focus first on the broader organizational issues of appraisal systems, HR planning and the relationship of staff with their longer-term goals, and, second on the provision of models which can be used with individual employees on topics such as individual learning, motivation, teamwork, empowerment and self-development.

Almost every company's annual statement claims that its staff are its most valuable asset and this chapter provides a number of models on staff development which would suit not just those companies but all those who recognize that trained and well-motivated employees are better able to contribute to the business goals and have a role in its short- and long-term success. For those investing in staff training and development it will be beneficial to have an understanding of how individuals approach and have a preference for different learning experiences to support their development. The role of management in this people-focused performance chapter can be seen in John Adair's overlapping three circle model on action-centred leadership. In addition a typical performance management process of objective setting, monitoring and recognition is provided together with some general models on staff motivation including the still widely recognized hierarchy of needs by Abraham Maslow and Frederick Hertzburg's work on motivation theory.

An important feature of obtaining performance from employees relies on regular communication and the development of trust. Having considered the individual this chapter also offers some models on teamworking and leadership including the organizational leadership style as a function of its focus on results or people as seen in the Leadership grid produced by Blake and Mouton.

A MODEL OF HUMAN RELATIONS

This 'onion ring' concept is shown in this model which it can be used to explore the issues and makeup which affect individuals.

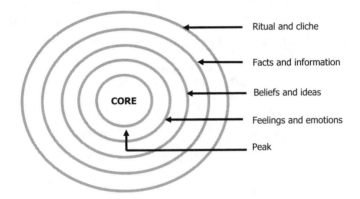

This diagram can be used to illustrate individual and team-work actions and those beyond the control of both.

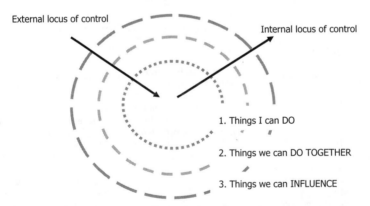

INDIVIDUAL LEARNING

This model called the 'learning cycle' shows a process for learning from experience and while cyclical it has four stages. This similar model comes from work by Honey and Mumford in the 1980s which looks at individual learning styles and classification of individual learning preferences.

This is still very much applicable today. It should be noted that an individual will usually have a strong preference for one learning style although will use others to a lesser extent depending on the learning situation.

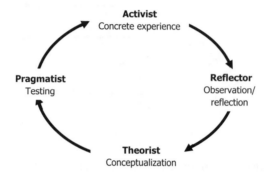

Reproduced with kind permission of Peter Honey Publications *The Learning Styles Questionnaire, 80-item version,* 2006.

The model below is a detailed development of the above learning cycle.

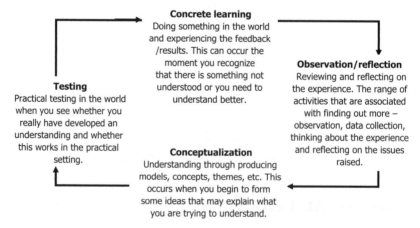

Reproduced with permission of John Wiley & Sons, from David Kolb and Roger Fry, 'Towards an applied theory of experimental learning', in Cary Cooper (ed.), *Theories of Group Processes,* 1975.

SELF-MANAGED LEARNING

Self-managed learning is regarded as the process whereby individuals determine what they learn and how they learn with
others in the context of their unique situation. As shown below
there are a number of options by which this learning may be
facilitated.

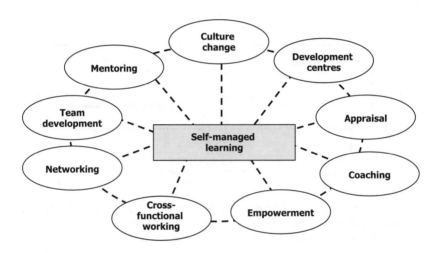

It should be said that while there are a number of advantages
to SML such as empowering the individual with responsibility,
the encouragement of independence, and that the learning equips
individuals with 'life skills' so too are there some drawbacks.
SML can appear vague, it is not structured and often does not
have clearly defined goals.

ACHIEVEMENT OBJECTIVE

The extent to which objective setting between managers and staff may be mandatory or discretionary. Some objectives will be mandatory themselves by their very nature (health and safety, budget targets, for example) but how they are to be achieved may be largely discretionary subject to agreement between the two parties.

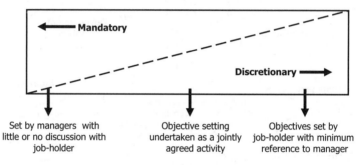

| Set by managers with little or no discussion with job-holder | Objective setting undertaken as a jointly agreed activity | Objectives set by job-holder with minimum reference to manager |

Model taken from *The Handbook of Management*, page 904, 3rd edition, Gower Publishing, 1992. Reproduced with kind permission of the editor Dennis Lock. Copyright Dennis Lock.

ACTION-CENTRED LEADERSHIP

The leadership task is to effectively undertake three inter-related activities, in John Adair's Action-Centred Leadership model this is represented by three circles representing Adair's identified three core management responsibilities: achieving the task; building and managing the team or group; and finally managing the work and development of individuals. While the team leader will have to assign tasks, build the team and play a role in the development of staff, it should also be noted that high performing teams exhibit the same regard for task, teamworking and self- and group development opportunities.

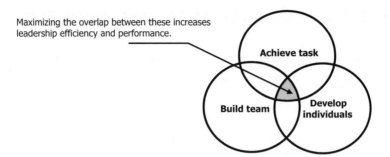

Maximizing the overlap between these increases leadership efficiency and performance.

Three circles model reproduced with permission of John Adair from *Effective Leadership*, 1988, Pan.

COACHING AND MENTORING

This model provides the rationale for the choice of coaching or mentoring based upon the intensity of the support and the role of the individual or organization in supporting this style of development.

Organization decides

Traditional coaching	Traditional mentoring
Counselling	Developmental mentoring/ coaching

Specific focus   Broad focus

Individual decides

Model reproduced with kind permission of Julie Hay, modified from her article published in *Effective Consulting*, August 2002.

HUMAN RESOURCE PLANNING PROCESS

This model shows the organization's business plan in relation to its resources requirement as part of its HR strategy.

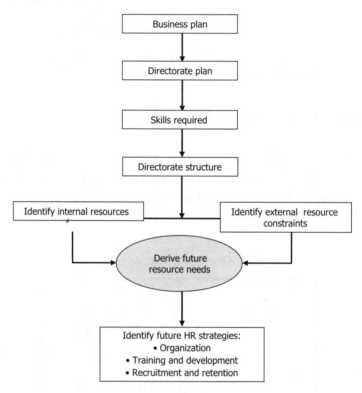

From Tony Dawson, *Principles and Practice of Modern Management*. Reproduced with kind permission of Liverpool Academic Press, 2000.

CORE SKILLS FOR PERFORMANCE MANAGEMENT

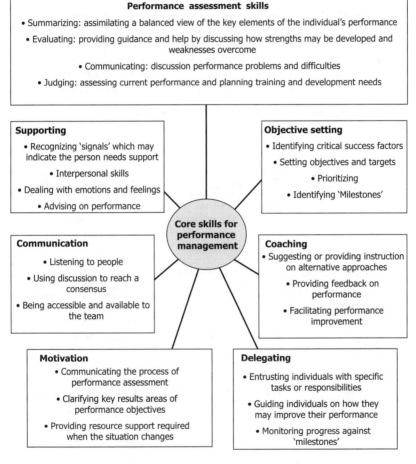

Performance assessment skills

- Summarizing: assimilating a balanced view of the key elements of the individual's performance
- Evaluating: providing guidance and help by discussing how strengths may be developed and weaknesses overcome
- Communicating: discussion performance problems and difficulties
- Judging: assessing current performance and planning training and development needs

Supporting

- Recognizing 'signals' which may indicate the person needs support
- Interpersonal skills
- Dealing with emotions and feelings
- Advising on performance

Objective setting

- Identifying critical success factors
- Setting objectives and targets
- Prioritizing
- Identifying 'Milestones'

Core skills for performance management

Communication

- Listening to people
- Using discussion to reach a consensus
- Being accessible and available to the team

Coaching

- Suggesting or providing instruction on alternative approaches
- Providing feedback on performance
- Facilitating performance improvement

Motivation

- Communicating the process of performance assessment
- Clarifying key results areas of performance objectives
- Providing resource support required when the situation changes

Delegating

- Entrusting individuals with specific tasks or responsibilities
- Guiding individuals on how they may improve their performance
- Monitoring progress against 'milestones'

Reproduced with kind permission of Michael Armstrong, from Lawrie Philpott and Louise Shepherd in *Strategies for Human Resource Management*, Michael Armstrong (ed.), 1992, Kogan Page Limited.

EMPOWERMENT

This table examines the incentives and controls in an empowered company contrasting with those of a traditional organization.

	TRADITIONAL	EMPOWERED
Executives	• Make decisions • Review results • Control firm's responses	• Delegate decisions • Plan for the future • Develop vision
Managers	• Supervise people • Monitor activity • Make work assignments • Report to the top	• Support team building • Manage systems • Coach teams • Report to the top
Rewards are	• Primary extrinsic (money and benefits) • Little intrinsic possible	• Lean to intrinsic (but extrinsic often equal to traditional) • Business results
Basis for pay	• Job duties performed • People supervised	• Team output • Variable salary
People receive	• Fixed salary • Small bonuses (pay for behaviour)	• Large bonuses (pay to performance) • Critical activity
Vision setting	• Limited activity	• Bottom-up process
Goal setting	• Top-down activity	• Customers have input
Performance appraisal	• Supervisor/manager only • Closely guarded process • One-to-one assessment	• Team mates may share • May have team assessment • Uses results-based performance data
Choosing leaders	• Relies on managerial judgement • Boss/bosses appointed to lead work groups • Critical management activity	• Leadership rotates inside a work team • Personal control is much less important

While individual teams may have a degree of empowerment from their immediate manager it is clear that for full empowerment covering rewards, goal setting, appraisals, etc. empowerment needs to be driven from the top to become part of the company culture and business philosophy.

TYPICAL PERFORMANCE MANAGEMENT PROCESS

This typical performance management process is widely used for setting and monitoring staff objectives and is often used as part of a formal performance appraisal system.

1. Objective setting

- Individual clear when to perform and what is expected
- Performance targets, measures and standards exist
- Seen as attainable by individual

6. Recognition

- Positive if performance is as expected
- If performance is not up to standard identify problem and communicate need for improvement

2. The individual

- Capability to perform as desired – skills and knowledge
- Willing to perform

5. Performance monitoring

- Interim reviews of performance
- Identify interim targets
- Take action to remedy poor performance as necessary

4. Feedback

- Relevant, immediate and frequent
- Constructive, balanced and specific
- Focused on critical success factors of task behaviour

3. Resources

- People
- Equipment, materials
- Information
- Plans
- Money

This cyclical process is often used either on an annual basis or on a task basis as appropriate. Although setting realistic and achievable objectives can be used to improve performance the task needs to be periodically reviewed and monitored.

CONTINUUM OF LEADERSHIP STYLES

This model shows the full range of the use of authority in decision making. It is unusual to find examples purely at either end of the continuum and even within the 'middle ground' the amount of authority/freedom can change with respect to situations, individuals and team dynamics.

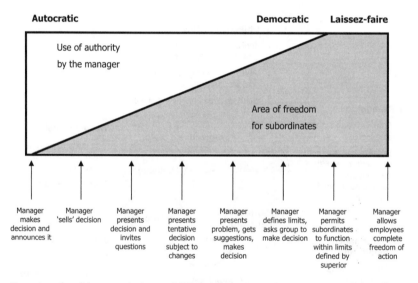

| Manager makes decision and announces it | Manager 'sells' decision | Manager presents decision and invites questions | Manager presents tentative decision subject to changes | Manager presents problem, gets suggestions, makes decision | Manager defines limits, asks group to make decision | Manager permits subordinates to function within limits defined by superior | Manager allows employees complete freedom of action |

Reprinted with permission of *Harvard Business Review*. An exhibit from 'How to choose a leadership pattern' by Robert Trannenbaum and W. H. Schmidt (May–June 1973). Copyright by the President and Fellows of Harvard College, all rights reserved.

THE BASIC MOTIVATIONAL MODEL

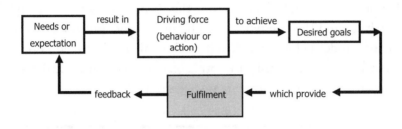

UNDERSTANDING CONFLICT – FIVE LAYERS

- Misunderstandings – these occur by accident and arise from misconceptions about what is said or intended; they are fairly easy to resolve once recognized.
- Differences in values and beliefs – as people have their own principles and sets of values differences can lead to disagreements about organizational objectives and decisions. These are often witnessed when organizations undergo a merger.
- Differences of interest and ambition – groups and individuals have different interests and ambitions, which result in competition for limited power, status and resources within organizations; in turn this can lead to conflict.
- Interpersonal differences – for whatever reason some people have difficulty in working with others and conflict can arise from such personality clashes.
- Feelings and emotions – these can also be intertwined with conflict, and often are disguised as 'the principle of the matter'. Conflict can arouse strong emotions that lead to further conflict and once emotions are aroused, the sense of proportion can be lost and the conflict escalates.

MODEL OF CONFLICT BEHAVIOUR

Resolving conflict depends on the behaviour of the people involved, and their responses can be one of five categories shown in the model below, which reflect the balance between cooperation (attempts to satisfy the other person's concerns) and assertion (attempts to satisfy your own concerns).

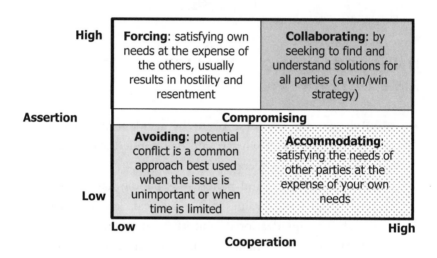

This article was published in *Organizational Behaviour and Human Performance* (now known as *Organizational Behaviour and Human Decision Processes*), Volume 16, by Thomas L. Ruble and Kenneth W. Thomas, 'Support for a two-dimensional model of conflict behaviour', pages 143–155, 1976. Copyright Elsevier. Reproduced with permission.

THE ALIGNMENT MODEL

Organizational alignment means creating a culture in which strategies, values and day-to-day behaviours are consistent and compatible.

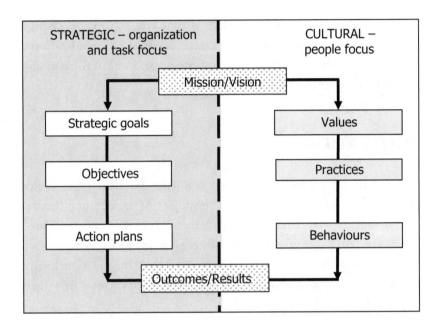

The model shows two interdependent paths for providing direction for helping move from the global statement of the organization's mission and vision to specific business results.

- **The strategic path** emphasizes what needs to be done and the broad strategic goals the organization will work towards; the objectives that groups and individuals must accomplish to carry out those strategies and the activities that must be performed to meet those objectives.
- **The cultural path** emphasizes how things will be done and the values implied by the mission and vision; the practices that reflect those values and the specific day-to-day behav-

iours that will represent the values and practices to others as people go about their work. Note that these values have to do with the way the organization conducts its business, not with people's personal values about home, family, religion, relationships, etc.

The key implication of this model is that any significant change whether strategic or cultural must take account of organizational alignment, compatibility between strategic and cultural paths and consistency within them.

MOTIVATION

The work on motivation theory was first published by Victor Vroom over 40 years ago under the subject of expectancy theory. This proposes that behaviour results from conscious choices aimed at maximizing pleasure and minimizing pain. However, Edward Lawler and Lyman Porter later suggested that the relationship of work behaviour and goals was not as simple as was first imagined by other scientists.

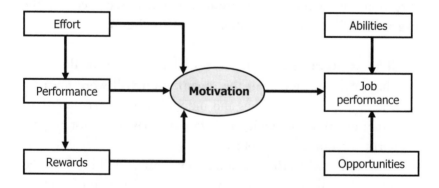

NEEDS AND EXPECTATIONS OF PEOPLE AT WORK

Managing the needs and expectations of staff is not just providing more economic rewards such as salary, bonuses, etc. but is a balance between other inter-related activities such as job satisfaction and social relationship with other members of the organization.

This model can also relate to creating commitment as shown in Chapter 2 and also provides a link to individual and team motivation.

CULTURE AND PERFORMANCE

This model illustrates how both employee and employer behaviour, values and culture play a joint role in converting the organization's desired performance targets into meeting and supporting longer-term strategic objectives. It can be used to gain an understanding and match both sides of the equation: from the employees' viewpoint in understanding their capabilities, level of involvement and individual values compared and linked to the employer's position on organizational design, reward and corporate values including the 'soft' issues. Such knowledge will provide a better match between individual capability and the organization's performance targets.

© Professor S. A. Burtonshaw-Gunn, unpublished model.

MUTUAL OBJECTIVE SETTING AND PERFORMANCE MANAGEMENT

While this model is cyclic it does not follow the plan-do-review approach, instead it shows progression from agreeing the objectives to discussing performance with joint actions which managers and staff need to instigate with a view to improving performance.

It is suggested that the following actions are necessary:

- Ensure clarity on overall goals.
- Make task lists independently.
- Discuss and agree on a mutually acceptable list.
- Clarify objective of each task.
- Describe: action-result-standards.
- Ensure understanding and agreement.

From Dr Tim Hannagan, *Management Concepts and Practices*. 2005. Reproduced with permission of Pearson Education.

COMMUNICATIONS

Six steps to good communications:

- Perceive difficulties as opportunities for creating something new.
- Accent the positive: state your outcome in positive terms.
- Create an evidence procedure: how will I know it when I see it.
- Institute a measurable outcome.
- Use assumptions: when doubt and distrust are present, check assumptions.
- Get curious, ask questions to gain new information.

Six steps to active listening with the use of paraphrasing, clarifying, giving feedback, openness and awareness:

- Concentration
- Acknowledgement
- Responding
- Exercising emotional control
- Sensing underlying issues
- Structuring and sequencing a response

MASLOW'S HIERARCHY OF NEEDS – MOTIVATION MODEL

In 1943 the behavioural scientist Abraham Maslow wrote a paper called 'A theory of human motivation' which put forward what has become the most widely accepted model on the subject. Maslow proposed that satisfying human needs is continuous and as soon as one need is satisfied another takes its place. This implies that there is a hierarchy of importance. Maslow divided these 'needs' into the following groups:

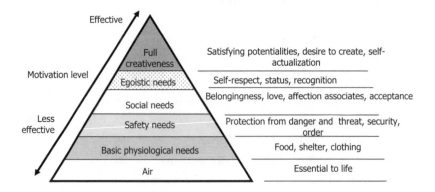

If a lower level need is not satisfied or at risk then a higher one will be given up as the hierarchy reasserts itself. In using this model for motivation, concentrating on the motivation factor has only a temporary effect if it is already sufficiently satisfied. While it was originally published in *Psychological Review* in 1944, there are many management and business books that cover Maslow's hierarchy of needs in detail as it is widely used when studying motivation. The version below shows how the activity of work can be mapped on to this model. In addition Marketing experts use this model to help them understand customer motives and behaviour when buying goods and services. It then allows them to design promotion approaches that harness or awaken specific needs to add psychological support to their advertising campaigns.

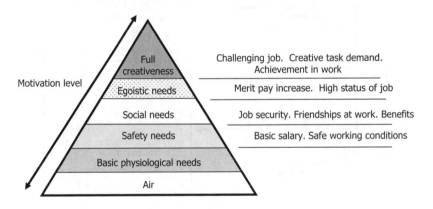

ANOTHER MOTIVATION MODEL – HERZBERG'S TWO-FACTOR THEORY

In 1966 Frederick Herzberg researched the topic of motivation by focusing his study on professional engineers and accountants where they were asked to describe incidents in their jobs which gave them strong feelings of satisfaction or dissatisfaction. He divided these answers into two categories or factors.

One he called 'Motivators' which he said provided workers with job satisfaction such as recognition for effort and in turn made them more efficient. However, he recognized that this was not guaranteed as other factors also affected productivity.

The other group he called 'Hygiene Factors' which lead to dissatisfaction of the workforce. Improving the hygiene factors could reduce or remove dissatisfaction, for example better canteen facilities. He suggested that an improvement in hygiene factors alone would not be likely to motivate an individual, but if they were not met then a fall in productivity was likely to result.

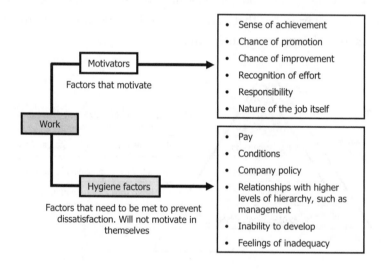

Herzberg's ideas are frequently linked to job enrichment often encouraging workers to become more involved and motivated and gain a greater sense of achievement.

THEORY X AND THEORY Y – DOUGLAS MCGREGOR

Douglas McGregor believed that the way that organizations were run was as a direct result of their managers and published his famous book *The Human Side of Enterprise* in 1960. The research behind Theory X and Theory Y suggested that Theory X assumes that people are lazy, dislike work and need a mixture of 'carrot and stick' to perform; that they are basically immature, need direction and are incapable of taking responsibility. Theory Y assumes the opposite – that people actually have a psychological need to work and want to achieve and have responsibility.

He formulated six basic assumptions for Theory Y:

- The expenditure of physical and mental effort on work is as natural as play or rest. The average human being does not inherently dislike work. Depending upon controllable conditions, work may be a source of satisfaction (and will be voluntarily performed) or a source of punishment (and will be avoided as possible).
- External control and the threat of punishment are not the only means for bringing effort towards organizational objectives. People will exercise self-direction and self-control in the service of objectives to which they are committed.
- Commitment to objectives is a function of the rewards associated with their achievement. The most significant of such rewards, e.g. the satisfaction of ego and self-actualization needs, can be direct products of effort directed towards organizational objectives.
- The average human being learns, under proper conditions, not only to accept but to seek responsibility.
- The capacity to exercise a relatively high degree of imagination, ingenuity and creativity in the solution of organizational problems is widely distributed in the population.
- Under the conditions of modern industrial life, the intellectual potentialities of the average human being are only partially utilized.

McGregor pointed out that these assumptions had a deep implication for management.

REVIEWING COMMUNICATION EFFECTIVENESS

This model shows that there are seven key areas to be considered when preparing for communication. For most of the time the approach to communication is a repeat of what has already worked in the past. The benefit of this model is to prompt the communicator to consider the aspects when non-routine communications are necessary, for example of company announcements.

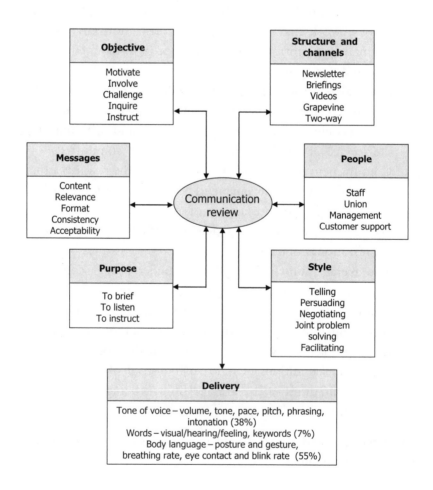

TYPES OF STAFF

This model shows how people may be viewed against their potential and current/past performance; this is very subjective and often varies over a period of time, i.e. people have off days and other moments of high performance. While it may be possible to turn all employees into stars the cost and time associated with this may be prohibitive.

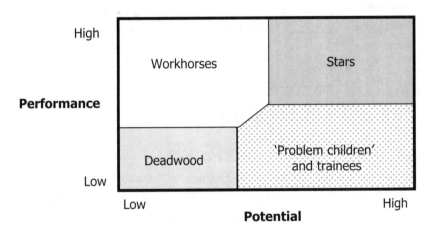

COMPETENCIES

To provide a fully effective job performance, people need to be effective in three areas: **knowledge** (what we know), **skills** (what we can do) and **competencies** (how we go about it). These three areas can be applied to a number of competencies within an organization such as customer focus, teamworking, innovation and problem solving, communications, etc. These competencies are linked into individual performance as shown below:

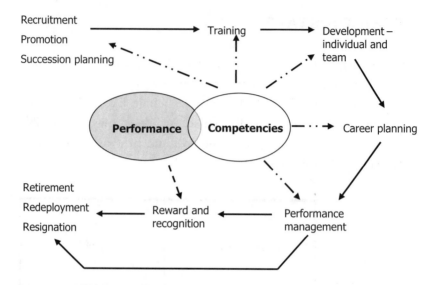

THE JOHARI WINDOW

The Johari Window is named after the first names of its inventors, Joseph Luft and Harry Ingham, and is one of the most useful models describing the process of human interaction. A four paned 'window' divides personal awareness into four different types: open, hidden, blind, and unknown.

	Behaviour known to self	**Behaviour unknown to self**
Behaviour known to others	Open	Blind
Behaviour unknown to others	Hidden	Unknown

- The 'open' quadrant represents free activity or public area and refers to behaviour and motivation that both I know about myself, and that you know about me.
- The 'blind' quadrant represents where others can see things in ourselves of which we are unaware.
- The 'hidden' quadrant represents things that I know about myself, that you do not know. As we get to know and trust each other, I will then feel more comfortable disclosing more intimate details about myself (e.g. a hidden agenda, or matters about which we have sensitive feelings). This process is called 'self-disclosure'.
- The 'unknown' quadrant represents areas of unknown activity, in which neither the individual nor others are aware of certain behaviours or motives. Yet, we can assume their existence because eventually some of these behaviours and motives were influencing our relationship all along.

	Customer's view	
Individual's view	**Explicit/ Contractual** We both know	**Hidden** Your customer knows, you don't
	Opportunity You know, your customer doesn't	**Latent** Neither of us knows

Customer's view

The same concept can be used to understand how your views and that of your customers can be used to improve communications and your relationship. This is shown in this version of the Johari model.

TEAMWORK AND LEADERSHIP

This model shows the behaviour types linked to teamwork and their management. It is from the work of Paul Hersey and Kenneth Blanchard who first published their work leadership in an article in *Training and Development Journal* in May 1969 under the title 'Lifecycle theory of leadership'. Since then it has featured in many publications including their own books on *Situational Leadership* in 1982, *Organizational Behavior* in 1993 and *Leadership and the One Minute Manager* published in 1994.

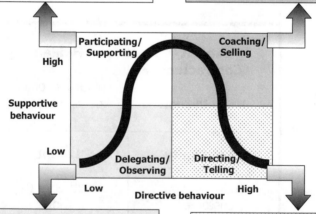

- Team leader has high level of interaction with the team
- Most communication from the team leader is positive feedback and emotional support, leader will protect them from attack and any criticism of the team's performance
- Team members chair meetings, although leader may take over these functions if others are too busy or pressured
- Team members trust the leader

- Leader takes a high level of interest in the development needs of the team and its members, identifying opportunities to help members realize their own ambitions
- Communication from the team leader is often to the individual, with support for new learning opportunities and experiences. The leader will protect the individuals from attack and any criticism of their performance
- The team leader will encourage members to participate in meetings

Participating/ Supporting

Coaching/ Selling

High

Supportive behaviour

Low

Delegating/ Observing

Directing/ Telling

Low   **High**

Directive behaviour

- Team leader has low level of interaction with the team
- Most communication from the team leader is responding to proposals and suggestions from the team
- Team members chair meetings, allocate work, give one another feedback and seek feedback directly from outside the team
- Team members feel respected by leader

- Team leader has high level of interaction with the team
- Most communication from the team leader is giving information and directions
- Team leader chairs meetings, allocates work, is the main source of feedback for the team
- Team members respect and rely on leader

Reprinted with permission of HarperCollins Publishers Ltd. © Kenneth Blanchard, 1994.

THE TEAM LIFE CYCLE

The original model published in 1965 by Dr Bruce Tuckman in the article 'Development sequences in small groups' (*Psychological Bulletin*, Volume 63, Number 6) only covered the first four of these stages. He added the fifth stage in the 1970s.

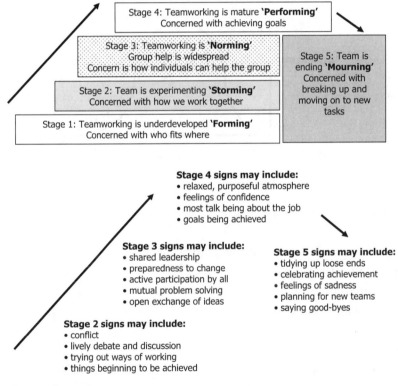

From Bruce W. Tuckman and M. A. C. Jenson, 'Development sequences in small groups', *Psychological Bulletin*, Volume 63, Number 6, 1977. The American Psychological Association. Reprinted with permission.

STRESS MANAGEMENT

The typically expected relationship between stress and performance is shown in the dashed straight line; however, the actual
relationship is shown in the solid line indicating that an acceptable level of stress aids performance.

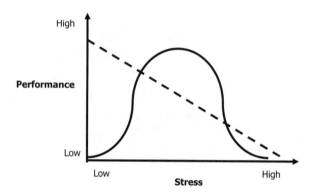

Common causes of stress are:

- Responsibility for the work of others
- Innovative functions
- Integrative or boundary functions
- Relationship problems
- Career uncertainty
- Role-based stress
  - Role ambiguity
  - Role incompatibility
  - Role conflict
  - Role overload or underload

From Tony Dawson, *Principles and Practice of Modern Management*. Reproduced with kind permission of Liverpool Academic Press, 2000.

THE LEADERSHIP GRID

This is a widely known management style model comprising five types depending on whether the focus is on people or performance, as is discussed below.

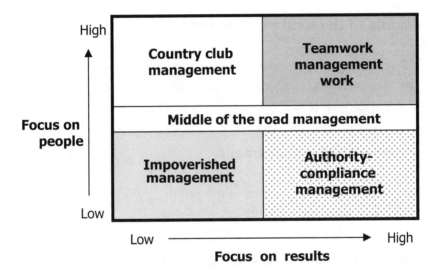

Country club management

Thoughtful attention to the needs of people for satisfying relationships leads to a comfortable, friendly, organization atmosphere and work tempo.

Team management work

Accomplishment is from committed people; interdependence through a 'common stake' in organization purpose leads to relationships of trust and respect.

Middle of the road management

Adequate organization performance is possible through balancing the necessity to get out work with maintaining morale of people at a satisfactory level.

Impoverished management

Exertion of minimum effort to get required work done is appropriate to sustain organization membership.

Authority-compliance management

Efficiency in operations results from arranging conditions of work in such a way that human elements interfere to a minimum degree.

This article was published in the *New Management Grid: the key to leadership excellence* by Robert R. Blake and Jane S. Mouton, 2nd edition, pages 11–12, 1978. Copyright Elsevier.

GIVING AND RECEIVING FEEDBACK

Performance measures

- Employee related – employee satisfaction, attendance, turn-over, safety, suggestions, etc.
- Operational – reliability, delivery, processing times, lead times, stock turnover, errors, cost of rework.
- Customer satisfaction – overall index, retention and complaints.
- Market and financial – market share, cash, profit, ROA, ROS, sales per employee.

TRUST

'To be **persuasive** we must be believable; to be **believable** we must be credible; to be **credible** we must be **truthful**.'
Edward R. Murrow (American journalist, 1908–1965)

Building trust between people is an important business requirement and one that needs to be worked at; it can be both frustrating and time consuming but offers rewards for both individuals and organizations. Indeed some would suggest that a strong trusting relationship between people from different organizations is a source of competitive advantage and a route to improved business performance. Often trust development takes place across four stages and progress from one stage needs success at the previous stage for the relationship to move forward:

- Stage 1: Don't ever trust anyone.
- Stage 2: Don't trust anyone until they prove themselves.
- Stage 3: Trust people but only until they make a mistake.
- Stage 4: Trust people even after they make a mistake.

The principles of building a trust-based relationship are:

- Go first, lead the relationship by example.
- Illustrate the topic by drawing on relevant examples, don't tell.
- Listen for what's different, not for what's familiar.
- Be sure your advice is being sought.
- Earn the right to offer advice.
- Say what you mean.
- When you need help, ask for it.
- Show an interest in the person and what is important to them.
- Respect other cultures if different to your own.
- Use compliments not flattery.
- Show appreciation.

Recommended further reading: *The Trusted Advisor* by David Maister, 2002, Free Press.

OBJECTIVE SETTING

Objectives must be:

• Defined	• **S**pecific
• Agreed AND Be 'SMART' . . .	• **M**easurable
• Written	• **A**chievable
	• **R**ealistic
	• **T**ime bound

CHAPTER 10

PROCESS IMPROVEMENT

P rocess improvement is the systematic effort to understand every aspect of a process in order to reduce rework, variation, and needless complexity, therefore contributing to a organization's performance through effectiveness and efficiency. While the obvious starting point is to gain an understanding of an organization's current processes in order to identify where waste and/or rework occurs it is also possible to take a more 'visionary' approach and look to producing new processes without the constraints or inhibitions imposed by an organization's current operations and capabilities. This envision stage exists in a standard business process re-engineering methodology and will then require a match to be made between the 'to be' processes of the organization and those of the current 'as is' position. One of the tools that can be used to compare and contrast similar processes in an organization, even if undertaken at different locations, is the POLDAT approach first used by the American Computer

Services Corporation. In addition to this internal comparison is the growing use of 'benchmarking' where comparison is made with similar and dissimilar industries and companies to mutually seek improvement in process operations.

One of the well-known and widely used models in Europe is the EFQM Business Excellence model which itself has similarities to the American 'Malcolm Baldrige National Quality Award' both of which prompt organizations to look at their processes and in particular question how they are developed, used, reviewed and updated. At a higher level the Business Excellence model also promotes the use of benchmarking with other companies and places great emphasis on performance measurement over time. This performance measurement can be customer or employee feedback (qualitative data), or financial reports, defect rates, etc. (quantitative data) and used to re-examine the alignment of company processes to business and customer requirements.

To be effective from a business viewpoint, process improvement needs to be regarded as a continual activity, as without such commitment it is likely that the company's performance will fail to keep pace with its competitors and larger change will then be required. In addition process improvement is in many cases the starting point of a much larger business improvement programme and can incrementally develop into a large-scale change management programme.

Companies may wish to address process improvement through the establishment of virtual teams or, at the other extreme, have dedicated staff charged with undertaking process improvement activity across an organization. For some companies process improvement arises from other business activities such as problem solving; however, one of the most used tools in this area is that of process mapping which encourages detailed investigation and analysis of how the company discharges its work. In this chapter some guidance notes are provided on process mapping which is a powerful visual tool for showing the sequence of activities, flow of information, decision points and the range of possible process outcomes. Process maps are usually presented in the form of a flow diagram and often have their own drawing convention; in widespread use is the internationally recognized Unified Modelling Language. Another area covered in this book which is applicable to those undertaking process improvement is the use of workshops.

THE RE-ENGINEERING SPECTRUM

A range of process improvement initiatives are available. This model suggests that a measure of the different ways in which organizations have interpreted the concept of re-engineering lies in a range of ambition of those who are applying it. The choice is dependent upon factors around the extent of the change required.

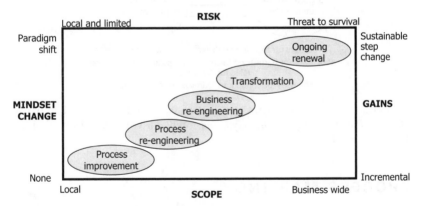

Reproduced by kind permission of Professor Colin Coulson-Thomas. Model by Rohit Talwar in *Business Process Re-engineering: myth and reality*, ed. Colin Coulson-Thomas. Kogan Page, 1996.

BUSINESS PROCESS RE-ENGINEERING STAGES

With this model its author suggests that the best form of long-term insurance against failure or irrelevance and protection against errors of judgement or perception is to build learning loops into processes and create a learning community. Adding that many who talk about the learning organization fail to identify the processes that enable an enterprise to match its vision, goal and capability to the changing requirements of customers and other stakeholders.

Processes for focusing on delivery of value to customers.
Processes for harnessing talents of groups and teams to add value for customers.
Processes for continuous learning and improvement.

Reproduced with kind permission of Professor Colin Coulson-Thomas in *Business Process Re-engineering: myth and reality* ed. Colin Coulson-Thomas, Kogan Page, 1996.

PROCESS MAPPING

Process mapping is a workflow diagram to provide a clear understanding of a business process or series of parallel processes. It is used as part of a process improvement activity and often follows seven main steps to construct the process flowchart. The text below offers some guidance.

Step 1: Determine the boundaries
Where does a process begin?
Where does a process end?

Step 2: List the steps
Use a verb to start the task description.
The flowchart can either show sufficient information to understand the general process flow or detail every finite action and decision point.

Step 3: Sequence the steps
Use Post-it notes so you can move tasks.
Do not draw arrows until later.

Step 4: Draw appropriate symbols
Start with the basic symbols:

• Ovals show input to start the process or output at the end of the process.
• Boxes or rectangles show task or activity performed in the process.
• Arrows show process direction flow.
• Diamonds show points in the process where yes/no questions are asked or a decision is required.

Usually there is only one arrow out of an activity box. If there is more than one arrow, you may need a decision diamond. If there are feedback arrows, make sure feedback loop is closed; i.e. it should take you back to the input box.

Step 5: System model
Draw charts using system model approach:

• Input – use information based upon people, machines, material, method, and environment.

- Process – use subsets of processes in series or parallel.
- Output – use outcomes or desired results.
- Control – use best in class business rules.
- Feedback – use information from surveys or feedback.

Step 6: Check for completeness

Include pertinent chart information, using title and date for easy reference.

Step 7: Finalize the flowchart

Ask if this process is being run the way it should be.
Are people following the process as charted?
Is there a consensus?
What is redundant; add what is missing.

Reproduced with kind permission of Christopher Ahoy, Associate Vice President, Facilities Planning and Management, Iowa State University.

PROCESS IMPROVEMENT

There are a number of approaches for business process re-engineering, this is a typical four stage approach:

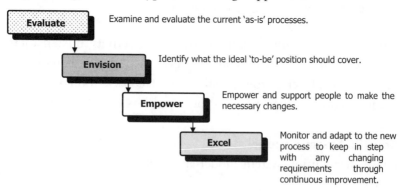

Evaluate — Examine and evaluate the current 'as-is' processes.

Envision — Identify what the ideal 'to-be' position should cover.

Empower — Empower and support people to make the necessary changes.

Excel — Monitor and adapt to the new process to keep in step with any changing requirements through continuous improvement.

The American Computer Services Corporation (CSC) developed this hexagonal 'POLDAT' model which has seen widespread use and is a good tool to use when comparing similar processes in different organizations or in different parts of the same organization.

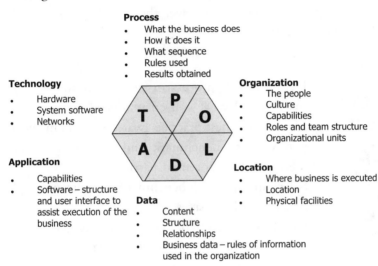

Process
- What the business does
- How it does it
- What sequence
- Rules used
- Results obtained

Technology
- Hardware
- System software
- Networks

Organization
- The people
- Culture
- Capabilities
- Roles and team structure
- Organizational units

Application
- Capabilities
- Software – structure and user interface to assist execution of the business

Data
- Content
- Structure
- Relationships
- Business data – rules of information used in the organization

Location
- Where business is executed
- Location
- Physical facilities

STAGES IN THE RE-ENGINEERING PROCESS

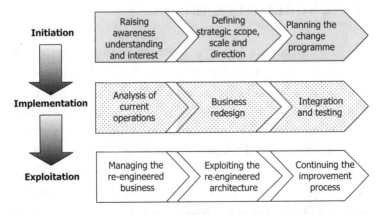

Reproduced with kind permission of Professor Colin Coulson-Thomas. Model by Rohit Talwar in *Business Process Re-engineering: myth and reality*, ed. Colin Coulson-Thomas, Kogan Page, 1996.

STAGES IN BENCHMARKING

Comparing an organization's performance by benchmarking with others has grown in popularity over the last 10 years and often follows these five stages:

Define

Identify

Approach

Conduct

Use

- Define which process or practice is to be benchmarked and what you currently do
- Identify any best practice award winners in the area you wish to benchmark and list contact persons who could be potential partners
- Select and approach benchmark partners and explain benefits to both sides
- Conduct benchmark visit and identify learning points and provide feedback to benchmark partner
- Use learning points to create benchmark report and options and agree next steps and implement

EFQM EXCELLENCE MODEL

The EFQM Excellence Model is based on nine criteria: 'Enablers' which cover what an organization does and 'Results' what an organization achieves. The two sets are interlinked as the 'Results' are caused by 'Enablers' and feedback from 'Results' suggests areas for improvement of the 'Enablers' through innovation and organizational learning. In looking at the two groups the Business Excellence Model is constructed on the premise that excellent results (People, Customers and Society leading to delivery of a businesses Key performance results) are achieved by Leadership and its relationship with Policy and Strategy, People, and Partnerships and Resources.

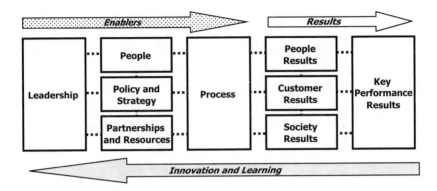

The fundamental concepts which underpin the EFQM Excellence Model are:

- Results that delight all the organization's stakeholders.
- Customer focus in creating sustainable customer value.
- Strategic leadership with a clear shared vision.
- Process management through a set of interdependent and inter-related systems, and processes.
- People development and involvement to maximize employee contribution through continuous learning, development and involvement to create innovation and improvement opportunities.
- Partnership with development and long-term involvement of value-adding partnerships.
- Social responsibility where the organization's operation is in harmony with its surroundings and meets their stakeholders' expectations.

EFQM Excellence Model © reproduced with kind permission of EFQM (www.efqm.org)

CHAPTER 11

PRODUCT MANAGEMENT

A good start to understanding product management is to consider the three traditional classes of production:

- Primary production is the earliest stage in the production process such as that witnessed in mining, farming, oil extraction, tree-felling, etc.
- Secondary production involves converting the primary production raw materials into finished or part-finished goods either through constructing or manufacturing.
- Tertiary production describes the activities of the services sector of the economy with examples such as retail, insurance, banking and direct services to the public such as policing, nursing, etc.

Product management can be undertaken as a management activity in any of the three classes of production and is regarded as a collective term used to describe the broad sum of diverse activities performed in the interest of delivering a particular product to market. The tasks involved with this can cover product planning or the marketing of a product or products at all stages in its life cycle. Indeed from a practical perspective, product management can comprise two professional disciplines: product planning and product marketing although some companies perceive them as being one discipline, which they call product management. Organizations depend on the abilities of their product management team to perform activities to satisfy customer's requirements utilizing five main areas of product management of people, product, process, plant and programme with the objectives of balancing the need to minimize cost and maximize quality; maximize the use of the plant yet minimize inventory and stock holding levels; and satisfy identified requirements to efficiently and effectively meet customer needs. This is often achieved through a joint marketing/engineering effort depending on the stage of the product life cycle.

The relationship between marketing and engineering is illustrated in the technical life cycle which aligns the relative effort of both disciplines with the product life cycle ranging from conception and cutting edge through to maturity and decline. Indeed the management of the design model suggests that it is three disciplines which are linked together through the development of a new product, these being production, marketing and industrial design where each function has a valid contribution to bring to the design process. As companies look for improved performance one method of supporting this is to identify and eliminate waste, look to lean production principles developed by Japanese industry, primarily in Toyota, and examine products from a number of interpretations of the term 'value'. Having mentioned minimizing costs a list of wastes is given in this chapter together with a model on lean production.

The final model in this section again brings together production and marketing in the product life cycle graph combined with the product performance matrix. Product management is not a stand-alone topic and some of the models within supply chain management are applicable to those involved in this management topic.

THE TECHNOLOGICAL LIFE CYCLE

Phases and features of a product life cycle.

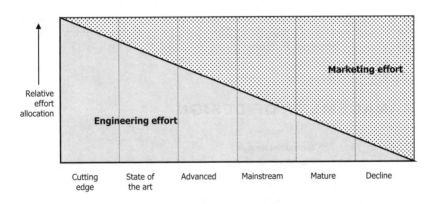

Cutting edge	• Technology marketed without specific application • No target market • Sell on technology markets
State of the art	• Adopt cutting edge to meet wider market needs • Sell on technological benefits • Begin to sell on benefits
Advanced	• 'Product' concept adopted • Sell on benefits

Mainstream	• Low cost, high quality standard product • Sell on benefits • Segmented market
Mature	• Reduced product differentiation (commodity market) • Shift from segmentation to customer service
Decline	• Displaced by new technologies • Price competition

From 'Industrial market behaviour and the technology lifecycle', in *Industrial Management and Data Systems*, Nov/Dec 1986. Reproduced with kind permission of Emerald Publishing.

MANAGEMENT OF DESIGN

Industrial design
• Aesthetic knowledge
• Social and cultural backgrounds
• Environmental relationships
• Ergonomic requirements
• Insight into aspects of marketing and production
• Visual trends

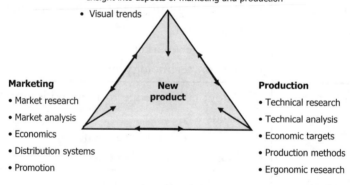

Marketing
• Market research
• Market analysis
• Economics
• Distribution systems
• Promotion

New product

Production
• Technical research
• Technical analysis
• Economic targets
• Production methods
• Ergonomic research

TYPE OF DESIGN	REASON
Design for distinctiveness	The development of innovation design (not necessarily technology).
Design for production	To ensure that component parts are made easily and economically in the manufacturing process itself; here, the designer must be aware of the production processes, technology, alternative methods and their costs.
Design for function	Value in use implies quality and reliability (the product must satisfy the customer in its prime function over the expected life period).
Design for aesthetic appeal/appearance	To appeal to the eye and attract customers.
Design for distribution	To facilitate easy low cost packaging, and a reduction of handling and storage space.

From Edgar P. Hibbert, *International Business – strategy and operations*, 1997, Macmillan Business. Reproduced with permission of Palgrave Macmillan.

LEAN THINKING – WASTE

Waste in lean thinking terms is anything that does not add value to a product or service for the customer. Toyota Production Services identified the following seven wastes as '*muda*':

- Overproduction
- Defects
- Unnecessary inventory
- Inappropriate processing
- Excessive transportation
- Waiting
- Unnecessary motion

EMBODIMENT AND DESIGN

Embodiment design begins with a preferred concept and ends with a fully developed, tested and working prototype. The top half of the model shows the inputs and outputs involved in the embodiment design process. This leads into the detail design process which takes these outputs to determine how the product will be made and where the design principles become progressively more specific in terms of the materials and manufacturing processes involved.

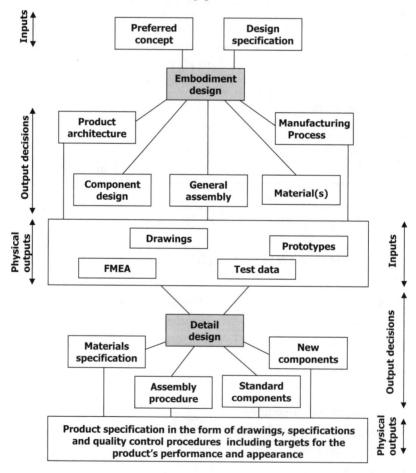

Reproduced with kind permission of Dr Mike Baxter, from *Product Design: a practical guide to systematic methods of new product development*, Nelson Thornes (Publishers) Ltd, 1995.

OPERATING EFFICIENCY:
CYCLE OF PRODUCTION

The cycle of production can be applied to any sector to illustrate the process whereby cash is used to purchase raw materials, which are processed in some way (work-in-progress) to produce the company's output (finished goods), which are finally sold for cash or used to create accounts receivable, which return to the start of the cycle with this new cash.

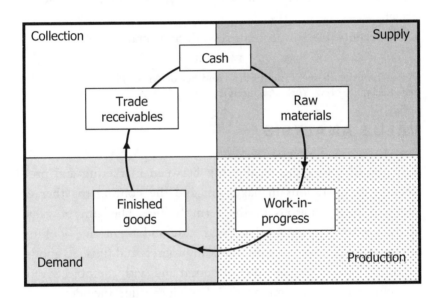

SEVEN WASTES

It is suggested that there are seven major wastes typically found in mass production, as categorized by Taiichi Ohno:

- **Overproduction** – producing ahead of what is actually needed by the next process or customer. The worst form of waste because it contributes to the other six.
- **Waiting** – operators standing idle as machine cycles, equipment fails, or needed parts fail to arrive.

- **Conveyance** – moving parts and products unnecessarily, such as from a processing step to a warehouse to a subsequent processing step when a second step instead could be located immediately adjacent to the first.
- **Processing** – performing unnecessary or incorrect processing, typically from poor tools or production design.
- **Inventory** – having more than the minimum stocks necessary for a precisely controlled 'pull' system.
- **Motion** – operators making movements that are straining or unnecessary, such as looking for parts, tools, documents, etc.
- **Correction** – inspection, rework and scrap.

For further details see Taiichi Ohno and Setsue Mito, *Just in time for Today and Tomorrow*, New York Productivity Press, 1998.

VALUE ANALYSIS

This model shows the relationship between marketing and production or operations management and the coming together of different interpretations of the term 'value'. The aim of value analysis is to examine products with care and attention – looking at raw materials, components, work in progress and finished goods, placing emphasis on the value of design and with the objective of reducing costs. The components of product value include:

- The fact that customers with money and unsatisfied wants comprise a market sector.
- That utility must be provided to such customers, and products must fit the sector.
- Scarcity or exclusivity, reflected in a limited range at a high price.
- Total cost to the customer.
- The customer's other options.

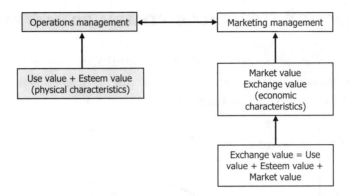

Use value is the price the purchaser will offer in order to ensure that the purpose or function of the product is achieved.

Esteem value is the price that is offered for the product over and above the use value on the basis of competitive advantage (in many cases this goes hand in hand with superior quality).

Exchange value is the conventional purchase price.

Market value is the price the purchaser will offer in the light of the scarcity of the product. Understanding market value helps to avoid reducing cost at the expense of customer acceptance.

From Edgar P. Hibbert, *International Business – strategy and operations*, 1997, Macmillan Business. Reproduced with permission of Palgrave Macmillan.

PRODUCT LIFE CYCLE COMBINED MATRIX

This model combines the Boston Consultancy Group product performance matrix with the product life cycle and was developed by Barksdale and Harris in 1982.

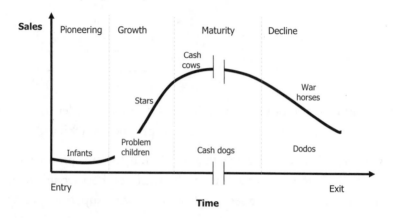

Infants are in a position where R&D costs are being recovered with high promotional expenditure in terms of educating the market.

Problem children or question marks are in a high growth situation but low market share. They are costly to maintain and market action should be taken to move them to a 'star' or 'cash cow' position.

Stars have high promotional costs but good future potential once the product/service has been accepted by the market.

Cash cows earn money in high market growth/low growth situation. Promotional costs are lower as the market is familiar with the product or service.

Cash dogs are products with a low market share in a saturated market and have a flat cash flow.

War horses are products in a declining market but which still have a relatively high market share probably as a result of competitors departing the market.

Dodos are products that are in a declining market with a low market share and a negative cash flow. They should be deleted.

This article was published in *Journal of Long Range Planning*, No. 15 by H. C. Barksdale and C. E. Harris, 'Portfolio analysis and the product life cycle', pages 74–93. Copyright Elsevier.

LEAN PRODUCTION

The five Japanese relative terms beginning with an 'S' sound describe workplace practices conducive to visual control and lean production:

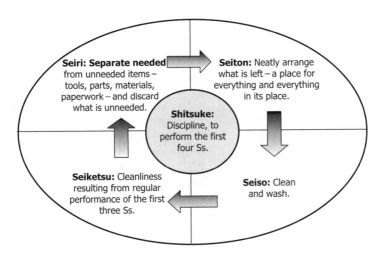

The above Japanese terms are often translated into English as:

- **Sort** → Seiri
- **Straighten** → Seiton
- **Standardize** → Shitsuke

- **Shine** → Seiso
- **Sustain** → Seiketsu

In addition some lean practitioners also add **Safety** to this list.

CHAPTER 12

PROJECT MANAGEMENT

*T*here are many approaches to managing production activities and by their nature some of these are repetitive such as mass production work; however, for one-off projects, i.e. those that have a natural start, middle and an end such as the construction of a building, then the use of adopting a project management approach is often used for organizing and managing resources (money, people, materials, space, provisions, communication, etc.) to deliver the required output against an agreed scope of work. Within the project management constraints and requirements are traditionally three key variables of time, cost and quality. However, in addition to these three parameters the management of customer expectations through communications is also essential to achieve the desired levels of customer satisfaction and possibly develop a longer-term relationship.

Whilst project management can be said to be about managing non-routine projects, and that many would say that no two projects are the same, this does not mean that this is also carried out in a non-routine or *ad-hoc* way; indeed project mangement is the application of good management practice in the form of allocating, planning and controlling resources as the project covers its life cycle. This life cycle will typically comprise identification of need, feasibility considerations, development of a suitable specification, design of required solution, building, procurement and installation through to commissioning and final operations. With a greater emphasis on understanding through-life operational costs of projects, an added task is placed on project managers to provide the most efffecient lifetime solution although this inevitably has to be balanced with the cost of the initial project and budget limitations. In addition to completion of a project there is also a growing interest in learning from experience as part of a process of continued improvement aimed to increase organizational performance.

The role of the project plan, which describes how the project management task will be executed, is widely used in connection with an organization's quality procedures as part of an overall wider governance role. The typical contents of a project plan are described in this chapter together with some models covering the control, measurement and feedback necessary to ensure that the project is delivered as required. There are a number of planning tools which can assist in the project management process to logically arrange and monitor activities against a generated programme. Some examples of project planning approaches are also shown in this chapter.

One of the key activities of project management is to identify, plan for and manage dangers and problems. While the topic of risk management is shown as a separate chapter in this book it is an integral part of project management and on large-scale projects this may be undertaken by an allocated risk manager on behalf of the project manager. As such, for those undertaking a project management role reference should also be made to Chapter 14.

A final point on project management is that, having said that this is about allocating, planning and controlling resources, it must be remembered that projects only become successful when the main people asset is professionally managed, whether this is the organization's own staff, that of the supply-chain members, other suppliers or staff within the customer's organization.

TRADITIONAL PROJECT MANAGEMENT VARIABLES

There are three main parameters of project management: time, cost and quality – these will always be in conflict. In addition to these is the need to achieve a desired level of customer satisfaction.

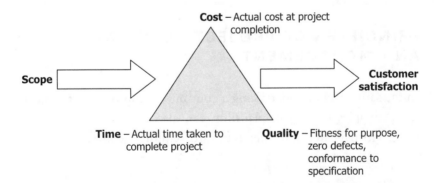

PROJECT MANAGEMENT PARAMETERS AND BENEFITS

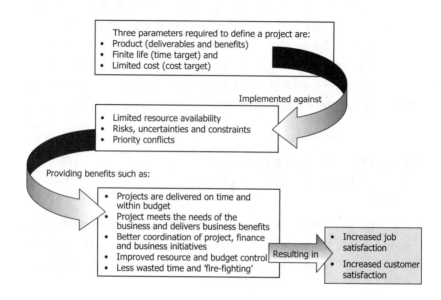

Three parameters required to define a project are:
- Product (deliverables and benefits)
- Finite life (time target) and
- Limited cost (cost target)

Implemented against

- Limited resource availability
- Risks, uncertainties and constraints
- Priority conflicts

Providing benefits such as:

- Projects are delivered on time and within budget
- Project meets the needs of the business and delivers business benefits
- Better coordination of project, finance and business initiatives
- Improved resource and budget control
- Less wasted time and 'fire-fighting'

Resulting in

- Increased job satisfaction
- Increased customer satisfaction

PRINCIPLES OF PROJECT PLANNING AND MANAGEMENT

In the same way as undertaking a continuous improvement project the principles of project planning can also use the lessons from the English writer and poet Rudyard Kipling, who wrote:

> *I keep six honest serving-men,*
> *(They taught me all I knew),*
> *There names are What and Why and When,*
> *And How and Where and Who.*

Why?

- To report that the business needs are understood including customers' needs for the project, its viability and that business policies and strategies can be satisfied by the project.

What?

- The project plan shows clearly defined project objectives: statement of requirements, scope of work, key performance indicators, priorities and time, cost and quality targets.

How and when?

- The plan reports on the agreed strategy and approach with work breakdown structure, organizational structure and resourcing plan with defined roles and responsibilities, payment schedule, cash flow forecast, vendor strategy and plans, contingency plans.

Project plan

How well?

- Suitable control and reporting systems for time and budget, risk management plan, quality assurance plan, vendor compliance, claims and variations, change management system are shown in the project plan.

What if?

- As part of the plan a section on risk assessment and contingency plans describing actions to avoid and mitigate, responsibility for monitoring threats and contingency planning should be included.

PROJECT PLANNING CHARTS

Project planning also makes use of vertical bar charts and hori-zontal Gantt charts (named after Henry Gantt) as shown below.

Gantt charts are usually sequenced in activity order and show percentage progress complete against planned duration; they also show the start and end position relative to one another.

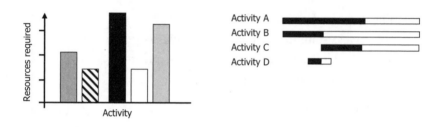

Bar charts can be used to illustrate a number of related vari-ables such as resources against activities, time against payments, project resource demand against available resources, etc.

TIME AND COST RELATIONSHIP

A typical 'S' type budget planned cost curve shows at 'Time now' the cost value of the work done compared to the budgeted expen-diture and the actual costs incurred. At the 'Time now' point shown below, although the planned costs are not exceeded by the actual costs they do not significantly exceed value. This position would suggest that while the project is not exceeding the planned rate of spend, it is also not achieving the expected progress for the costs incurred at this time. Conducting a series of regular project reviews it is possible to predict the project cost overrun and overspend and examine options to rectify the situation.

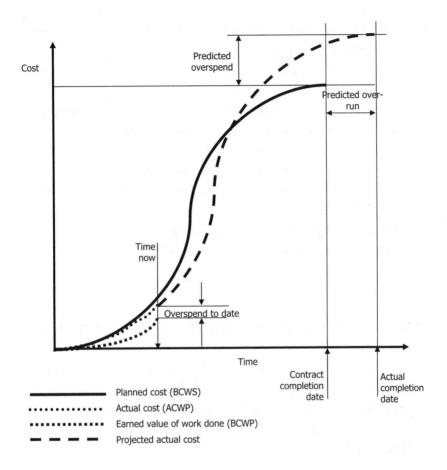

Planned cost (BCWS)

Actual cost (ACWP)

Earned value of work done (BCWP)

Projected actual cost

PROJECT MANAGEMENT – PROJECT ACCOUNTING TERMINOLOGY

In conjunction with the model on time and cost relationship opposite are the following terms:

- Budget at completion (BAC) = The total budgeted cost of the project

- Estimate to completion (ETC) = The costs still to be spent to complete the project
- Estimate at completion (EAC) = The total estimated costs of the project
- Earned value analysis = Measure of progress, monitoring cost and programme achievement against budget
- Actual cost of work performed (ACWP)
- Budget cost of work performed (BCWP)
- Cost variance (cost performance indicator) = BCWP minus ACWP
- Budget cost of work schedule (budget) = BCWS
- Schedule performance indicator = BCWP minus BCWS

MONITORING AND CONTROL PROCEDURE

This is a typical project control cycle. Looking backwards at each stage can be used to compare actual with projected progress and to review and potentially revise targets. Looking forward at each stage can be used to establish extra activities required to attain existing targets.

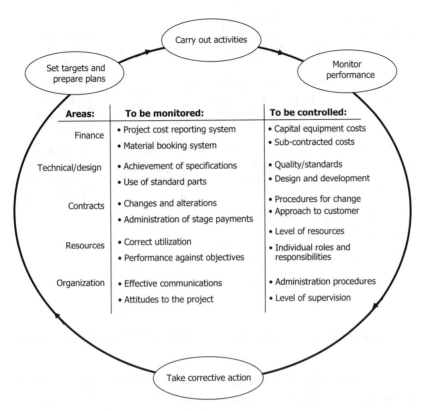

Areas:	To be monitored:	To be controlled:
Finance	• Project cost reporting system • Material booking system	• Capital equipment costs • Sub-contracted costs
Technical/design	• Achievement of specifications • Use of standard parts	• Quality/standards • Design and development
Contracts	• Changes and alterations • Administration of stage payments	• Procedures for change • Approach to customer
Resources	• Correct utilization • Performance against objectives	• Level of resources • Individual roles and responsibilities
Organization	• Effective communications • Attitudes to the project	• Administration procedures • Level of supervision

Reproduced with kind permission of Jean Harris from *Sharpen your Team's Skills in Project Management*, McGraw-Hill, 1997.

THE LIFE CYCLE OF A PROJECT

This model covers the steps involved in a new project through to operation and eventual disposal and demolition. Learning from the project experience can influence future projects in terms of life cycle costs, use of materials and processes.

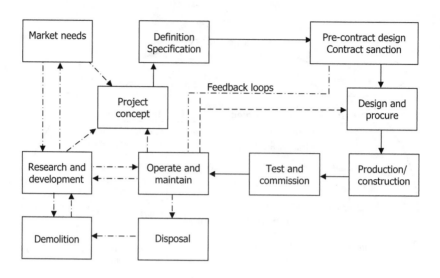

THE PROJECT AS A CONVERSION PROCESS

In this model, while the vertical input to output through a project is shown, this relies on input mechanisms to addresses specific project constraints.

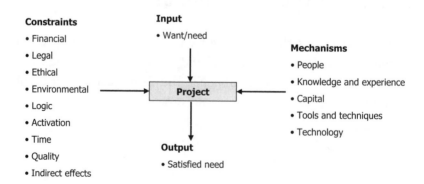

PROJECT CASH FLOW PROFILE

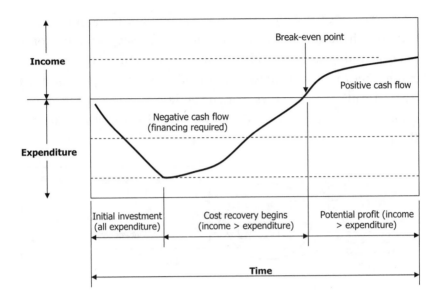

NETWORK ANALYSIS

Project programmes can use a range of network systems to assist in the planning and delivery of projects. Some of the typical conventions are shown below where the dotted line is a 'dummy' with no work done but acts as a logic link to other activities. Activities 2 and 4 can only start when 1 is complete, activity 6 needs activities 3 and 5 to be completed before it can start. The number on the line represents the time duration.

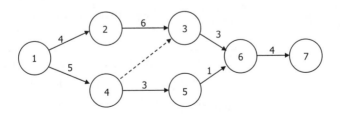

NETWORK NOTATION

The precedence system of notation is common usage for project activity scheduling and it is well suited to be supported by computer planning software. The advantage of detailing the start and finish times is that it allows the calculation of the programme's 'critical path' which shows that any additional times spent on the critical path activities will delay the overall completion date for the project.

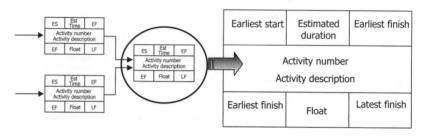

NETWORK LOGIC

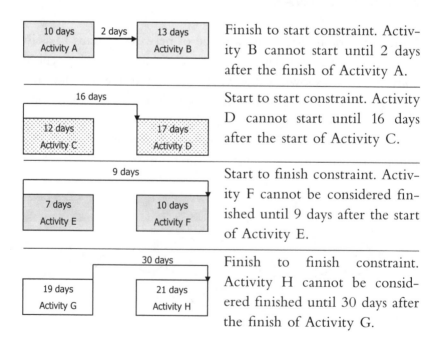

Finish to start constraint. Activity B cannot start until 2 days after the finish of Activity A.

Start to start constraint. Activity D cannot start until 16 days after the start of Activity C.

Start to finish constraint. Activity F cannot be considered finished until 9 days after the start of Activity E.

Finish to finish constraint. Activity H cannot be considered finished until 30 days after the finish of Activity G.

PROJECT PLANNING NETWORKS

The first example below shows the traditional arrow-based network, below this is the same project programme in a precedence format with logic start and finish nodes convenient for computer processing because they simplify the placing of target project start and finish dates and avoid ambiguity in time analysis. The start and end nodes are virtually dummy activities.

Arrow-based network diagram

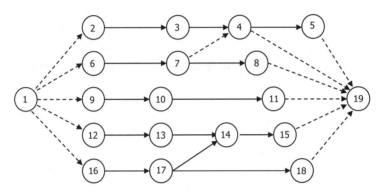

Precedence network diagram

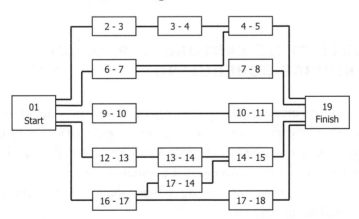

Models taken from Dennis Lock *Project Management*, page 232, 6th edition, Gower Publishing, 1996. Reproduced with kind permission of Dennis Lock. Copyright Dennis Lock.

CONTROLLING THE PROGRAMME – CLOSED LOOP FEEDBACK SYSTEM

While planning sets the goals to be obtained, the function of control regulates the actions necessary to achieve the progress. Any control system requires measurements to be taken to allow comparison against required standards and to justify appropriate actions to be taken. Once again this is an example of a model not just for project management but also for controlling the business planning objectives as part of an organization's performance.

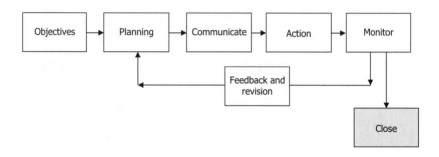

CONFLICTING FACTORS IN PROJECT RESOURCE SCHEDULING

A range of competing factors which influence the final working schedule is shown in the model below. These factors are usually so great that the scheduling process can be regarded as an intuitive task. The job of professional planners is to replace intuition with scientific resourcing using a logic sequence and eliminate the variables in easy steps.

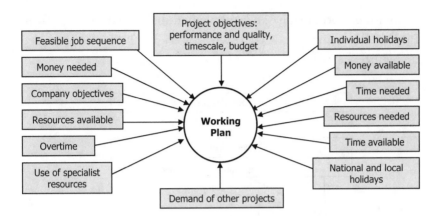

Model taken from Dennis Lock *Project Management*, page 213, 6th edition, Gower Publishing, 1996. Reproduced with kind permission of Dennis Lock. Copyright Dennis Lock.

PRINCE® AND PROJECT ORGANIZATION

PRINCE® – '**PR**ojects **IN** **C**ontrolled **E**nvironments' – was first developed in 1989 by the Central Computer and Telecommunications Agency of the UK government (now part of the Office of Government Commerce) as the standard approach for Information Systems and Information Technology projects for central government projects. This has subsequently been developed into PRINCE2™ which offers a more generic approach to project management through three elements: Organization, Management and Control of projects and is widely used in both the public and private sectors.

In the model below the Project Board embraces three senior management responsibilities each of which represents a key stakeholder: the Executive provides overall guidance and assessment; the Senior User represents the users of the project deliverables and the Senior Supplier represents those who have responsibility for the supply of technical and/or specialist services and skills. This encompasses the 'interests of those designing, developing, facilitating, procuring and implementing' (text taken from PRINCE2™ manual, © Crown copyright 2005. Reproduced under licence from OGC).

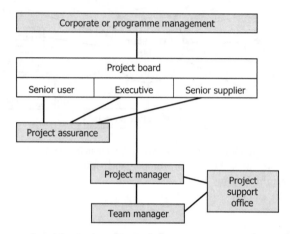

Diagram © Crown Copyright 2005. Reproduced under licence from OGC.

PRINCE2™, like other project management methodologies, comprises a number of high level processes from directing a project, planning, project initiation, controls, managing product delivery and stage boundaries through to project closure. The advantage of a standard project management method is witnessed in the use of a uniform method of working together with a common suite of terminology which offers cross project comparisons and best practice transfer.

PRINCE® is a registered trade mark and a registered community trade mark of the Office of Government Commerce, and is registered in the US Patent and Trademark Office. PRINCE2™ is a trade mark of the Office of Government Commerce.

CHAPTER 13

QUALITY MANAGEMENT

T he management of quality is widespread across all organizations – whether focused on product or services delivery. At one
time the term quality was associated with only the end result –
the product that the customer paid for and indeed quality often
was associated with price. Today the term quality is regarded as
an integral part of the management process covering product
design through to after-sales services including people and financial processes and the interrelationship of all of these into the
organization's long-term strategic plans. What was once regarded
as quality management is today only part of the inspection and
quality control process which aims at sustaining set quality
requirements through measurement and control. The disadvantage of quality control was that it was unable to improve the
performance, reliability and desirability of the finished goods as
the focus was solely on achieving a consistent level of repeatabil-
ity. With a recognition of the limitations of quality control came

a move towards the development of quality assurance which focused on the company's systems and processes rather than on the actual product and hence quality was then regarded as a function of modern management. This approach is seen in the plan-do-review quality cycle which covers documented organizational structure and the allocation of responsibilities. The next development stage in quality management came in the concept of total quality management (TQM) which extends to consider external influences such as the customer and suppliers; it also spans after-sales service to customers and encourages external process improvement to meet customer feedback comments.

As mentioned in the Introduction of this book, quality management is one of those topics that has links to all other aspects of management and is seen as an appropriate approach to question processes and seek efficiency and effectiveness aimed at improving an organization's competitive position. While it is true that a quality management philosophy alone will not provide an organization with a competitive advantage, the reverse of not having a coherent approach to quality will certainly result in a weaker long-term performance and place an organization at a disadvantage when compared to competitors. In this chapter are a number of models showing quality improvement processes. One of these is from the USA, a 12 step quality process improvement model which is shown as a circle to emphasize the importance of looking at everything as a continuous process. In addition is the pan-Europe EFQM 'Excellence Model' which is shown in Chapter 12; this provides a well-tested and widely accepted framework for TQM. This model comprises nine elements divided into two groups: enablers and results. These nine key areas are important to all organizations, whether business, charity, services or product centred.

Quality management as a basic tool for efficiency and effectiveness improvements must be regarded as a key management tool and even if not fully embraced by organizations is demanded by some customers as part of their supplier selection process. The implementation of a formal TQM system offers advantages such as:

- Better planning of activities,
- Correct interpretation of customer requirements,
- Early resolution of problems,
- Reduced level of remedial work and wastage, and
- Feedback of customer problems.

DEMING CYCLE

The following simple diagram was created by Dr W. Edwards Deming to illustrate a continuous process, commonly known as the PDCA cycle for Plan, Do, Check, Act:

Plan methods of reaching goals. Design or revise business process components to improve results, plan performance goal and targets.

Plan

Decide on changes needed to improve the process and take appropriate action.

Act

Do

Implement the plan and measure its performance. Engage in education and training. Implement improvement.

Check

Assess the measurements and report the results to decision makers. Check the effects of implementation.

KEY ELEMENTS IN THE CONCEPT OF QUALITY

As shown in this model aspects of quality also have implications for customer care and marketing of the quality of the organization's product or service as viewed by the customer.

Reproduced by kind permission of Thomson Learning, from Gerald A. Cole, *Strategic Management*, 1997. Imprint DR Publications Ltd.

QUALITY AND PROFIT – THE PRICE PERFORMANCE GRAPH

This graph shows the relationship between relative quality and price.

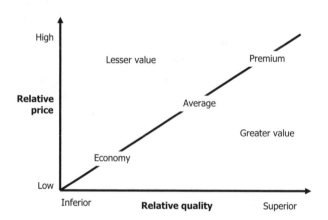

QUALITY AND PROFIT – BALANCING OPERATIONAL AND STRATEGIC EFFECTIVENESS

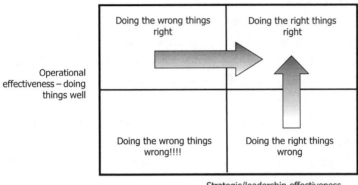

DEMING'S 14 POINT LIST

While 'quality' is part of everybody's job, it must be led by top management and the 14 points as proposed by Deming as being their responsibility.

- Create constancy of purpose toward improvement of product and service, with the aim of becoming competitive and to stay in business, and to provide jobs.
- Adopt the new philosophy. We are in a new economic age. Western management must awaken to the challenge, must learn their responsibilities, and take on leadership for change.
- Cease dependence on inspection to achieve quality. Eliminate the need for inspection on a mass basis by building quality into the product in the first place.
- End the practice of awarding business on the basis of price tag. Instead, minimize total cost. Move toward a single

supplier for any one item, on a long-term relationship of loyalty and trust.

- Improve constantly and forever the system of production and service, to improve quality and productivity, and thus constantly decrease costs.
- Institute training on the job.
- Institute leadership. The aim of supervision should be to help people and machines and gadgets to do a better job. Supervision of management is in need of overhaul as well as supervision of production workers.
- Drive out fear, so that everyone may work effectively for the company.
- Break down barriers between departments. People in research, design, sales, and production must work as a team, to foresee problems of production and use that may be encountered with the product or service.
- Eliminate slogans, exhortations, and targets for the work force asking for zero defects and new levels of productivity. Such exhortations only create adversarial relationships, as the bulk of the causes of low quality and low productivity belong to the system and thus lie beyond the power of the work force.
- (a) Eliminate work standards (quotas) on the factory floor. Substitute leadership.
  (b) Eliminate management by objective. Eliminate management by numbers, numerical goals. Substitute leadership.
- (a) Remove barriers that rob the hourly worker of his right to pride of workmanship. The responsibility of supervisors must be changed from sheer numbers to quality.
  (b) Remove barriers that rob people in management and in engineering of their right to pride of workmanship. This means abolishment of the annual merit rating and of management by objective.

- Institute a vigorous program of education and self-improvement.
- Put everybody in the company to work to accomplish the transformation. The transformation is everybody's job.

From W. Edwards Deming in *Out of Crisis*, pages 23–24, 2000. Reproduced by permission of W. Edwards-Deming Institute. Published by The MIT Press.

CONTINUOUS IMPROVEMENT

Continuous improvement in services is seen by the UK government as a responsibility of local authorities such as national parks, police authorities, etc., and the Local Government Act of 1999 states that 'a best practice authority must make arrangements to secure continuous improvement in the way in which its functions are exercised having regard to a construction of economy, efficiency and effectiveness'. This relationship of the three 'Es' is shown in the model.

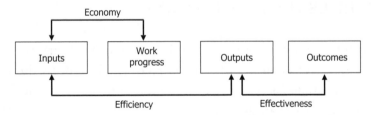

Reproduced with kind permission of the Institute for Sport, Parks and Leisure, from *101 ways to Approach Value Review*, ILAM Best Value Working Group, 2001.

PERFORMANCE DETERIORATION

While this model aligns to the subject of quality it can be seen to support other models in Chapter 2 on how this performance deterioration may be addressed.

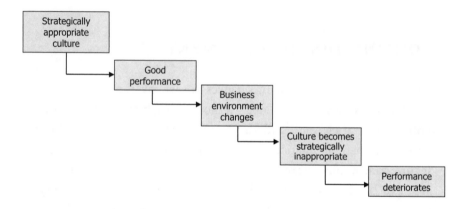

FOUR LEVELS OF QUALITY

This listing illustrates the historical development of quality from its early stages as an inspection and rectification process through to organizational acceptance as a business philosophy on the form of total quality management.

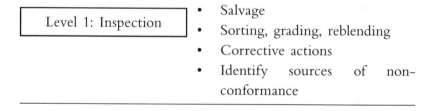

Level 2: Quality control	• Develop a quality manual • Process performance data • Self inspection • Product testing • Basic quality planning • Use of basic statistics • Paperwork controls
Level 3: Quality assurance	• Develop systems development • Advanced quality planning • Comprehensive quality manuals • Use of quality costs • Involvement in non-production operations • Failure mode and effects analysis • Statistical process control
Level 4: Total quality management	• Policy development • Improved suppliers and customers • Process management • Performance measurement • Teamwork • Employee involvement

THE QUALITY IMPROVEMENT PROCESS MODEL

This model originated from the Information Technology Services Agency and is drawn as a circle to emphasize the vital importance of looking at everything as a continuous process and can be seen as a guide to look at all stages of the quality process. The elements of the Deming 'Plan-Do-Act-Review' cycle can be seen again in this model.

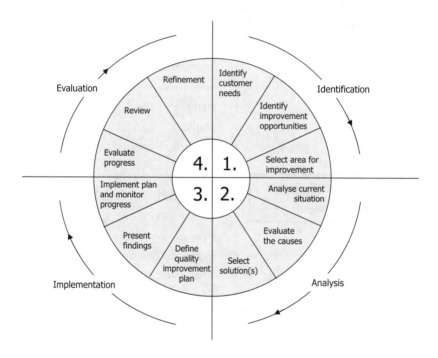

The quality improvement model should be seen as a guide to examine all of the stages of this suggested quality improvement process. More detail on each of the steps is provided in the following pages.

This model comes from a UK Government *Total Quality Booklet* in 1993 and is reproduced with kind permission of the Information Management and Archives Team.

THE QUALITY IMPROVEMENT PROCESS MODEL, QUADRANT 1 DETAILS: IDENTIFICATION

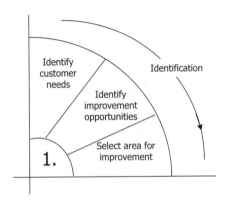

Step 1: Identify customer needs and requirements:
- Identify your key customers
- Identify your suppliers
- Plan how you will identify what internal and external customers want
- Determine needs versus wants
- Determine customer service level agreements
- Capability check – how capable are we of delivering what our customers wants?

Step 2: Analyse current situation:
- Seek customer feedback
- Examine operational performance (KPI)
- Conduct benchmarking
- Examine industry competitors
- Identify cost factors

Step 3: Select area for improvement:
- Customer specification/service level agreements
- Identify key criteria
- Decide plans and objectives
- Team outputs

THE QUALITY IMPROVEMENT PROCESS MODEL, QUADRANT 2 DETAILS: ANALYSIS

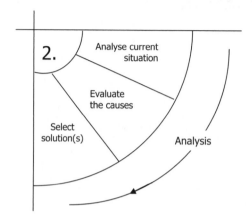

Step 4: Analyse current situation:
- Discuss with customer(s)
- Conduct customer survey
- Conduct benchmarking
- Examine operational performance (KPI)

Step 5: Evaluate the causes:
- Conduct customer survey
- Discuss the team's experience
- Observations
- Discuss with other members of the team and your customers

Step 6: Select solution:
- Examine needs versus wants
- Prioritization of what customers want
- Capability check – can we deliver what customers want?
- Financial considerations – can we afford to deliver what customers want?
- Measurement systems – what systems should we use?

THE QUALITY IMPROVEMENT PROCESS MODEL, QUADRANT 3 DETAILS: IMPLEMENTATION

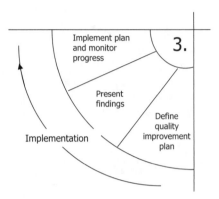

Step 7: Define quality improvement plan:
- Determine main tasks
- What, who, when, who will do what?
- Methodology – how your plan will be rolled out
- Costings – fully cost your plan
- Contingency plans – have you considered what will happen if it does not work?
- Measurement plans – finalize

Step 8: Present findings:
- Decide – who to include/exclude
- Decide – what to include/exclude
- How and by whom (what will happen in the presentation?)

Step 9: Implement plan and monitor progress:
- Customer agreement – how will you secure customer agreement?
- Progress versus plan
- Milestone check – plan regular reviews of how you are proceeding

THE QUALITY IMPROVEMENT PROCESS MODEL, QUADRANT 4 DETAILS: EVALUATION

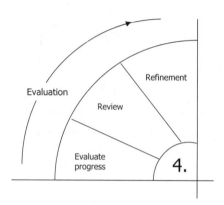

Step 10: Evaluate progress:

- Actual versus plan – are you proceeding according to your plan?
- Qualitative research
- Quantitative research

Step 11: Review:

- Team review – how did the team feel it went?
- Customer reviews – what are the customer's views?

Step 12: Refinement:

- Fine tuning – can we make it better?

This model comes from a UK Government *Total Quality Booklet* produced by a now disbanded organization called 'Information Technology Services Agency'. It was published in 1993 and is reproduced with kind permission of the Information Management and Archives Team, Department for Work and Pensions, Room 114, Adelphi, 1–11 John Adam Street, London WC2N 6HT.

EFQM THE EXCELLENCE MODEL

As mentioned in the Introduction there are a number of management tools applicable to a range of situations or subject areas; the EFQM Excellence Model is one of these tools. While it is undoubtedly a 'quality management' concept it also provides a strong framework for overall business analysis and as such is also shown in Chapter 10. The EFQM Model is based on nine criteria: 'Enablers' which cover what an organization does and 'Results' what an organization achieves. The two sets are inter-linked as the 'Results' are caused by 'Enablers' and feedback from 'Results' suggests areas for improvement of the 'Enablers' through innovation and organizational learning.

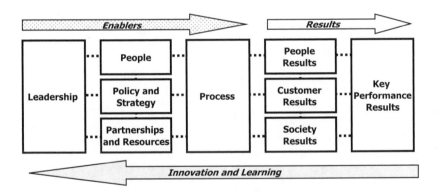

The fundamental concepts which underpin the EFQM Model are:

- Results that delight all the organization's stakeholders.
- Customer focus in creating sustainable customer value.
- Strategic leadership with a clear shared vision.
- Process Management through a set of interdependent and inter-related systems, and processes.
- People development and involvement to maximize employee contribution through continuous learning, development and

involvement to create innovation and improvement opportunities.

- Partnership with development and long-term involvement of value-adding partnerships.
- Social responsibility where the organization's operation is in harmony with its surroundings and meets their stakeholders' expectations.

EFQM Excellence Model © reproduced with kind permission of EFQM (www.efqm.org).

CHAPTER 14

RISK MANAGEMENT

*I*n life there are risks: driving a car, crossing the road or playing various sports. So too in business although in many cases such risk uncertainties are naturally associated with a financial risk compared to the market volatility and hence the ability to realistically provide expectations based upon a risk versus reward trade-off. While the management of corporate financial risk is undertaken through a very specialist risk discipline this chapter looks at the subject of risk management from a project, business or operational viewpoint where such risks can be internally or externally driven and may impact on the project's stated scope, schedule and cost objectives.

Risk management has evolved into a formal systematic process of identifying potential risk or uncertainties and developing, selecting and managing options for addressing the risks through the life of the project. While risk management may be a proactive approach it cannot control future events but allows decisions to be made and actions to be taken if such identified risks become reality. An understanding of risk comes from a realistic understanding of what can go wrong, the likelihood of the event occurring and the consequences of such an event, seen in Professor Clare Brindley's triple definition. On the basis of a good understanding of what can go wrong a number of actions are open to companies to manage the risk and to a large extent such management response will be a function of the probability and quantified consequences of the risk occurring. A matrix of probability and risk is provided in this chapter together with practical definitions of risk impact on scope, cost, quality and time.

Although the way risk management is operationalized varies from one company to another, one common approach is a staged approval of risk identification followed by employment of a number of strategies for its management. Typically this approach covers 'risk identification' to capture all of the potential risks which could arise within the project followed by 'risk classification' where risks are grouped into internal risks (which reside within the company or organization) and external risks (those factors that condition the environment or are conditional on the environment in which the organization has to operate) which are outside its direct control. The next step would often be to undertake a 'risk analysis' to quantify and evaluate the risk on the project leading to the final stage of 'risk response' which addresses how the risk will be managed. This final activity is likely to cover a range of actions including risk reduction, risk avoidance, risk transfer and risk retention.

Within this chapter are models of approaches to risk management, considerations on probability versus impact and ways to respond to identified risk through selection of the appropriate response. One action open to clients of construction projects is to use a suitable procurement method and the choices on contract selection are described here together with an example of a typical prime contact and how it would consider risk management as part of its commercial management role.

Although there is a chapter on international business (Chapter 6) the risks which need to be considered before undertaking or even bidding for an international project are described in a hexagonal model and while this has a focus on international projects many of the risk areas identified also need to be addressed in home-market projects.

RISK MANAGEMENT – THE TRIPLE DEFINITION

The model offers three inter-related questions and the processes that facilitate the answers to these are at the core of risk analysis.

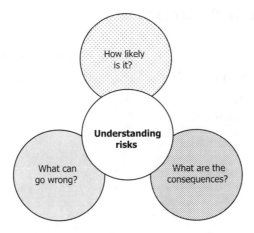

From *Supply Chain Risk*, editor Professor Clare Brindley, 2004. Reproduced with permission of Ashgate Publishing.

CONSEQUENCES OF FAILING TO MANAGE RISK

The list leads to the suggestion that the consequences of failing to manage risk has an impact not only on the project and the project manager's organization but also on the PM as an individual.

- Significant overruns
- Schedule delays
- Inability to achieve stated technical objectives in terms of delivery, functionality, cost, etc.
- Project de-scoping
- Project cancellation
- Penalties and fines
- Personal and or organizational liability
- Loss of credibility for company and for individual as project manager

RISK MANAGEMENT

Here project risks are analysed and the probability of occurrence is assessed. This probability is then used in the table showing the degree of impact and on this basis appropriate actions can then be taken to manage the risk.

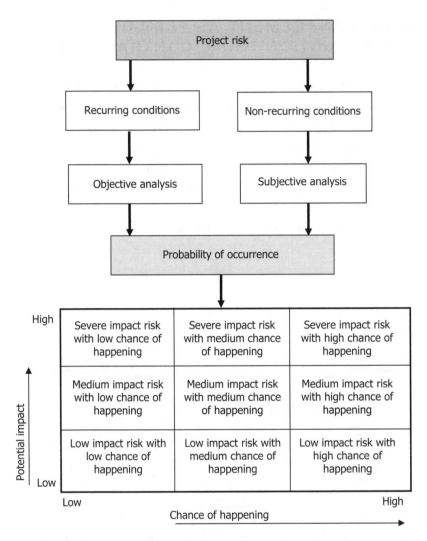

Project Management Institute, *Project & Program Risk Management: a guide to managing project risks and opportunities*, Project Management Institute, Inc., 1992. Copyright and all rights reserved. Material from this publication has been reproduced with the permission of PMI.

RISK MANAGEMENT AS PART OF CONSTRUCTION PRIME CONTRACTING

The model shows the relationship between the attributes of a single point responsibility of prime contracting and risk management considerations. In executing a typical development and operation project arrangement through a prime contracting procurement method, one of the key advantages is the opportunity for the risks associated with the project to be devolved to the party best able to deal with them: this delegated authority could be the client or the contractor, or indeed a member of the supply chain.

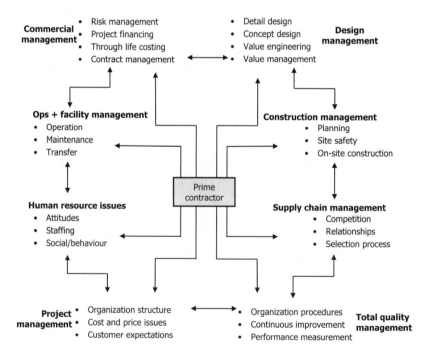

It is widely accepted within the industry that the number of client/customer interfaces and the imprecise allocation of risks have long-hampered traditional procurement and as such the use of a prime contracting framework provides a degree of confidence with respect to project uncertainty together with a reduction in the amount of required contingency typically witnessed with traditional procurement methods.

From *Considerations of Pre-contract Risks in International PFI Projects* by Professor S. A. Burtonshaw-Gunn, 2005. Reproduced with kind permission of the Salford Centre for Research and Innovation, University of Salford, UK.

THE STAGES OF RISK ANALYSIS AND MANAGEMENT

The main purpose of risk analysis is to inform the decision makers about risks. The sequential order in the model is usually cyclical and often begins with problem identification and formulation through to data collection, analysis process, conclusions and recommendations on the way forward.

INTEGRATING RISK MANAGEMENT WITH OTHER PROJECT MANAGEMENT FUNCTIONS

Risk management can be seen to be at the centre of a project by undertaking an integration role bringing together the project management constraints of time, cost and quality with the project management functions of HR, contract management, PM life cycle integration, and information management.

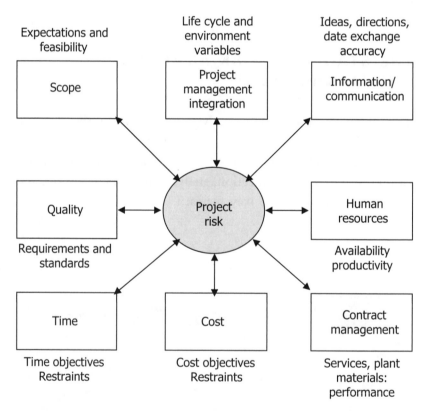

Project Management Institute, *Project & Program Risk Management: a guide to managing project risks and opportunities*, Project Management Institute, Inc., 1992. Copyright and all rights reserved. Material from this publication has been reproduced with the permission of PMI.

RISKS ON CONTRACT CONSIDERATIONS

In the model below I have identified six areas which need to be considered before undertaking or bidding for international projects. Some of these risks lie outside the direct control of the organization but nevertheless still need to be managed.

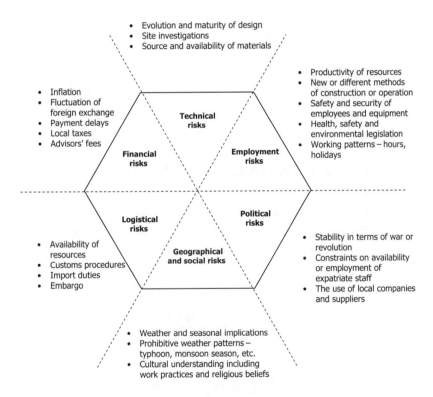

- Evolution and maturity of design
- Site investigations
- Source and availability of materials

- Inflation
- Fluctuation of foreign exchange
- Payment delays
- Local taxes
- Advisors' fees

Technical risks

Financial risks

Employment risks

- Productivity of resources
- New or different methods of construction or operation
- Safety and security of employees and equipment
- Health, safety and environmental legislation
- Working patterns – hours, holidays

Logistical risks

Political risks

Geographical and social risks

- Availability of resources
- Customs procedures
- Import duties
- Embargo

- Stability in terms of war or revolution
- Constraints on availability or employment of expatriate staff
- The use of local companies and suppliers

- Weather and seasonal implications
- Prohibitive weather patterns – typhoon, monsoon season, etc.
- Cultural understanding including work practices and religious beliefs

Model developed from text: 'The importance of pre-contract risk assessment and management in PFI international projects', Professor S. A. Burtonshaw-Gunn, from *Supply Chain Risk: a handbook of assessment, management and performance*, Springer International Publications, 2008.

BALANCING RISK AND CONTROL

The diagram illustrates the difficulty of balancing risk taking with risk management, in reality these two forces cause the project to osculate around the optimum approach.

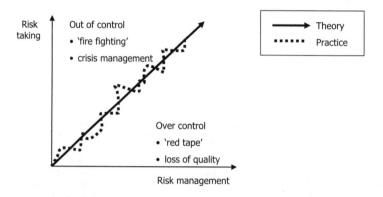

BUSINESS CONTINUITY PLANNING

The first activities in business continuity plans are to identify the risks and assess the probability and impact. The plan is to ensure continued operations in case of a catastrophic event.

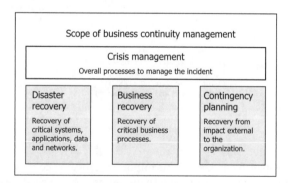

Reproduced with kind permission of the Chartered Management Institute, UK, *Business Continuity and Supply Chain Risk*, 2002.

PROBABILITY VERSUS IMPACT

There are a number of probability and impact assessment methods that follow a common format. Examples given will vary for each project in terms of cost and programme.

Impact \ Probability	Low	Medium	High	Very high
Critical				
High				
Medium				
Low				

Example impact definitions:

PROJECT OBJECTIVE	LOW	MEDIUM	HIGH	VERY HIGH
Cost	Less than 5% cost increase	5–10% cost increase	10–20% cost increase	More than 20% cost increase
Programme	Project schedule slips by 5%	Project schedule slips by 5–10%	Project schedule slips by 10–20%	Project schedule slips by 20%
Scope	Minor areas of scope affected	Major areas of scope affected	Scope reduced, not acceptable to client	Project End. Item is useless
Quality	Only demanding areas are affected	Quality reduced with client acceptance	Quality reduced, not accepted by client	Project End. Item is useless

Example risk definitions:

AREAS OF RISK IMPACT	LOW	MEDIUM	HIGH	CRITICAL
Cost	Acceptable level cost increase	Major cost increase	Significant cost increase	Massive Cost increase
Programme	Delay less than 2 months	Project delay up to 2 months	Delay 2 to 6 months	Significant delay >6 months
Quality	Only demanding areas are affected	Quality reduced with client acceptance	Failure to meet key criteria solution not identified	Failure to deliver to acceptable standard

RESPONSE TO RISK

The response to an identified risk must be appropriate to its severity and cost effective. There are four main actions which may change the characteristics of a risk.

Avoidance

Risk avoidance is changing the project plan to eliminate the risk or to protect the project objectives from its impact. Although not all risks can be eliminated some may be avoided by taking this pre-emptive action.

Transfer

Risk transfer is seeking to move the consequence of a risk to a third party together with ownership of the response. Transferring the risk does not eliminate it; it simply gives another party responsibility for its management. This is the most effective way of dealing with financial risk exposure and can be by a contract to another party or by payment of a premium in the case of insurance.

Mitigation

This strategy seeks to reduce the risk probability or its impact by taking early action to reduce the occurrence of the risk to an acceptable limit. Risk mitigation may take the form of implementing new processes, undertaking more preliminary work or selecting more stable suppliers. Risk mitigation can also include changing conditions so that the probability of the risk is reduced, by adding resources or time to the programme.

Acceptance

This strategy indicates that the project has decided not to change the project plan and to deal with a risk or is unable to identify any other suitable strategy to adopt. Risk acceptance may also occur when the cost of dealing with it would not be so effective. In this event the development of a contingency plan to execute should the risk occur is a natural step.

CONSIDERING RISKS FOR CONTRACT SELECTION

The contract strategy contributes to the ownership of risk. This risk associated with a 'cost plus' contract rests with the customer and the supplier is not encouraged to save costs, in this way the customer obtains the highest quality work. This works when time is important as the supplier can start work without lengthy negotiation and knows at what level its profit will be. At the other extreme are 'fixed firm price' contracts where the supplier takes all of the risk. This needs more management and encourages the customer to keep to its original scope of work as any changes will still attract a price increase from the supplier.

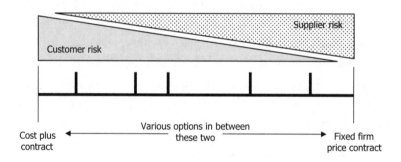

In between these two extremes are a variety of contract types. These can cover:

- **Target cost** (expected cost). Based on measuring performance.
- **Target profit** (expected profit). Negotiated profit in the contract.
- **Profit ceiling** and **profit floor** with maximum and minimum values of the total profit for the supplier.
- **Price ceiling** that the customer will pay and is usually a percentage of target cost.

- **Sharing arrangement** (sharing formula). This is a balance of cost responsibility between the customer and the supplier for each £/$ spent.
- **Point of total assumption**. This occurs at the point where the supplier assumes all responsibility for additional costs.
- **Supplier incentive contracts** are used when the customer wants to motivate the supplier performance and can cover allocation of a great profit percentage if total costs are reduced or performance improved. On the other hand the supplier will earn less profit if costs are allowed to increase or performance targets are not achieved.

CHAPTER 15

STRATEGIC MANAGEMENT

Many works on strategic management treat the subject as consisting of several component parts such as goal formulation, strategic evaluation, strategy implementation and strategy control but advise that these are components of a framework and may not exist as discrete orderly steps in a strategic management decision-making process. It is further suggested that there are a number of characteristics of strategic decisions concerned with the scope of an organization's activities, the matching of the organization to the environment and the matching of the organization's activities to its resource capability.

Within this chapter are a number of major well-known business models, many of which help to achieve a comprehensive analysis of the business in order to help determine its future direction, or at least make decisions based on informed choice and then plan how this can be best put into effect. In addition the words 'strategy' and 'strategic management' relate to a number of levels within an organization and a hierarchy of these together with inter-related strategies are shown in this chapter. The lowest level of strategy is often referred to as 'functional strategy' which focuses on the day-to-day operational activities that the organization is involved in. Within a business there are often a number of functional strategies which take their lead from the next level, 'business strategy'. This intermediate level covers the aggregation of the functional strategies for a single business unit or organization with a concentration on the tactics that the business will use to address its threats from competitors and opportunities with customers. The business strategy reflects the higher level, 'corporate strategy'. This highest strategy level refers to the overarching strategy of the business which addresses questions concerning the arena in which it should compete and how the organization's activities contribute to its competitive advantage and longer-term aspirations. It also reflects the organization's mission, vision and objectives seen in its business plan.

Strategic management involves not just trying to exploit the strengths of the organization and minimizing any weaknesses but requires that the organization also considers the external environment in which it operates, typically looking for opportunities and threats which it may have to react to. The universally used 'SWOT' analysis is often used for this initial examination and as part of the strategy formulation process. In looking externally at the threats to the business Professor Porter's model of the impact of Suppliers, Buyers, Substitutes and New Entrants is also in common use and included in this chapter.

In any one organization there are a number of interconnected and inter-related influences so that for strategic management and strategic plans to have any productive benefit these need to have a strong fit between soft issues on the organization as seen in the '7S' model and the linkages to the lower level planning activities around HR and marketing. These interconnecting plans will detail the actions on how the organization will develop further its strengths and react to anticipate changes in the external customer and competitor environment. In addition to the competitive or business factors there will be a need to comply with state legislation as a minimum and perhaps reflect a social responsibility expectation as part of an organization's desired or actual brand reputation.

INTER-RELATED STRATEGIES

This is another example of the model above showing the relationship between the external facing business strategy and the internally focused product strategy which is concerned with how the overall corporate strategy can be met by the business.

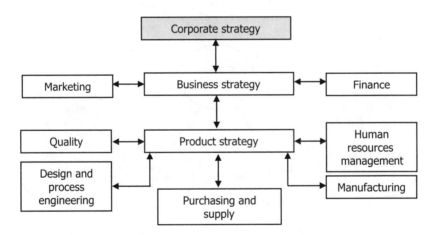

A SUMMARY MODEL OF THE ELEMENTS OF STRATEGIC MANAGEMENT

This model is the main proposition for strategic management shown in the textbook on corporate strategy by Professors Gerry Johnson and Kevan Scholes. This summary model of the strategic management process concerns three major elements: strategic analysis; strategic choice and strategic implementation with each having its own inter-related subsets of supporting considerations/actions.

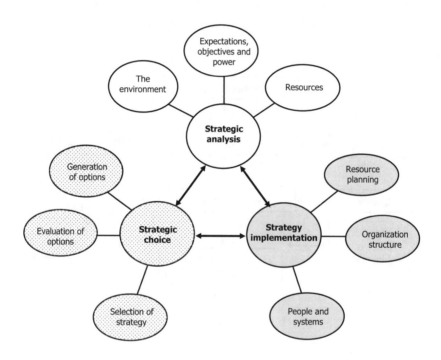

Each of these inter-related elements is crucial in defining and succeeding in establishing a robust strategy to take an organization forward. The supporting parts of strategic analysis identify the company's circumstances. The topics with Strategic choice will prompt an assessment of the suitability and rationale based on strategic logic, research evidence and cultural fit. Finally the Strategic implementation elements need to be considered and addressed in translating the selected strategy into action.

From Professor Gerry Johnson and Professor Kevan Scholes, *Exploring Corporate Strategy*, 2002, 6th edition text and cases. Reproduced with permission of Pearson Publishing.

THE FAMILY OF PLANS

As seen in other models, strategic management covers the bringing together of other areas of the business as shown in this model through a master strategic plan and a series of supporting operational plans.

From H. Igor Ansoff, *Corporate Strategy*, 1968. Reproduced with kind permission of Penguin Publishing.

SWOT ANALYSIS

Almost every book on management strategy uses the SWOT tool for establishing the company's strengths, weaknesses, external opportunities and threats. It is helpful for generating a summary of a strategic situation. Strengths and weakness can include skills, expertise or technological know-how, particular organizational resources, competitive capabilities or potential advantages. Opportunities and threats typically stem from a company's external competitive environment.

- Strengths usually cover factors such as product or service quality, lower costs than the competition, effective processes and well-trained staff.
- Weaknesses also tend to be internal to the organization such as relative size compared to the competition, size of operation, amount of experience in particular geographic region when looking at new markets.
- Opportunities are usually derived from factors outside of the organization such as new export market opportunities, difficulties that competitors face, etc.
- Threats are also external in nature and often take the form of competitor actions such as launch of new products rendering your goods obsolete or unfashionable.

In a number of circumstances the same feature will appear in more than one of the SWOT quadrants.

Internal to organization	**Strengths**	**Weaknesses**
External to organization	**Opportunities**	**Threats**

The SWOT analysis tool can be used by individuals or as a group exercise where it can bring up areas for discussion; however, the simplicity of the tool can be a trap and care needs to be taken in using this for two main reasons:

- Do not assume that completing each quadrant is the full analysis – while an organization may have 10 strengths and only two weaknesses it is not the volume of each but the severity. Indeed two major weaknesses may easily outweigh 10 strengths.
- The factors used to populate the matrix must be seen as a 'snap-shot' at a particular moment in time; as the world changes new opportunities and threats emerge. Additionally what are internal strengths today may not be tomorrow.

The output of the SWOT analysis is to examine the internal and external actors on the business. Its use is in strategic management, people development, marketing, change management and business planning as it provides a clear indication of where a business is performing well and the areas it needs to address. It can be used as part of a change programme to convert threats into opportunities and internal weaknesses into competitive strengths.

SWOT ANALYSIS – POTENTIAL FEATURES

Potential internal strengths

- Leading manufacturing capability – plant and equipment
- Good customer relationships with repeat sales
- Long-term contracts
- Skills and knowledge in key areas
- Strong financial results and retained profits
- Recognized as the market leader
- Integrated strategies throughout organization
- Leverage from economies of scale
- Proprietary and patented technology
- Low cost/efficient operations
- Recognized brands through advertising campaigns
- Effective marketing approach and good sales team
- Experienced long-term management teams
- Encouragement of innovation
- Superior products through R&D investment

Potential internal weaknesses

- Limited R&D work – trend is to follow rather than lead product design
- Limited or outdated product range Obsolete facilities and processes
- Limited managerial skills and experience
- Undefined or communicated strategic direction
- Strategy implementation poorly executed or implemented
- Low profit margins or low profitability compared to competitors
- Market reputation poor
- Distribution and logistics network underdeveloped
- Marketing skills below those of competitors

- Absence of key skills or competencies
- Operating problems with plant and equipment

Potential external opportunities

- Potential to embrace new technologies
- Good prospects for further market development
- Potential to expand into new markets or segments
- Ability to transfer skills and technological knowhow to new products or business
- Product line has extension capacity to expand to meet changing customer needs
- Availability of new markets through removal of trade barriers in attractive foreign markets
- Forward and backward integration through supply chain management
- Growth potential due to increased market demand

Potential external threats

- Foreign competition aided by lower cost of entry to market
- Foreign exchange rates and trade policies of foreign governments affecting overseas markets and value of income
- Changes in demographics; consequential impact on product demand
- Increase in sales of substitute products
- Slower market growth than production requirement
- Threat of market recession
- Failure to deliver new products and/or poor product reliability
- Increasing bargaining power of distributors, wholesales and retailers prior to selling to customers
- Buyer more aware of competitors' products that match their needs/tastes

PORTER'S 'DIAMOND' THEORY

In his book *The Competitive Advantage of Nations* Professor Porter argues that there are four attributes that shape the economic environment faced by domestic firms, and that they have a direct impact on the firm's ability to compete globally.

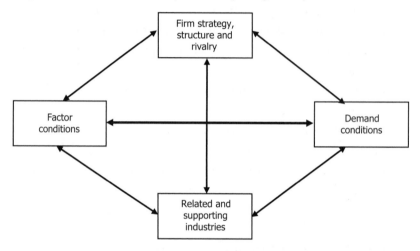

He also made four conclusions from this study:

- The nature of competition and the sources of competitive advantage differ widely among industries (and even among industry segments).
- Successful global competitors perform some activities in the 'value chain' outside their home country and draw competitive advantages from their entire worldwide network rather than from just their home base.
- Firms gain and sustain competitive advantage in modern international competition through innovation.
- Firms that successfully gain competitive advantage in an industry are those that more early and aggressively exploit a new market or technology.

Reprinted with the permission of The Free Press, a Division of Simon & Schuster Adult Publishing Group, from *The Competitive Advantage of Nations* by Professor Michael E. Porter. Copyright © 1990, 1998 Michael E. Porter. All rights reserved.

A MODEL FOR STRATEGIC ANALYSIS

This is a major model covering the elements of industry structure. For those involved in strategic management it is widely used to understand a company's strategic position.

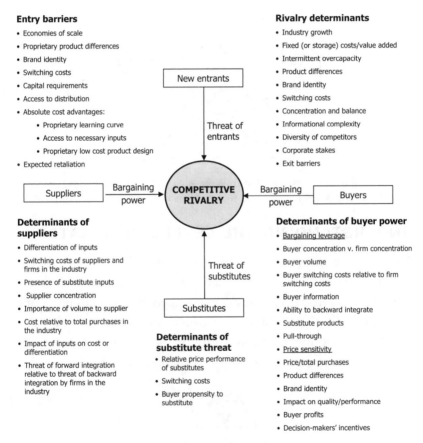

Entry barriers

- Economies of scale
- Proprietary product differences
- Brand identity
- Switching costs
- Capital requirements
- Access to distribution
- Absolute cost advantages:
  - Proprietary learning curve
  - Access to necessary inputs
  - Proprietary low cost product design
- Expected retaliation

Rivalry determinants

- Industry growth
- Fixed (or storage) costs/value added
- Intermittent overcapacity
- Product differences
- Brand identity
- Switching costs
- Concentration and balance
- Informational complexity
- Diversity of competitors
- Corporate stakes
- Exit barriers

New entrants

Threat of entrants

Suppliers — Bargaining power → **COMPETITIVE RIVALRY** ← Bargaining power — Buyers

Determinants of suppliers

- Differentiation of inputs
- Switching costs of suppliers and firms in the industry
- Presence of substitute inputs
- Supplier concentration
- Importance of volume to supplier
- Cost relative to total purchases in the industry
- Impact of inputs on cost or differentiation
- Threat of forward integration relative to threat of backward integration by firms in the industry

Threat of substitutes

Substitutes

Determinants of substitute threat

- Relative price performance of substitutes
- Switching costs
- Buyer propensity to substitute

Determinants of buyer power

- Bargaining leverage
- Buyer concentration v. firm concentration
- Buyer volume
- Buyer switching costs relative to firm switching costs
- Buyer information
- Ability to backward integrate
- Substitute products
- Pull-through
- Price sensitivity
- Price/total purchases
- Product differences
- Brand identity
- Impact on quality/performance
- Buyer profits
- Decision-makers' incentives

Reprinted with the permission of The Free Press, a Division of Simon & Schuster Adult Publishing Group, from *Competitive Advantage: creating and sustaining superior performance* by Professor Michael E. Porter. Copyright © 1985, 1998 Michael E. Porter. All rights reserved.

STRATEGIC MANAGEMENT AND ENVIRONMENTAL PRESSURES

This model shows the pressures on an organization from external sources.

The location of human resource management is shown as a major link to organizational structure and the company's mission and overall strategy.

Reproduced with permission of John Wiley & Sons Inc. from Charles Fomburn, Noel Tichy and Mary Devanna in *Strategic Human Resources Management*, 1984.

UNDERSTANDING THE LEVELS OF STRATEGY

The hierarchy of the various levels of strategy is important for all staff in an organization to understand and reflect in their plans at whatever level in the company. This model is also applicable to a business planning approach which could cover **functional strategy** (the value activities engage in); **business strategy** (how to fight competition – tactics) and **corporate strategy** (what business should I be in?).

STRATEGY FORMULATION PROCESS

This model provides an approach by which business strategy can be developed and implemented. Again this can be seen to consist of other management areas including business planning and market research.

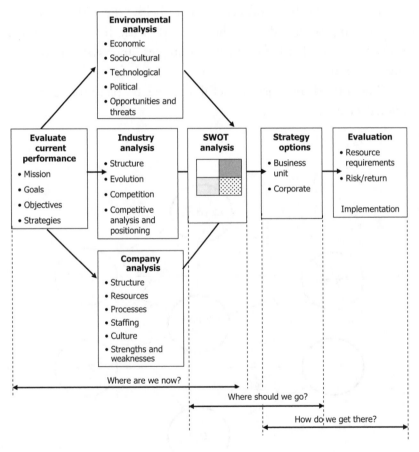

From deKluyver, Cornelis A., *Strategic Thinking: An Executive Perspetive*, © 2000, page 8. Reproduced by permission of Pearson Education Inc., Upper Saddle River, NJ.

7S FRAMEWORK (SOMETIMES CALLED MCKINSEY 7S MODEL)

The 7S framework provides some guidance on which to undertake an analysis of seven 'soft' and 'hard' issues on an organisation. The hard elements are easy to recognize in strategy documents, organizational plans and other documents; the four soft Ss are more difficult to identify and describe, as capabilities, values and culture are continually developing and undergoing change. As such these soft elements are below the surface and are not easy to plan or influence; however, they can have a significant impact of the hard structures, strategies and systems of the organization.

The model also has a useful linkage to planning organizational change.

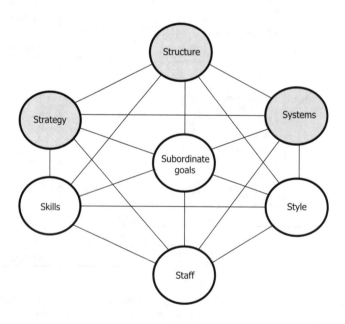

Strategy: A set of actions that you start with and must maintain

Structure: How people and tasks/work are organized

Systems: All the processes and information flows that link the organization together

Style: How managers behave

Staff: How you develop managers (current and future)

Subordinate goals: Longer-term vision, and all that values stuff, that shapes the destiny of the organization

Skills: Dominant attributes or capabilities that exist in the organization

From an article entitled 'Structure is not an organization' by R. H. Waterman, Tom D. Peters and I. R. Philips, published in *Blue Horizons*, Volume 23, Issue 3, 1980. Reproduced with kind permission of Elsevier.

IMPLEMENTING STRATEGY – KEY FORCES

The key forces that influence strategy selection are shown in Cole's first model; below this the second model illustrates how strategy may be implemented.

IMPLEMENTING STRATEGY – A WORKING MODEL

Reproduced with kind permission of Thomson Learning, from Gerald A. Cole, *Strategic Management*, 1997. Imprint DR Publications Ltd.

THE LINK BETWEEN STRATEGY AND PLANNING

The activities involved in strategy development may start broad but narrow as the process matures; conversely the planning phase covers the expansion of the organization's identified strategy in the production of detailed operation plans reflecting the corporate objects, budgets, operational targets and how these will be reviewed, monitored and reported. This model reflects the task of business planning seen earlier in this book.

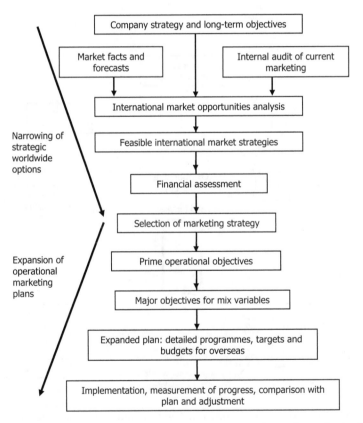

Adapted by Edgar P. Hibbert from L. Fisher, 'Industrial marketing', in *International Business − strategy and operations*, 1997, Macmillan Business. Reproduced with permission of MacMillan Palgrave.

A PERSPECTIVE ON BUSINESS STRATEGY AND HR STRATEGY INTERDEPENDENCE

The model of interdependence proposes that demand for skills and employees is a function of the competitive strategy and an organization's ability and readiness is a product of the HR strategy. However, they are related as the HR strategy conditions the competitive strategy.

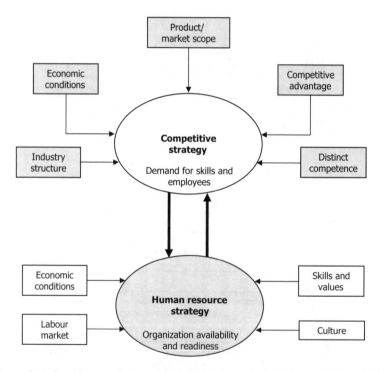

Reproduced with permission, from Cynthia and Mark Lengnick-Hall, 'A perspective on business strategy and human resource strategy interdependence', *Academy of Management Review*, Volume 13, Number 3, Pages 454–470, 1988.

MOTIVES FOR GOING 'GREEN'

The basic reason for accepting environmental responsibility is to stay within the law. As environmental legislation becomes more stringent such conformance will affect an increasing number of companies. On this basis 'society' has increased expectations or demands on larger companies partly based on the perception that the larger organizations should lead by example and that in proportion to their turnover or profit they are better able to afford to invest in meeting more environmental requirements.

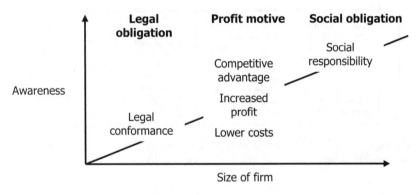

Reproduced with kind permission of Kit Sadgrove, from *The Green Guide to Profitable Management*, Gower Publications, 1994.

The 'Green Grid' below is a simple way to assess a company's environmental performance as the company can only adopt one of the four positions. Such identification can assist in its future plans on meeting its environmental obligations.

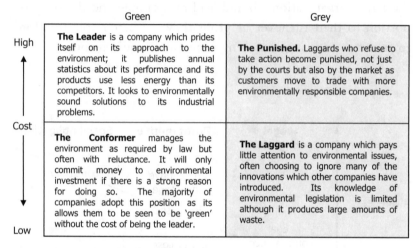

	Green	Grey
High	**The Leader** is a company which prides itself on its approach to the environment; it publishes annual statistics about its performance and its products use less energy than its competitors. It looks to environmentally sound solutions to its industrial problems.	**The Punished.** Laggards who refuse to take action become punished, not just by the courts but also by the market as customers move to trade with more environmentally responsible companies.
Low	**The Conformer** manages the environment as required by law but often with reluctance. It will only commit money to environmental investment if there is a strong reason for doing so. The majority of companies adopt this position as its allows them to be seen to be 'green' without the cost of being the leader.	**The Laggard** is a company which pays little attention to environmental issues, often choosing to ignore many of the innovations which other companies have introduced. Its knowledge of environmental legislation is limited although it produces large amounts of waste.

(Cost axis from High to Low on the left side)

Reproduced with kind permission of Kit Sadgrove, from *The Green Guide to Profitable Management*, Gower Publications, 1994.

CHAPTER 16

SUPPLY CHAIN
MANAGEMENT

Supply chain management (SCM) has, for many companies, developed from the older purchasing function to now embrace planning, implementing, and controlling all of the suppliers into the organization with a view to delivering a more integrated service to its customers. Typically the management of the supply chain covers raw material ordering, storage, work-in-progress inventory and finished goods. This is often achieved through a set of product and production processes. Another way to consider supply chain management is that it offers organizations a systematic approach to the management of the entire value-added chain; from the component level supplier to the main manufacturer, then to the retailer who in turn exchanges the goods for money with the end customer. However, this management function is not without some challenges and there are risks in supply chain management which need to be considered and addressed. These risks are covered both in this chapter and in Chapter 14 and occur at various stages in the buyer/supplier interface.

The relative power of the supplier in relation to the buyer's business and vice versa also needs to be considered as the performance of each has a direct impact on the other's business. While many companies will not wish to have a plethora of small suppliers with all of the associated administration that this necessitates, equally they will be reluctant to be reliant on a sole supplier arrangement and as a compromise organizations often select a small number of suppliers with which they will develop a close relationship. The changes made from a simple purchasing function into SCM have witnessed a cultural change where much closer cooperation is seen between the supplier and the buyer; this is very evident in the UK's retail, manufacturing and to a lesser extent construction sectors. The latter has previously been known for its adversarial relationship; however, over the last 15 years there have been dramatic changes resulting in more collaboration through 'partnering' where both parties commence their business relationship by agreeing a set of mutual objectives, have an agreed process for problem resolution and decision making and have a joint commitment to continuous improvement and performance measures. Well-established supply chains provide many parties in the arrangement with a security of future work and hence a confidence to commit investment to staff development through training – in plant and equipment and finally in business processes to support the SCM relationship. Developments in supply chain management typically centre on reducing inventory, increasing the transaction speed by exchanging data in real time, and increasing sales by implementing customer requirements more efficiently.

Supply chain management continues to grow in importance with the globalization of business operations and use of worldwide suppliers. As such it is an important feature that needs to be considered by those companies seeking growth throug international operations. As with many management topics supply chain management is not an isolated discipline – indeed it can be seen to have links to other sections in this book: for example, in customer relationship management, decision making, risk management, project management and finally people-focused performance management which itself covers teamworking, trust and conflict resolution.

A SUMMARY MODEL OF THE ELEMENTS OF SUPPLY CHAIN MANAGEMENT

This model examines the developments of the supply chain characteristics and suggests that this is influenced by changes in both the supply chain and the changing relationships within the industry structure and the global market. Understanding these relationships is important to productivity and efficiency within the organization and looking externally at how the company can use its supply chain strengths to leverage markets and gain improved business performance.

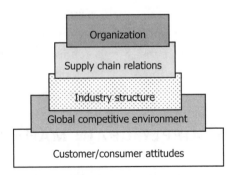

From Professor Clare S. Brindley in *Supply Chain Risk*, editor Professor Clare Brindley, 2004. Reproduced with permission of Ashgate Publishing.

ADVERSARIAL VERSUS PARTNERSHIP APPROACHES

The adversarial model → ← **The partnership model**

The adversarial model	The partnership model
• Adversarial hostile attitudes	• Cooperative attitudes
• Arm's length approach with heavy reliance on formal communication	• Exhibits a high frequency of both formal and informal communications
• Lack of trust	• A developed trusting relationship
• Aggressive win/lose approach in negotiations with emphasis on price	• Emphasis placed on problem solving, win/win negotiation styles with emphasis on managing total costs
• Focus on individual transactions and short-term contracts	• No blame culture, looking for solutions rather than reasons
• Little direct contact and reduced involvement in design activities	• Development of long-term business agreements
• Reluctance to share information	• Open sharing of information by multifunctional teams
• Reliance on reactive goods inspection and defect rectification rather than proactive approach	• Vendor certification and defence prevention approaches

RISKS AND SUPPLY CHAIN MANAGEMENT

Establishing good, close and strong supply chain relationships is the ideal for any company; however, this is not without risk and the risks of supply chain management and collaborative working are shown in this model – these cover the main features of

environmental risks, competitive risks, client and supplier relationship and project attractiveness. As can be seen the competitive
risks reflect the elements of Professor Porter's strategic analysis
model. Understanding these risks can be used to develop the
relationships within the supply chain whether at the client, lead
consultant or specialist contractor positions as each party can have
an appreciation of the risks that the other supply chain partners
face and have to deal with.

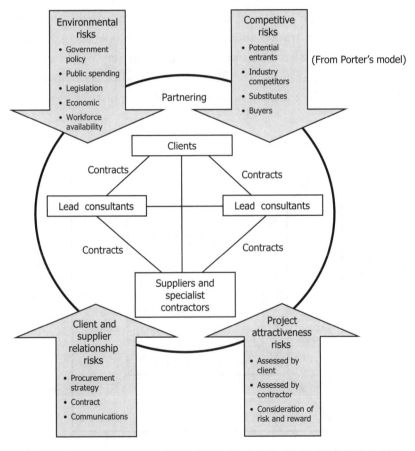

From Professor S.A. Burtonshaw-Gunn in *Supply Chain Risk*, editor Professor Clare Brindley, 2004. Reproduced with permission of Ashgate
Publishing.

ENVIRONMENTAL FRAMEWORK FOR THE SUPPLY CHAIN

The model below illustrates the relationship between the environment and factors outside of the control or influence of the organization – its aim is to show the supply chain in an extended framework. Some conditions of the wider environment impose constraints on the feasibility of strategies while others may provide opportunities. The author, Malcolm Saunders, suggests that while the product strategies partly determine the nature of the task of the supply chain, it is the strategic 'make or buy' decision which determines the division of tasks around internal and external operations. Finally decisions about what to manufacture or what services to provide within an organization actually locate the company in its supply chain and in effect draw boundaries around the organization.

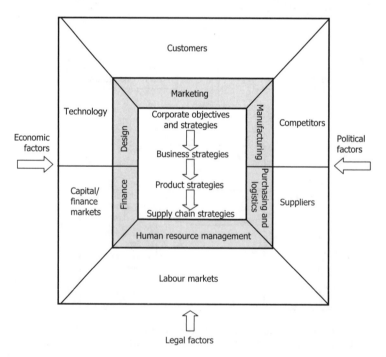

From Malcolm Saunders, *Strategy Purchasing and Supply Chain Management*, 1994. Reproduced with permission of Pearson Publishing.

FACTORS ON THE DESIGN OF A LOGISTICS SYSTEM

This model shows the factors that play on developing a logistics strategy. While this must be linked into the organization's main corporate strategy it also requires the organization to reflect the external environment with respect to customer requirements, competitors, technology, etc. balanced with the organization's competencies.

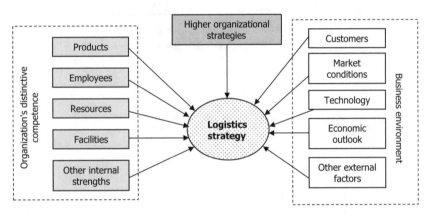

From *Logistics – An Introduction to Supply Chain Management* by Professor David Walters, 2002. Reproduced with permission of Palgrave Macmillan.

SUPPLIER/BUYER RELATIONSHIP

This model shows the relative position of customer/supplier dependence based on the value that each has on one another's business performance. This information can be useful to companies to recognize the strength or vulnerability of their supplier relationship and may assist in setting business or operational strategies.

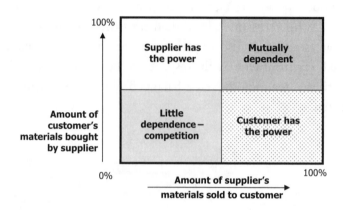

STOCK ORDERING STRATEGY

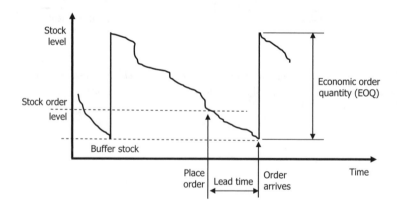

$$EOQ = \sqrt{\frac{2 \times R \times O}{C}}$$

R = Annual units required

O = Cost of placing an order

C = Cost of holding a unit of stock per period

VARIATION OF COST WITH ORDER SIZE

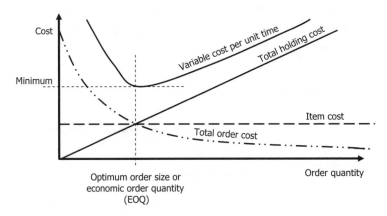

Model taken from *The Handbook of Management*, page 428, 3rd edition, Gower Publishing, 1992. Reproduced with kind permission of the editor Dennis Lock. Copyright Dennis Lock.

TYPES OF STOCK

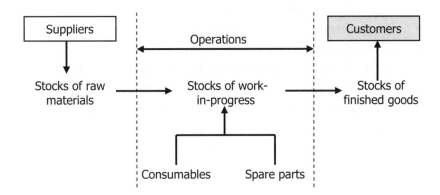

JUST IN CASE STOCK

While there has been a widespread use of just in time (JIT) delivery systems, traditional stock control is sometimes referred to as just in case stock and is used to provide protection when things go wrong.

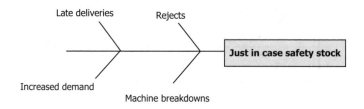

This approach is a luxury and comes at a cost, including the cost of processing this stock held in stores or as work progresses, the money invested as well as cost of operating the stores. Other supply chain costs are:

- Costs of processing goods or the purchase price of goods.
- Set-up or changeover costs.
- Costs of materials handling.
- Costs of transport and internal transit.
- Costs of packaging.
- Costs of administration and communication.
- Costs of failure – stockouts and failure to deliver on time.
- Cost of tariff duties where international movements are concerned.

SUPPLY CHAIN ANALYSIS

The two models below have been developed to identify different classes of problem and to apply different procurement approaches. They each consider the relative purchasing importance to the conditions in the supply market.

Purchase portfolio matrix – this compares levels of importance of purchasing with the levels of complexity.

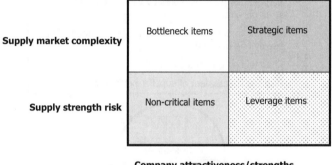

Bottleneck items	Strategic items
Non-critical items	Leverage items

Supply market complexity

Supply strength risk

Company attractiveness/strengths →

Procurement positioning matrix – this is a similar model to the one above and has been developed to understand the relationship between supplier vulnerability and value or profit potential.

High	Strategic – security	Strategic – critical
	Tactical – acquisition	Tactical – profit
Low		

Supply exposure/ vulnerability

Low   **Profit/value potential**   High

Both of these approaches can provide a guide to the allocation of time and effort required to be allocated by the supplier and the selection of the most appropriate course of action.

TYPICAL RESULTS OF A SUPPLIER REALIGNMENT PROCESS

This model illustrates some of the areas where benefits can be gained when organizations come together to realign their joint processes in order to gain market advantage.

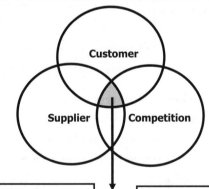

- Identification of key customer needs (both demand and supply) and their importance and satisfaction
- Segmentation of customers by value, profit, and strategic direction
- Analysis to determine highly leverageable needs (both supply and demands)
- Channel and geometric analysis
- Baseline assessment of supplier performance

Customer

Supplier **Competition**

- Identification of internal barriers and issues
- Assessment of strategic alignment
- Comparison versus new customer-required capabilities
- Deployment of resources, customer opportunities
- Process and organization period assessment
- Assessment of information technology capability

- Benchmarking of customer perceptions against major competitors
- Identification of competitive business intentions
- Assessment of performance in specific customer-related programs
- Establishment of best practices

From Charles C. Poirier, *Advanced Supply Chain Management*, 1999. Reproduced with permission of Berrett-Koehler Publishers Inc.

SUPPLY AND DEMAND MISALIGNMENT

The diagram below illustrates the usual misalignment that can occur between supply and demand as a product proceeds through its economic life cycle. Demand is typically highest around the date of product launch when supplies are elusive because the manufacturer is uncertain as to how well the introduction will proceed. During this period distributors and retailers often over-order as a way of hedging against shortages in the event that the introduction is successful and can then satisfy customer demand.

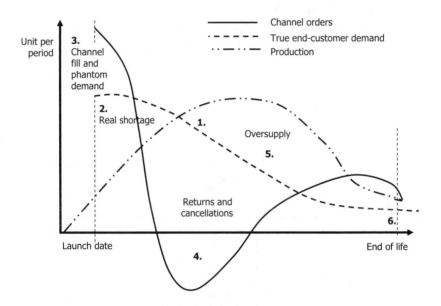

1. True end-customer demand is unknown, must be anticipated.
2. Production cannot meet initial projected demand, resulting in real shortages.
3. Channel partners over-order in an attempt to meet demand and stock their shelves.
4. As supply catches up with demand, orders are cancelled or returned.

5. Financial and production planning are not aligned with real demand therefore production continues.
6. As demand declines, all parties attempt to drain inventory to prevent losses.

From Charles C. Poirier, *Advanced Supply Chain Management*, 1999. Reproduced with permission of Berrett-Koehler Publishers Inc.

INPUTS INTO MASTER PRODUCTION SCHEDULE

This model illustrates the importance of considering all sources of demand. The master production schedule is regarded as the most important planning and control scheme in a business and provides an input to the materials requirements planning (MRP).

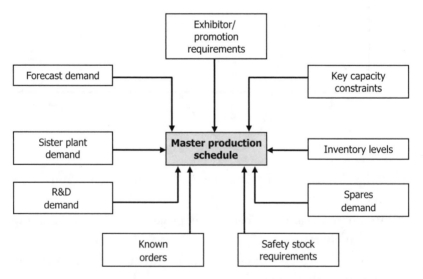

From Nigel Slack, Stuart Chambers and Robert Johnston, *Operations Management*, 1995. Reproduced with permission of Pearson Education.

SUPPLY CHAIN POSITIONING MATRIX

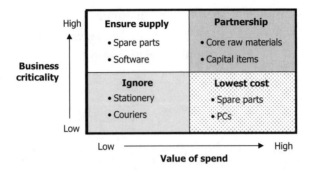

MATERIAL REQUIREMENTS PLANNING

This links into the model shown on the previous page and covers the elements of a typical MRP system.

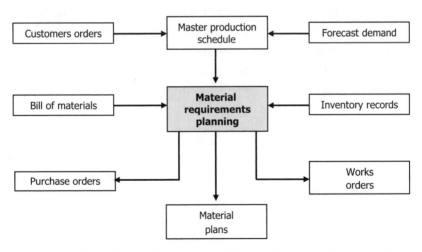

From Nigel Slack, Stuart Chambers and Robert Johnston, *Operations Management*, 1995. Reproduced by permission of Pearson Education.

STAGES IN THE BUYER/SUPPLIER RELATIONSHIP LIFE CYCLE

While this model is shown here in supply chain management it also has clear links to other areas of Management depending on the stage of the buyer/supplier relationship.

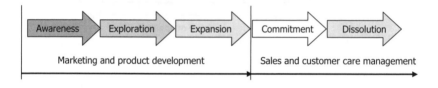

THE PURCHASING CYCLE

The author of this model suggests that the normal cycle of events for a single project purchase is not unlike that of a manufacturing project, and that the purchase of any item can be regarded as a mini-project in itself Activities in the cycle can vary according to the type of goods or services involved but this model is fairly typical of goods that must be specially ordered.

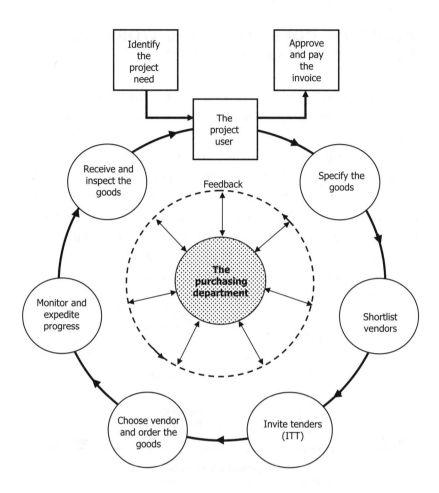

Model taken from *Project Management* by Dennis Lock, Gower Publications, 8th edition, page 381, 2003. Reproduced with kind permission of Dennis Lock. Copyright Dennis Lock.

MODEL OF COLLABORATIVE WORKING/ PARTNERING COMPONENTS

My own research into partnering provided this model, showing a number of key components analogous to the construction of a building.

Those components represented below the ground level are the foundation components necessary to support the partnering relationship for the duration of the project and potentially beyond, especially if considering a more strategic partnering arrangement. It is suggested that the absence of sufficiently robust foundations would constrain the success of the partnering relationship and the achievement of the potential benefits from the outset.

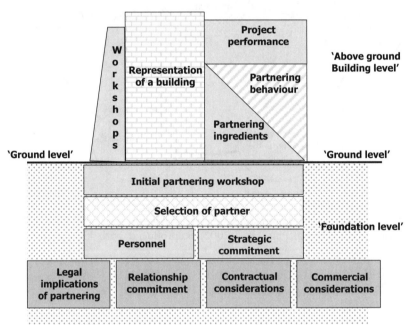

The foundation components possess a common theme of the selection stages between the customer and client/contractor organizations. The main groups of components include:

- **Legal implications** – for example, changes to the contractual relationship consequent on partnering.
- **Relationship commitment** – to achieve full potential is more than simply making a longer-term commitment to work together. Realizing the full potential in terms of risk reduction and joint profit margins requires a more immediate and also a lasting commitment by both organizations to developing a robust relationship.
- **Contractual considerations** – recognition and resolution of disputes by a mutually agreed process, which only as a last resort refers to the contract, is viewed as one of the cornerstones of the partnering philosophy.
- **Commercial** – performance incentives incorporating rewards and penalties (e.g., maximum value for money, improved quality and safety, timely completion, reduction in fixed overheads and shortened learning curves) are 'an essential aspect of partnering . . . the opportunity for participants to share in the rewards of improved performance'.
- **Personnel** – one of the most significant consequences of partnering is the impact on people and the change in behaviour that such a closer relationship necessitates. The personnel must possess the appropriate technical skills, experience, attitudes and a genuine commitment towards the partnering approach and philosophy.
- **Strategic commitment** – to develop a strategic relationship, fully endorsed by the senior management of both organizations.
- **Selection of Partner** – most partnerships originate through the competitive tendering process; however, the partnership philosophy should not look merely at price and delivery, but concentrate on other attributes such as culture, level of technology, production flexibility, commercial awareness, innovation and ease of communication.

- **Initial partnering workshop** – provides the opportunity to understand and agree how the relationship will work, how the parties will interact with one another and what each expects of the other at the strategic and operational levels.

'Above ground' components

The above ground components are shown as a building with 'buttresses' on each side to show that the building project is supported by the three features below together with addition workshops as the project progresses.

- **Partnering ingredients** – incorporating three crucial ingredients: establishment of mutual objectives; development of a process for problem resolution; and an all-party commitment to continuous improvement.
- **Partnering behaviour** – gaining agreement on the behavioural attributes (e.g. commitment, trust and mutual advantage) to support and engender success between the organizations and the individual team members.
- **Project performance** – reflects the composite improvements in performance from all of the components (e.g. lower costs, improved quality, fewer over-runs, fewer disputes and improved working experience for employees).

Prior to the commencement of the project, the client organization is primarily in control of the foundation components; but the relationship should evolve to become bilateral, or multilateral, such that client and contractors have more equal influence on the overall project development and performance.

From Prof. S.A. Burtonshaw-Gunn and Prof. R.L. Ritchie, in *ESRC People and Culture in Construction Series*, Prof. A. Dainty (ed.), 2007. Reproduced with kind permission of Taylor & Francis Publishing.

MODEL OF PARTNERING IN ACTION

The focus of this model relates to the phase following the award of a contract where the partnering philosophy is being utilized – 'partnering in action' – providing a more interactive representation of the issues likely to be encountered in the implementation and continuing management of the process.

Each of the four primary components – project management, total quality management, supply chain management and human resource issues – is represented by a quadrant together with the associated main sub-components. The discussion of the sub-components is focused towards the implications for closer collaborative working practices and relationships.

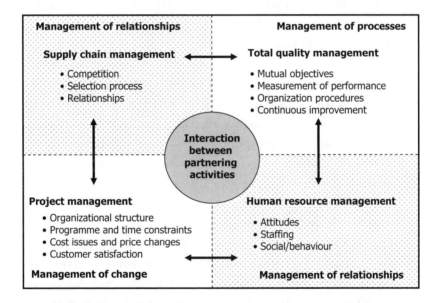

* **Human resource management**

    The emphasis on relationships within the partnership suggests the need for effective human resource strategies and policies, designed to inculcate the appropriate attitudes and behavioural traits among those employees directly involved. Selection and training of the key senior staff concerned may be critical to the partnering relationship's eventual success. These requirements apply to both contractor and client organizations and there may be merit in hosting joint staff development programmes (e.g. team building).

- **Project management**
  Organizational structures and processes are important issues to be settled at the outset to define roles and responsibilities and to establish agreed communication channels. The project manager remains primarily responsible for delivering the project within the requirements of specification, time and budget, often regarded as the cornerstones of project management, together with achievement of client satisfaction. Establishing effective structures, processes, communication channels and relationships should discourage the adversarial approach, providing benefits in terms of efficiency (e.g. costs, work flow and flexibility) and effectiveness (e.g. meeting the client's needs and funding additional project requirements).

- **Total quality management**
  Partnering and total quality management may be viewed as highly complementary philosophies including the establishment of mutual objectives, the shared commitment towards continuous improvement and the need for mutually agreed measures of performance.

- **Supply chain management**
  The characteristics of the evolution towards strategic partnering relationships require a move away from selection on lowest tender price to consideration of life cycle costs and value for money. Important features of supply chain management include the initial selection of partners in the chain, building and developing effective relationships, and agreeing arrangements for the nature of competition both within the partnership and with other suppliers/customers. In some

industries, it is important that relationships are forged not only between the customer and the first-tier main contractor but also between the second-tier subcontractors and the prime contractor. Evidence from the manufacturing sector suggests that maximum benefit is gained by early and full involvement of all the key partners in the supply chain.

The other important feature of the model is the dynamic interaction between the subcomponents within each of these four main groups and between the sub-components in the other groups. For example, staff selection and appropriate attitudes (i.e. human resource issue sub-components) will influence simultaneously relationship development (i.e. a supply chain management sub-component) and the effectiveness of continuous improvement (i.e. a total quality management sub-component).

From Professor S. A. Burtonshaw-Gunn and Professor R. L. Ritchie, in *ESRC People and Culture in Construction Series*, Professor A. Dainty (ed.), 2007. Reproduced with kind permission of Taylor & Francis Publishing.

ELEMENTS OF A PURCHASING ORGANIZATION FOR A CAPITAL PROJECT

This model shows some of the important elements typically found in a project purchasing organization. The client is shown dealing only with the managing contractor or prime contractor who in turn deals with the rest of the purchasing process either through the use of the prime contractor's own resources or through other organizations if the prime contractor is acting solely in the capacity of the project manager. The benefit in understanding these relationships is to allow a matrix of required tasks against those best placed to undertake the activity and hence derive a set of agreed project roles and responsibilities.

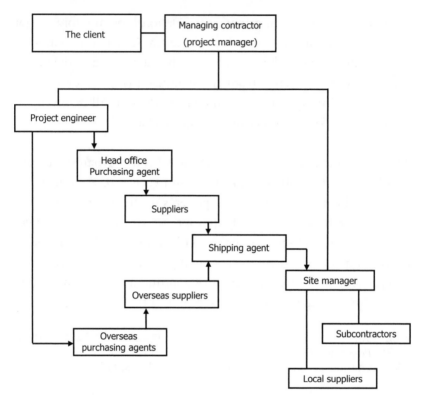

Model taken from *Project Management* by Dennis Lock, Gower Publications, 8th edition, page 412, 2003. Reproduced with kind permission of Dennis Lock. Copyright Dennis Lock.

CHAPTER 17

TIME MANAGEMENT

*I*n many ways this chapter would appear to be different from the others in this book as it focuses more on the individual manager than a particular management discipline. However, organizational skills in time management provide benefits not just to the individual but also to the company. Furthermore this chapter also differs in that rather than trying to provide a model associated with time management, the concentration here is on possible time management related problems and their suggested solutions.

Whether a student or established manager, the use of time will likely be of concern to both. It should be remembered that as individuals we each have all of the time in the world. Even being the most wealthy person on the planet does not provide any more time – we all have to make do with 168 hours each week.

In looking at the causes of lost time and potential remedies it is possible to identify links to other management disciplines and topics covered elsewhere in this book. The topics of project and risk management together with individual performance management models can be seen to be related to some of the text in this chapter.

Some of the causes of inefficient working resulting in poor time management identified in this chapter may assist in seeking process improvements at one level or bringing about an organizational change programme at a higher level. In both cases the starting point of examining how we and others identify which activities inhibit our performance can often be covered at an early facilitated workshop aimed at improving individual and organizational performance.

The text of this chapter concentrates on 17 key issues which inhibit personal performance through demands on time which in turn create inefficiency such as:

- Poor delegation
- Inability to finish things
- Unclear responsibilities
- Personal disorganization
- Too much paper
- The telephone/email
- Poor meetings
- Fire-fighting
- Interruption by visitors
- Too much reading
- Communication
- Too much routine
- Lack of self-discipline
- Involved too much
- Can't say no
- Lack of priorities
- Indecision and delay

The chapter ends with a model to offer some guidance on the time required to address important and urgent demands.

'TIME STEALERS'

The causes of and solutions to these time stealers are described below:

Poor delegation

CAUSES	POSSIBLE SOLUTIONS
Insecurity – fear of failure	Bear in mind that you probably learnt most by your mistakes. Teach others to foresee and anticipate mistakes and pass on your own experience to them
Lack of faith in others	Train your staff, build up faith in them
Over-control	Measure your staff on the basis of results, not the detail of how they do the task
Inadequate instructions	Train yourself and your staff. Let your staff accept a task by repeating your instructions
Delegation of formal responsibility but not actual authority	Fix times for report back when decisions can be made
Fear of my staff doing a better job than me	Be grateful instead. The whole department will benefit. Nobody is expected to be equally good at everything. Remember your results depend on their performance
Involving myself in too much detail	Do nothing yourself, delegate to others
Can do job better myself	Don't try to be a perfectionist
I feel more comfortable doing than managing	Practise managing techniques. The better you master them, the more comfortable you will feel with them
Overworked staff	Help them make priorities. Make realistic demands. Always have an overview of your staff's workload

Inability to finish things

CAUSES	POSSIBLE SOLUTIONS
Lack of deadlines	Make it a rule to put deadlines on all jobs
Lack of respect for your time/interruptions by other people	Fix some regular time when you are not to be disturbed and inform 'others'
Overworked – too much to do	Drop old responsibilities when you accept new ones
Laziness	Impose deadlines on yourself – and tell 'others' about them
Things look too big to start on	Break down problems to manageable pieces, set milestones

Unclear responsibilities

CAUSES	POSSIBLE SOLUTIONS
Inadequate job description	Organization chart with key areas would be of great help
You have the formal responsibility but no actual authority	Show through your results that you can live up to authority
Power struggle/distrust in the organization	Key areas, goals and objectives need to be established in the whole organization
Job descriptions overlap each other	Identify overlapping. Eliminate them by establishing key areas.
Ambiguous instructions	Write down your understanding of what you have been asked to do and send it to them. Seek face to face clarification.

Personal disorganization

CAUSES	POSSIBLE SOLUTIONS
Lack of system	Use your secretary/diary, then you have the best basis for keeping everything organized
Giving people the impression that you are busy, of importance or indispensable	This may symbolize insecurity, lack of system, confusion or inability to meet deadlines
Cannot delegate	Accept that others have abilities and experience. Learn to delegate
Indecision	80% of tasks arriving at your desk can be handled immediately

Too much paper

CAUSES	POSSIBLE SOLUTIONS
Random circulation	Ask who needs to see what information and why. Stop people sending you things if you don't need to see them
Poor communications	Select the best method and most time-saving methods of communication
Poor administrative routines	Ask if things are done too elaborately or if the control is too strict or too formalized. Are the administration processes kept up to date?
Poor organization	Standardize written communication. See if the present paperwork can be improved. Establish a systematic approach to information processing

The telephone

CAUSES	POSSIBLE SOLUTIONS
Discussion too lengthy	Separate 'chat' from information
Wish or need to be available to outside interruptions	Train operator/secretary to be selective
No plans for privacy	Switch phone off and schedule periods in which you do not want to be disturbed. Set times for taking calls – or agree to call back
Unstructured conversations	Make a plan in advance by listing items you want to discuss
Wish to be involved	Divorce yourself from the details
Inability to terminate and shorten conversations	Preset time limits
Unrealistic time estimates	Have an egg-timer by your telephone
Lack of priorities – all calls get through	Discuss the problem with your secretary/ operator. Make a plan
No secretary	Ask a colleague to cover your telephone for a set number of minutes and do the same in return

Poor meetings

CAUSES	POSSIBLE SOLUTIONS
Purpose of meeting not clear	Draw up an agenda
Wrong participants	Invite only those needed the most
Too many meetings	Evaluate the results in relation to the time spent
Poor or no minutes produced	Make standard outline of minutes
Irrelevant talk	Firm chairing of meeting

Poor meetings (*continued*)

CAUSES	POSSIBLE SOLUTIONS
No conclusions	Agenda to clearly state decisions to be taken
No follow-up	Minutes to indicate who, what and when
Indecision	Invite a person with decision-making authority
Poor chairmanship	Train yourself and your colleagues in chairmanship
Not starting on time	Always start on time. By waiting for late-comers you reward them and penalize others
Too many interruptions	Allow no interruptions except for emergency. Let secretary/operator know when the meeting will be finished at the latest
Not sticking to agenda	Bring it back to the point
Failure to set ending time and/or time allocations for each subject	To begin with set time limit for meeting. Assign each subject specific time according to importance

'Fire-fighting'

CAUSES	POSSIBLE SOLUTIONS
Lack of priorities	Learn to distinguish between the urgent jobs and the important jobs. Establish priorities. What is your time mainly spent on?
Trying to do too much at the same time	Learn to say no. Do one job at a time. Have an outline of the tasks
Lack of planning	Think ahead. Have alternatives ready for unexpected situations. Expect the unexpected

Fire-fighting (*continued*)

CAUSES	POSSIBLE SOLUTIONS
Over-reacting and treating all small problems as a full crisis	Ignore the problems that are of minor importance. Delegate problems which your staff can handle, then you preserve the overview and control
Overlooking negative consequences of a decision	Analyse what can go wrong and establish alternative plans
Being purely reactive	Spend time on doing what is important – many urgent things will wait or go away

Interruption by visitors

CAUSES	POSSIBLE SOLUTIONS
No plans to avoid drop-in visitors	Design and implement a screening plan. Insist on appointments
My door is always open	Establish a quiet hour in which you are not to be disturbed. Find somewhere else to work at that time if necessary
People ask me to make decisions below my level of authority	Don't make decisions on something you can delegate. Refer to your staff in charge of such matters
Frequent interruptions by my staff	Manage by exception. Ask for information only concerning deviations from plans and budgets. Decide which tasks your staff can do without asking questions. Decide on which situations they may interrupt you with and which things can be postponed to be discussed at your regular meetings
Inability to terminate visits	You go to their office. Keep standing. Preset time limits for visits/meetings. Make it clear that the meeting is over, such as 'Before we finish, I would . . .'

Too much reading

CAUSES	POSSIBLE SOLUTIONS
Unclear and poorly edited material	Persuade your staff or your boss or your colleagues only to forward information in an acceptable form – and set a good example yourself
Poor reading skills	Undertake speed reading course
No priorities for what to read and how thoroughly	List things you must read. Give them priorities and assign time in your diary. Learn selective reading skills, i.e. skimming

Communication

CAUSES	POSSIBLE SOLUTIONS
Unaware of colleagues needs for information	Ask them what they need. Be aware of the requirements
Language difficulties	Create common expressions and terminology
Wrong media used	Agree when you should hold meetings, write emails, use the telephone, etc.
Poor timing	The timing of information should be chosen carefully so that the recipient will be open to the message
Overcommunicating	Define the aim of communication. Learn to express yourself clearly, unambiguously and completely
Recipient does not seem open and motivated	Discover the recipient's true motive and attitudes. Examine the attitude beforehand. Learn to decipher body language
Indecision or delay in providing answers	Use the 'unless I hear anything to the contrary . . .' technique. Find the actual reason for the indecision

Too much routine

CAUSES	POSSIBLE SOLUTIONS
Lack of priorities	Establish priorities
Fear of staff's mistakes	Train them
Fear of losing influence	Get an overview of what is really important
Can do the job better myself	Train your staff and have confidence in them
Too much detail	Ask what would happen if you didn't do it

Lack of self-discipline

CAUSES	POSSIBLE SOLUTIONS
Lack of performance standards	Set your own standards
Postponing the unpleasant	Recognize that it has to be done. It is not going to be easier later on. Do the unpleasant things first and the rest of the day will seem easier.
Lack of direction in your work	Say 'no' to unimportant matters
Responding to urgent matters, postponing the important	Ignore the problems that solve themselves. Delegate the problems that others can handle and attend to those that only you can resolve
Not following up unrealistic time estimates	A thing is not finished until it functions the way it was intended to. Monitor milestones in diary
I cannot say 'no'	Take the plunge and call a halt
Carelessness	If you haven't got time to do it right the first time, when will you have time to do it again?

Involved too much

CAUSES	POSSIBLE SOLUTIONS
Unclear priorities	Set clearly defined tasks and goals
I want to be important and involved in everything	Be selective. Use your time and energy on the 20% that produces 80% of the results
Unrealistic time estimates	Recognize that tasks take longer and build in some additional time based on this
Overwhelming pressure and larger piles of paper	Do not confuse activity with effectiveness.

Can't say no

CAUSES	POSSIBLE SOLUTIONS
Wish to help others	If you always say 'yes', others will take your help for granted. Break this habit
Need to feel important and involved in everything	Stake your efforts on something that matters and show results in this field
Fear of causing offence	Learn to say 'no' without offending. For example, 'I cannot do this but offer a suggestion which may help . . .'
Not knowing how to say 'no'	Train yourself to say 'no'. It will make it possible for you to concentrate on things that are important
Ambition, desire to be busy	It is better to do less well than a lot poorly
Others quite simply assume that you will say 'yes'	Probably your own fault because you never say 'no'!

Lack of priorities

CAUSES	POSSIBLE SOLUTIONS
No system	Establish a weekly 'to do' list
Lack of time to plan	Planning takes time initially but saves time in the long run
Lack of self-discipline	Task and plan activities in your diary for one month at a time
Would rather be doing than thinking	Those who know what to do succeed once. Those who know why will succeed again
No job description	Ask for one, write one and make sure it covers what you do

Indecision and delay

CAUSES	POSSIBLE SOLUTIONS
Lack of faith in decision-making process	Have a systematic approach to data collection and evaluate for more reliability
Paralysis by analysis	Know when to stop gathering information
Irrational decision technique	Train yourself and your staff in decision-making techniques. Think hard about the criteria
Fear of what may happen even when small mistakes are made	Distrust and power struggles must be cleared away. Learn from mistakes
Unrealistic deadlines	If everything takes longer than you think then build in additional time
Postponing the unpleasant and difficult	Do them first and you will feel much better afterwards
Ignorance of what the decision will lead to	Set goals and targets and relate the decisions to the key areas

MAKING TIME: IMPORTANCE VERSUS URGENCY

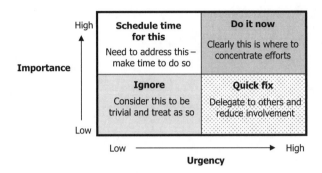

CHAPTER 18

UNDERTAKING RESEARCH

*M*any management courses involve project work which requires an element of research. In addition to this are research-based higher level qualifications where undertaking research is the fundamental basis of acquiring and sharing new knowledge. Within the business environment it would be odd to find a company that did not undertake research of some kind, whether in gaining customer satisfaction results or by proactive research such as part of market or product development. Within this chapter are a number of models designed to help those undertaking research to satisfy either management, education or wider business needs.

Without doubt there can be no set method or approach to undertaking research as it is often unique to the company (or student) objectives, the industry under review, the amount of time available and budget limitations. However, there are a number of research strategies that can be matched to the research objectives available. These, and a typical research process, are shown in this chapter.

As mentioned in the Introduction there are a number of management topics that are closely inter-related. Undertaking research can be used to support many of the topics covered by this book, from marketing or product development, process improvement, obtaining customer feedback to gaining an understanding of their requirements as part of customer relationship management. Research has a clear link to problem solving and problem resolution. The involvement of the researcher is also of key importance as this provides guidance on their research involvement ranging from interviews, questionnaires, and surveys to observation and more direct involvement. In addition to the ways that data may be collected is the consideration of a wider framework approach open to researchers such as case studies, action research, historical documentation and experimentation. Of course collecting the raw data is often regarded as the most interesting part of any research but careful consideration also needs to be undertaken before this stage so that the 'right' data is collected and a plan of how this data will be analysed is in place. This analysis can cover either a qualitative or quantitative approach, or both, as they should not be regarded as being mutually exclusive – good research rarely relies on just one approach to the exclusion of the other. The attributes of each of the qualitative and quantitative approaches are provided in this chapter.

While in the business environment, research may, for example, focus on customer views, perceptions and needs, it is less likely to require the researcher to undertake a review of any secondary data from the published literature to support the findings. This will not be the case for academic research where a review of the secondary data is almost mandated and even if this is not the case a review of the literature presents a good starting point to gain an understanding of what else has been done on the research subject, the limitations of the research undertaken and if lessons from other industries or countries would produce a different conclusion. Examples of secondary data are not limited to books and articles in journals, magazines and newspapers but can also include conference reports, published statistics, company's annual reports, electronic databases and of course the internet. Having undertaken a review of the available literature and then carried out some field work necessary for the collection of primary research data from interviews, questionnaires, etc., it is important that these two sets are brought together in any conclusions. In some cases the published literature will support the new field work findings, while in other cases new, differing views may be identified and provide a new understanding or knowledge applicable in a business or an academic environment.

TYPICAL RESEARCH PROCESS

Undertaking research is needed in many areas of management in additional to academic studies. The activity diagram below shows the main steps of a typical research processes. Following this staged approach will prevent wasted time, effort and perhaps reputation caused by commencing the data collection or field research work without having an understanding of its purpose and main objectives. Even when it comes to the data collection phase it is sensible to undertake and learn from a small pilot study before the main research is done. This pilot study will often confirm that the right data is being sought and will provide the research with an opportunity to test the quality of the data obtained and how it will be analyzed and used. For those conducting surveys such preliminary work will also provide a view on the practicality and sensitivity of the questions being asked. The benefit of the pilot study includes

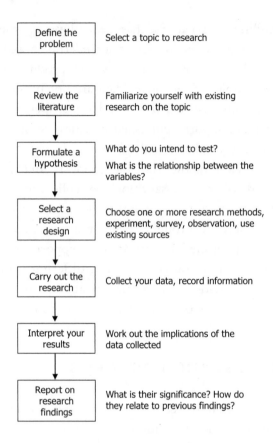

the opportunity to make changes without incurring large expense and effort.

Often after completing research further new areas may be identified which may warrant a separate study. In addition the scope of the research establishes boundaries which subsequently may expanded. It should be noted that having undertaken the data collection phase it is important to compare and contrast this with the literature review previously undertaken otherwise there will be a question as to how the new research supports or contradicts previously published views.

SELECTION OF RESEARCH STRATEGIES

The figure helps the researcher's selection of the most appropriate strategy based upon the number of studies to be undertaken and their involvement in the process. For research students this model is useful in helping to select a strategy/strategies based on their cost and timetable constraints. For consultants this can be used in discussion with a client to determine the scope of the research, how it can been undertaken and establish likely time and cost parameters.

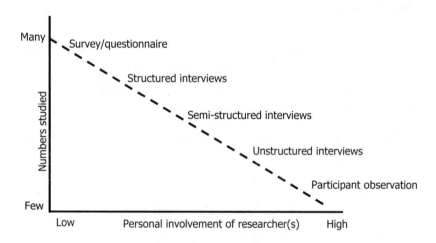

Graph of 'Researcher involvement' (page 89) from *The New Introducing Sociology* edited by Peter Worsely. First published as *Introducing Sociology*, Penguin Books, 1970, 3rd edition published as *The New Introducing Sociology*, 1987, 1992. Copyright Peter Worsley and contributors 1970, 1977, 1987, 1992.

SOURCES OF EVIDENCE

It is proposed that there are six sources of evidence used in research:

- Documentation
- Archival records
- Interviews
- Direct observation
- Participant observation
- Physical artifacts

SELECTING THE RESEARCH APPROACH

Quantitative

Quantitative data in social research has attractions because it uses numbers and can present findings in the form of graphs and tables; it conveys a sense of solid, objective research.

Quantitative research can be used if:

- You believe that there is an objective reality that can be measured.
- Your audience is familiar with/supportive of quantitative studies.
- Your research question is confirmatory, predictive.
- The available literature is relatively large.
- Your research focus covers a lot of breadth.
- Your time available is relatively short.
- Your ability/desire to work with people is medium to low.
- Your desire to structure is high.
- You have skills in the area(s) of statistics and deductive reasoning.
- Your writing skills are strong in the area of technical, scientific writing.

Qualitative

Qualitative data, whether words or images, is the product of a process of interpretation. Qualitative studies do not aim to quantify data, but use data as a means to increase understanding by careful analysis and interpretation.

Qualitative research can be used if:

- You believe that there are multiple constructed realities.
- Your audience is familiar with/supportive of qualitative studies.
- Your research question is exploratory, interpretative.
- The available literature is limited or missing.
- Your research focus involves in-depth study.
- Your time available is relatively long.
- Your ability/desire to work with people is high.
- Your desire to structure is low.
- You have skills in attention to detail and inductive reasoning.
- Your writing skills are strong in the area of literary, narrative writing.

Reproduced with kind permission of Blackwell Publishing, from Colin Robson, *Real World Research*, 2002.

SELECTING THE RESEARCH STRATEGY

The table below presents the relative situations for different research strategies.

STRATEGY	FORM OF RESEARCH QUESTION	REQUIRES CONTROL OVER BEHAVIOUR?	FOCUSES ON CONTEMPORARY EVENTS?
Experiment	How, why	Yes	Yes
Survey	Who, what, where, how many, how much	No	Yes
Archival analysis	Who, what, where, how many, how much	No	Yes/No
History	How, why	No	No
Case study	How, why	No	Yes

Reproduced with kind permission of Blackwell Publishing, from Colin Robson, *Real World Research*, 2002.

METHODOLOGICAL TRIANGULATION

The aim of this illustration is to show that a number of techniques can be used to provide research information and verify that obtained by other sources. While this figure is drawn from an academic research point of view it also shows that in business more than one approach can provide the organization with the ability to verify the situation, results and understandings.

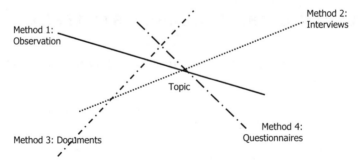

Reproduced with permission of the Open University Press, from Martyn Denscombe, *Good Research Guide*, page 85, 1998.

RESEARCH CONSIDERATIONS

There are some key decisions which need to be considered . . .

Relevance – Does it really matter whether the research takes place?
- Is the research significant in relation to current issues in society?
- Will the research build upon existing knowledge?
- Are specific theories to be used, tested and developed?

Feasibility – Can it be done?
- Is their sufficient time for the design of the research, collection of data and analysis of results?
- Will the resources be available to cover the costs of the research?
- Will it be possible and practicable to gain access to necessary data – people, events, documents?

Coverage – Are the right things included?
- Will the questions cover the full range of issues?
- Will an adequate number and suitable diversity of people, events, etc. be included?
- Will it be reasonable to make generalizations about the data collected?
- Is it likely that there will be adequate response data?

Accuracy – Will the research produce true and honest data?
- Will the data be precise and detailed?
- Are respondents likely to give full and honest answers?
- Will the investigation manage to focus on the most vital issues?

Objectivity – Will the research provide a fair and balanced view?

- Can I avoid being biased because of my values, beliefs and background?
- Will the research be approached with an open mind about what the findings might show?
- Am I prepared to recognize the limitations of the research approach that is adopted?

Ethics – What about the rights and feelings of those affected by the research?

- Can I avoid any deception or misrepresentation in my dealings with the research subjects?
- Will the identities and interests of those involved be protected?
- Can I guarantee the confidentiality of the information given to me during the research?

CHAPTER 19

WORKING AS A
MANAGEMENT
CONSULTANT

*I*t is widely accepted that management consulting typically involves the identification and cross-fertilization of best practices, analytical techniques, change management, technology implementations, strategy development and coaching skills. However, the above list are merely tools or competencies on which consultants may draw in order to provide sound advice to business about efficient management practices. On this basis therefore one of the attributes of management consultancy can be considered to be the practice of assisting companies improve their operational and hence financial performance through analysis of existing business problems together with the introduction of performance metrics by which the organization can then be incentively managed.

The decision for an organization to use a firm of management consultants can arise through a number of reasons; the first being that they can often provide an informed analysis by drawing upon their wider expertise and independent specialist skills than are available within the host organization. Second, it is often easier for an outsider to provide an objective appraisal by seeing the broader picture while realistically recognizing the organization's long-term requirements. The third reason arises where the use of a management consultant may be needed for the provision of additional temporary assistance to meet an unexpected increase in the management workload; this can often arise in conjunction with the implementation of a major change programme or from a new development in management responsibility.

Although it is hoped that the readers of this book may come from a wide management audience, from student, through to career managers and possibly to management consultants, this chapter is specifically written for the latter who rely on their knowledge and experience of management and employ both ethical and professional standards to initiate and implement technological, organizational and behavioural changes. In so doing these management consultants contribute to the increased performance of their own practises and that of their client's business. The aim of this chapter then is to provide some guidance on the role of the management consultant partly because one of the objectives of this book is to support the delivery of professional management consultancy courses as new entrants into the profession but also because companies use more of their staff to undertake an internal consultancy role either as a facilitator or as part of a company-wide change management initiative. Although it is recognized that internal consultancy has additional challenges for those in the consultancy role, often due to their perceived position in the company, this chapter nevertheless offers some useful checklists and steps to follow in the undertaking of both internal and external consultancy assignments. In addition the notes on workshop facilitation in Chapter 20 are also hoped to be of value for management consultant readers. For those students and managers who hold career ambitions of entering the management consulting profession, the tools on the following pages provide well-tested approaches that may be considered as a good starting position and many of the other chapters of this book will be useful in directly undertaking consultancy assignments or as an aid to discussing the implementation of ideas with clients.

Towards the end of this chapter are some suggestions on networking: again a widely used tool in business and in consultancy in particular. The use of networks can be linked to 'added value' which can provide benefits to both consultant and client organizations.

SEVEN C CONSULTING PROCESS

This model is constructed to show a consultancy life cycle with each stage comprising a number of elements. Each of the stages can be undertaken independently, jointly or in parallel with each other.

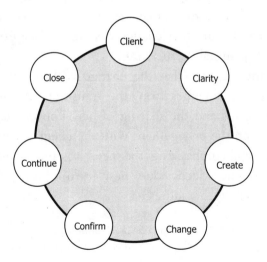

These seven stages are:

1. **Client:** Define the client's orientation of the work, their perceptions of the situation, what goals they have regarding the final outcome and who has the power to influence the outcome. The essence of this stage is to understand the person and problem and will provide a clear agreement as to what value is required to be delivered to the client.

2. **Clarify:** Determine the nature and detail of the problem to be addressed. The primary question to understand is 'What is really going on?'

3. **Create:** Use creative techniques to develop a sustainable solution that is measured against clear success criteria, takes as divergent a path as possible to find potential options and then chooses the best possible solution that meets the criteria.

4. **Change:** Understand the fundamental aspects that drive and underpin the change process and in particular the human factors that need to be managed to make it happen.

5. **Confirm:** Ensure that change has taken place using qualitative and quantitative measures.

6. **Continue:** Ensure that the change will be sustained using learning that emerges from the transition, the skills of the change agents and the sharing of new knowledge and skills.

7. **Close:** End the engagement with the client but maintain the relationship, emphasizing the need to understand the final outcomes, the added value, new learning and what further action needs to be addressed.

From Mick Cope, *The Seven Cs of Consulting: the definitive guide to the consultancy process*, 2003. Reproduced with permission of Pearson Education.

THE ROLE OF THE MANAGEMENT CONSULTANT

Authors Nees and Greiner suggested that the management consultancy role can be divided into the following five categories, although in reality consultants often perform a combination of these:

Mental adventurers. These analyse truly intransigent problem scenarios for country development, by adopting rigorous economic methods and leveraging their experience base. They identify with scholarly discipline, enjoy statistical analysis of specific areas and resist telling clients what to do but prefer sharing lengthy reports on newly discovered knowledge. They are useful when a client requires leading edge knowledge but not if the client wants firm recommendations.

Strategic navigators. This category bases its contribution on rich quantitative understanding of the market and competitive dynamics and then recommends course of action without too much regard for the client's own perspective. They rely on gathering large amounts of quantitative data on the economical aspects of making and selling products rather than industrial experience. They focus more on the environmental positioning of a client rather than the internal workings. Consultants in the category are useful if the client wants an economic overview of their industry to relate the firm to its competition. By contrast they are not useful if the client requires practical assistance in implementation of a new strategic direction.

Management physicians. This category derives its name from their recommendations based on a deep understanding of the internal dynamics of the client organization including its structure, culture, values, leadership capabilities, etc. They often take a generalist view making broad diagnoses and are deeply concerned with what is achievable. On this basis they are useful when a client wants a close working relationship and help with a complex organizational problem. They are not useful, however, if a client wants an external marketing study or work to determine the most profitable niche market in a particular industry.

Systems architects. These impact on the clients by helping redesign processes, routines and systems; they usually use a predetermined methodology and employ this in close cooperation with the client. They sometimes lack a broader business perspective and are useful when the client knows exactly what it wants and offer a narrowly defined project requiring a technical solution. The disadvantage of consultants in this category is that they are not very useful if the problem is more complex and cannot be cured by a particular method of technology.

Friendly co-pilots. This final category of management consultants occurs when they are able draw on their experience to counsel senior managers as a facilitator rather than as an expert, and have no ambition to provide new knowledge to the client.

This article was published in *Organizational Dynamics*, Volume 13, by Daniel Ness and Professor Larry Greiner, 'Seeing behind the look alike management consultants', pages 68–79, Winter 1985. Copyright Elsevier. Reproduced with permission.

VALUE ADDED OF CONSULTANCY TO THE CONSULTANT ORGANIZATION

While the techniques of value management and value engineering have long been in use in infrastructure projects to explore possible cost savings and assist decision making based on value for money over the life cycle of the facility, more recently there has been a growing interest in the wider concept of 'added-value'. Examples of added value for the consultant organization are given below.

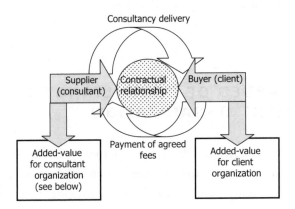

- Establish track record with client/industry/work type which can be used to market services to other potential clients.
- Potential to develop further work by having knowledge of client needs, experience of client's culture and hence a vastly reduced 'learning curve'. With overseas projects there will be the potential to develop work in the same geographic region based on some new local knowledge.
- Opportunity to use and manage own known supply chain to undertake work or support from specialist advisors, e.g. geotechnic consultants.
- Opportunity to use the consultancy tasks as a lead item for subsequent follow-on work as part of 'one-stop-shop' approach with knowledge of project and client organization already known to consultancy team.
- Consultancy can be marketed as business enabler with a multiplier affect on its impact on the client's business from decisions made and processes introduced and their impact on overall business operation.

- Used to develop knowledge of clients and other businesses as part of ongoing consultancy skills programme.

From Professor S.A. Burtonshaw-Gunn, 'Extending the concept of "added-value" to consultancy', *Professional Consulting*, Issue 14, August 2005. Reproduction with kind permission of the Institute of Management Consultancy.

VALUE ADDED OF CONSULTANCY TO THE CLIENT ORGANIZATION

While the techniques of value management and value engineering have long been in use in infrastructure projects to explore possible cost savings and assist decision making based on value for money over the life cycle of the facility, more recently there has been a growing interest in the wider concept of 'added-value'. Examples of added-value for the client organization are given below.

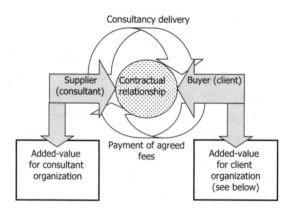

- Immediate use of required skills and experience to undertake task, no recruitment, training, or termination costs.
- Specialist advice, knowledge, processes, etc. transferred into client business as 'best practice' examples from other clients, industries, etc.

- Opportunity for other specialist consultants to be used to support project requirements without delays in further tendering, assessment and selection by client.
- Project risk reduction from gaining expert advice and opportunity for client to reduce risk contingency allocation.
- Clients can regard consultancy as a business enabler with a multiplier affect on its impact on the business, e.g. decisions made and processes introduced have impact on success of its larger-scale business operations.
- Client staff can learn from consultants through knowledge transfer and training.

From Professor S. A. Burtonshaw-Gunn, 'Extending the concept of "added-value" to consultancy', *Professional Consulting*, Issue 14, August 2005. Reproduction with kind permission of the Institute of Management Consultancy.

CONSULTANCY MODELS FOR HELPING ORGANIZATIONS

Work by Edgar Schien on the process of consultation published in 1969 gave the following three models which could be adopted by consultants for helping organizations. These are:

- Expert consulting.
- The patient/doctor model, and
- Process consulting.

Expert consulting is where a client purchases information or expertise and where ownership if the problem is passed to the expert. It can be used when the client has correctly diagnosed a problem and your capability to provide the expertise. It also requires the client to have thought through and accepted the potential consequences of obtaining the information or solution.

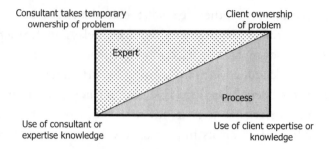

The doctor/patient model differs from the expert model in that it gives the consultant the additional roles of diagnoses and recommendation of what type of expertise will solve the problem. This is best employed when the diagnostic process is seen as being helpful to the client and information on the problem area will be freely provided in full and without exaggeration. The doctor/patient model can be used when the client will understand and correctly interpret the diagnosis provided by the consultant and will implement the prescribed solution.

Process consulting is founded on the premise that the client owns the problem and continues to do so throughout the consultation process. In this model diagnosis is part of the intervention and not a separate process. It can be used when the client has problems but does not know the source of the problem or how to address it. In the longer term the client will be capable of learning how to diagnose and solve their own organizational problems.

Further reading: Edgar F. Schein, *Process Consultation, its Role in Organizational Development*, Addison-Wesley Publishing Co., 1969.

TYPES OF CONSULTANT

This model shows that the consulting activity can be undertaken from either an advisory or an executive role and undertaken by external or by an organization's own in-house consultants.

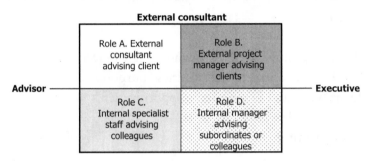

Role A. This is the conventional notion of an external consultant who provides specialist advice on contract for a time to clients.

Role B. This role has its origin in the construction and IT industries particularly where a project manager from an outside organization has responsibility for delivering an assignment but acts as a consultant to the clients and as a line manager in their own organization.

Role C. Here a full-time executive can act as a consultant to colleagues in a coaching and supporting way.

Role D. Many organizations employ internal consultants for their specialist advice such as health and safety, finance, marketing, legal, etc.

From *Managerial Consulting – a practical guide* by C. J. Margerison, 2000. Reproduced with permission of Gower Publications.

GENERIC CONSULTANCY PURPOSES

The International Labour Organization of Geneva suggests the following five broad generic consultancy purposes proposed by clients in using consultants irrespective of differences in technical area of intervention and in the specific intervention method used. These are:

- Achieving organizational purposes and objectives
- Solving management and business purposes
- Identifying and seizing new opportunities
- Enhancing learning
- Implementing changes

From *Management Consulting – a guide to the profession*, page 9, 1994, edited by Milan Kubr. Reproduced with permission of the International Labour Organization, Geneva.

CONSULTANT'S CHECKLIST FOR CONTRACTING

Margerson's book on managerial consulting uses this checklist which has been produced by Sue Morrell, an internal consultant for the Queensland State Public Service in Australia, and again follows the Rudyard Kipling 'Six honest serving-men' approach already covered in Chapter 4. For the consultant it offers a robust approach to understanding the client organization's issues and problems together with constraints and expectations. There are also similarities with the facilitator's checklist provided in Chapter 20.

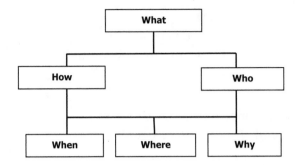

What

- What is the background to the request for a project?
- What is the client system?
- What are the objectives of the project?
- What does the client want from the consultant?
- What information is sought?
- What criteria will be used to measure results?
- What resources (staff, financial, materials) will the client commit to the project?
- What support does the consultant need to carry out the project?
- What checks will be made on progress?

How

- How long will the project take?
- How will the consultant and the project team work?
- How much time will the client commit to the project?
- How will information be communicated?
- How will confidentiality be maintained?

Who

- Who is the client?
- Who will be on the project team?
- Who must agree to the contract?
- Who should be involved in discussions?
- Who should be kept informed of progress?

When

- When will the project start and finish?
- When will the checks on progress occur?

Where

- Where will meetings be held?
- Where will the consultant work?

Why

- Why has the consultant been asked to assist?

From *Managerial Consulting – a practical guide* by Charles J. Margerison, 2000. Reproduced with permission of Gower Publications.

A RANGE OF CONSULTANCY SERVICES

It is proposed that both consultants and clients can choose among so many alternative types of services to be undertaken although most of the consulting assistance to management will be given in one or more of the following ways:

- Providing information and specialist resources
- Establishing business contacts and linkages
- Providing expert opinions
- Doing diagnostic work and developing action plans
- Improving systems and methods
- Training and development of management and staff
- Providing personal counselling

From *Management Consulting – a guide to the profession*, page 13, 1994, edited by Milan Kubr. Reproduced with permission of the International Labour Organization, Geneva.

THE CONSULTING PROCESS

This model shows a four stage process of organizational consulting and although presented in a sequential order the consultant and client may have to determine a different order to suit the situation, client requirements, timescale, resource limitations and constraints, etc.

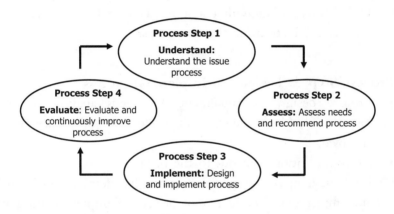

Process Step 1: Understand the issue process
- Source the issues through a proactive approach as strategic partner identifies opportunities or problems or reactive where client identifies an opportunity or problem.
- Discover underlying need through conversation about the issue to discover underlying need.
- Determine intervention by deciding if you should assess need in depth, implement and advice and follow-up.

Process Step 2: Assess needs and recommend process
- Identify what success would look like for this initiative and the barriers to success. Identify what is the preferred future

for the business, the organization and people processes and the individual and team performance.

- Engage in data collection analysis through interviews, documentation, surveys, observation, personal experience.
- Identify current reality with individual and team performance, organizational and team processes, business implications. Then determine gaps and recommend direction to overcome gaps. Determine metrics for evaluation of the entire initiative.
- Hold conversation with client on data analysis and recommendation. Determine the next steps.

Process Step 3: Design and **implement** process
- Prepare design to implement the needs analysis recommendations. Identify metrics for evaluation and secure client approval.
- Communication: roll out to the business.
- Implement in the simplest way possible, identify 'quick hits' and implement. Conduct pilot project of implementation in more complex situations.
- Implement project.
- 'Roll in' the change into the business so it becomes the business as usual.

Process Step 4: Evaluate and continuously improve process
- Hold conversation with client on desired outcome of evaluation.
- Design overall impact and evaluation analysis.
- Evaluate performance results based on metrics identified and agreed in the proposal.
- Determine areas of continuous improvement and shared learning and review with the client.

- Ensure that the project becomes part of the normal day-to-day business.

From *High Impact HR* by Dr David Weiss, 1999. Reproduced with permission of John Wiley & Sons.

TEN TIPS TO ENHANCE ORGANIZATIONAL CONSULTING SUCCESS

The list below also comes from David Weiss's book on HR as it offers these tips which are applicable to many consulting situations.

1. Find a 'shadow consultant' internally or externally to talk through assignments behind the scenes.
2. Build a network of external consultants to call upon as the need arises.
3. Be diligent in writing proposal letters and review them regularly before meeting with clients.
4. Know the pressure points for the client and tread carefully.
5. Be well prepared for clients at all times.
6. Suffer fools gladly – they have more influence than you think.
7. Always meet commitment and time lines.
8. Have a unique database but share it willingly.
9. Choose your timing and manage your impulse control.
10. Use organizational consulting experiences as an opportunity to learn and share learning.

From *High Impact HR* by Dr David Weiss, 1999. Reproduced with permission of John Wiley & Sons.

MAXIMIZING THE VALUE OF PROFESSIONAL NETWORKING MEETINGS

If you consider how much time is actually available to you to network, to meet new people and explore common interests, etc. when faced with other demands upon your time then selection of where, when and how often to network should be seen to be a serious decision. On the basis of available time you can next select which networking groups or events to target and attend; these can cover any one of the three types of professional networking groups which offer different benefits:

- Some groups provide opportunities to interact with prospective employers and clients, e.g. business breakfast meetings where smaller businesses are encouraged to share experiences and ideas to improve in-house knowledge.
- Some groups enable its members to keep abreast of the latest developments in your field, such as technical products or managerial processes. These are typical of many professional institute local branch meetings and special interest groups such as the Women in Management, Risk Management and Care Management groups.
- Some provide opportunities for career skills development that will enable attendees to learn more about themselves from activities such as self-marketing, interviewing, and making a successful transition. An example of this is an alumni association.

In addition to these overt networking groups is the use of a more informal casual network such as family and friends; local school PTA; Friends of Arts or Charity groups.

In looking at professional networking in practice the best opportunities for networking are typically before the start of the formal programme or immediately after the guest speaker's presentation. In limiting your attendance to just listening to the speaker attendees will miss out on much of the networking opportunity that the meeting can provide. Skilled networkers arrive in good time and use the expectation of the event as an introduction tool; equally late departers can make use of the presentation content, speaker's performance, or the announced forthcoming programme as a way to initiate an introduction of themselves to others.

Good networkers use the meeting as an opportunity to develop a relationship and then suggest a business meeting for a later date. A word of caution here is that having begun to establish a relationship and allude to a meeting it is important that this is followed through to show commitment and to begin to engender some degree of trust and reliability. It is also important in a practical way to follow up immediately while the person, the conversation and the issues discussed are fresh in both your minds; forgetting all about it until the next time you meet is unlikely to progress your relationship or business opportunity.

In addition to networking providing a real value it needs to be carefully managed and continually rationalized otherwise individuals run the risk of hoarding a myriad of contacts which are never interactive and can ultimately breed complacency over the need to attend networking events.

In addition to the outward facing external networking it is not surprising that we more easily develop our own internal networks often through proximity and organizational structure than by invitation. The purpose of these networks can be used to help members develop to their potential and for them in turn to contribute to the development of others. Membership of these advice networks contributes to both individual and organization capability enhancement. Finally the trust network is often the smallest of the internal networks and is developed over a long time-frame; its benefit, however, is to offer its members the safety to share delicate political information and a route to support one another in difficult circumstances.

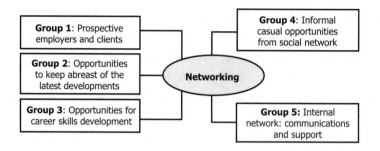

From a professional career development perspective networking is valuable and should be considered as an essential exercise in 'personal branding'; where such brand management and visibility can help to raise your industry profile, credibility and consequently an individual's 'brand value'. Whether the term 'networking' is a passing 'fad' its future success will continue to depend on individuals' commitment to a group and the results they obtain from it. For some consultants a professional network is one of their most valuable assets with networking meetings regarded as one of the best ways to continually keep up to date on industrial, commercial and professional developments and to revitalize and grow future business contacts.

While many advocate a highly structured approach to networking through contact mapping and customer relationship management frameworks one must not forget to seize those unpredicted opportunities which sometimes present themselves as they may prove serendipitous from a future development perspective.

The ability to network effectively is often considered to be one of the strongest predictors of managerial success, but to realize the optimum from an individual's network in whichever field of practice, there is always a need to sew the seeds of fruitful relationships carefully through networking, nurture them through demonstrable commitment and then harvest them – while appreciating that the equal and opposite role is being fulfilled by you in other people's networks.

Text extract from '*Networking – a personal view*' by Professor S. A. Burtonshaw-Gunn, published in *Professional Consulting*, Issue 20, 2007. Reproduction with kind permission of the Institute of Business Consulting, UK.

TWELVE STEPS OF CONSULTING

Consulting assignments go through various steps and stages and although the model below illustrates these in a sequential order, often real-life projects do not easily fall into such a pattern and may have to be undertaken in a different order or have some of the steps and stages combined.

Stage 1: Appraisal steps

1. Contact – initial meeting to discuss problem or opportunities.
2. Preparation – thinking and preparation, development of initial thoughts for in-depth discussion with client.
3. Contracting – production of outline proposal of what could be done, by whom, when, why and at what cost. This usually is a document issued to the prospective client.
4. Contract negotiation – client assesses proposal amendments on details of contract proposed.

Stage 2: Assessment steps

5. Data collection – collection of relevant data by interview, group meetings or questionnaires, etc. as appropriate to the task.

6. Data analysis and diagnosis – assessment of data and opportunity to review how it should be used and set up organizational and meeting arrangements.
7. Data feedback – presentation of data collected (orally or by written report).
8. Data discussion – discussion of the issues in terms of objectives and purpose. This also allows opportunity to clarify points and avoid misunderstandings.

Stage 3: Application steps

9. Proposal – following discussions held in steps 7 and 8 a proposal on solutions or changes should be produced.
10. Executive decision – here the client individually or collectively within the organization comes to a decision based on the data presented and the consultant's proposals.
11. Implementation of the decision – this is an executive function which sometimes may be delegated to the consultant. A vital aspect of consulting is giving advice on implementation of any proposed solutions.
12. Review – an objective assessment on how the assignment has been carried out in terms of factual results, as well as a subjective assessment in terms of people's feelings, needs to be undertaken and lessons learnt from it.

From *Managerial Consulting – a practical guide* by Charles J. Margerison, 2000. Reproduced with permission of Gower Publications.

CHAPTER 20

WORKSHOP FACILITATION

Within the larger organizations there is a growing acceptance of shared development through the use of group facilitation which can often be linked to business continuous improvement or as part of a change management process. The facilitation role may be delivered as part of a consultant/client relationship or internally as part of a corporate communication style. The term 'workshop' has itself emerged over the last decade or so to describe such a working group event although this term is not universally recognizable and some local knowledge is needed as to its applicability in some countries.

While there is a choice of using internal or external facilitators the aim will be to bring key decision makers together in order to gain 'buy-in' by a group to a new process, organizational change or product development. The role of a facilitator is covered in this chapter and can range from being effective outside of the workshop group to being engaged within the group process but always with the task of managing, encouraging, steering and in some cases curtailing the discussion and creativity in line with a broad planned outcome requirement.

The success of a workshop is knowing who is attending, who is able to make decisions or hinder the group's progress, what the workshop objectives are and finally what a successful outcome will consist of. Against this background a programme for the workshop can be developed and while the nature of the workshop is typically semi-structured to accommodate discussion, problem resolution, idea generation and to some degree an amount of deviation, the importance of a workshop plan is to guide the facilitator in meeting the workshop objectives. Workshops are like projects in that they have a start, a middle and an end. The start may be at the time of the workshop or before in the case of pre-workshop preparation, reading, questionnaire completion, etc. Starting the workshop correctly is important as this sets the scene of what is expected in the form of output, participation and group 'rules' of operating. Again the level of individual participation and involvement will vary in different cultures and this will need to be reflected in the workshop design.

Attendance at workshops is governed largely by the topic and the required level of involvement of the participants: some workshop topics are only effective in small groups where more time is available to get to know each other and where a large degree of flexibility is needed. On the other hand large group facilitation offers other advantages in bringing ideas forward, promoting wide involvement and in seeking to identify overlaps or shortfalls. This chapter provides some guidance for facilitating both small and large groups, together with a four stage checklist to help the facilitator plan a workshop event.

Many of the tools and models shown in this book can be used at workshops to stimulate discussion, explore new ideas, prompt the sharing of experience, utilize ready-proven techniques for adoption such as in decision making and problem resolution. Facilitated workshops can be used to support a number of areas of management such as change management initiatives; process improvement; business planning at corporate and/or functional levels; and organizational development.

THE THREE COMPONENTS OF FACILITATION

The roles that need to be undertaken by the workshop facilitator are outlined below. It is not just the matter of running a group meeting as the role demands specific facilitation skills and techniques such as:

- **Leadership**
  The ability to move from a directive, autocratic, hierarchical mode of operating through cooperation to an autonomous, standing back mode, depending upon the maturity level of the team and the demands of the specific situation at the time.

- **Discussion management**
  The ability to manage a discussion and all forms of communication through the use of appropriate interpersonal skills. This includes creating a safe environment in which people can fully participate, both when agreeing and disagreeing. Skills such as active listening, questioning, summarizing, linking and reflecting, along with self-disclosure when appropriate.

- **Structures (including tools and techniques)**
  Having a range of structures available and understanding their suitability, effect and operation. Covering ideas such as basic structures, large techniques, decision making and action planning.

THE ROLE OF THE FACILITATOR

Following the above activities this simple model of two triangles shows a paradigm shift where the expert and inexpert views are changed.

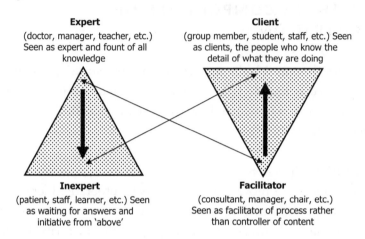

Expert	**Client**
(doctor, manager, teacher, etc.) Seen as expert and fount of all knowledge	(group member, student, staff, etc.) Seen as clients, the people who know the detail of what they are doing
Inexpert	**Facilitator**
(patient, staff, learner, etc.) Seen as waiting for answers and initiative from 'above'	(consultant, manager, chair, etc.) Seen as facilitator of process rather than controller of content

Model reproduced with kind permission of Nick Eve, *The Facilitator's Development Programme Course Manual*, Elements, UK.

THE ROLE OF THE WORKSHOP ATTENDEE

This '4P' model shows that the attendee's feelings about participation of a workshop or a meeting will fall into one of four categories. The model can be used with the group to establish the motivation of the attendees in a non-threatening way, allowing them to express their feelings in a simple way which can be checked as the workshop proceeds.

Passenger. This attendee is like being on a train travelling through interesting places with their feet up, enjoying the ride. They are protected from weather and local conditions, and as such like the journey but are not actively engaged. They like looking out of the window and taking a back seat.

Prisoner. This person is like the protestor only the dissent is less voluble. There is a sense of resignation, an acceptance that they are present but they only intend to give their 'name, rank and number'. This may be due to time of day, hunger, a need for a break or the feeling that a particular exercise or item has gone on for too long.

Protester. As this suggests the person is unhappy about being present and is voicing this dissatisfaction volubly. Often this is to do with outside pressures either at work or at home. There is the feeling that they should not be there as it's the wrong time, wrong place, the wrong content, etc.

Participant. This person is actively engaged in the event with their head, heart and body; they are interested and stimulated by what is coming. They want to be at the event and are keen to take part fully in whatever occurs to get as much as possible from the experience.

Reproduced with permission of Nick Eve, *The Facilitator's Development Programme Course Manual*, Elements, UK.

MODES OF FACILITATION INVOLVEMENT

This model has been developed by Nick Eve from the modes of facilitation described by John Heron in a number of his publications.

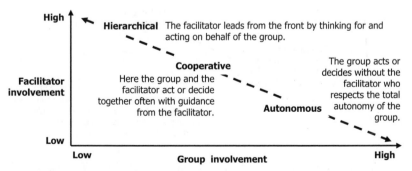

Reproduced with permission of Nick Eve, *The Facilitator's Development Programme Course Manual*, Elements, UK.

RELATIONSHIP BETWEEN FACILITATOR, GROUP AND THE TASK

In the model below the facilitator is observing and is aware of the whole situation (including their relationship with the group). They can observe the individual members and the task and the group's relationship to addressing the required task. Using this model facilitators often move between the positions in order to control the workshop and encourage participation.

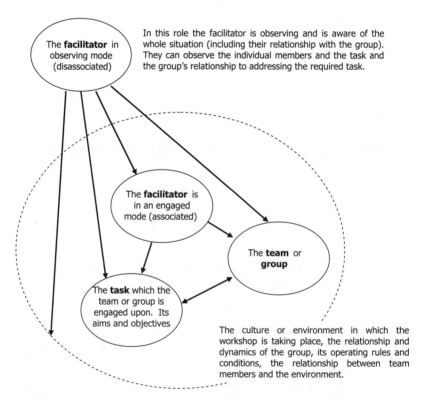

The **facilitator** in observing mode (disassociated)

In this role the facilitator is observing and is aware of the whole situation (including their relationship with the group). They can observe the individual members and the task and the group's relationship to addressing the required task.

The **facilitator** is in an engaged mode (associated)

The **team** or **group**

The **task** which the team or group is engaged upon. Its aims and objectives

The culture or environment in which the workshop is taking place, the relationship and dynamics of the group, its operating rules and conditions, the relationship between team members and the environment.

Model reproduced with kind permission of Nick Eve, *The Facilitator's Development Programme Course Manual*, Elements, UK.

FORCE-FIELD ANALYSIS

The principle of force-field analysis developed by the German born social scientist Kurt Lewin which is shown in Chapter 2 can also be used in workshops to encourage groups to visualize the problem in terms of a balance between those forces that drive a change and those of resistance. The steps involved in its construction are shown below and lend themselves to group work with opportunities for discussion of each issue and how the removal of barriers identified can best be managed.

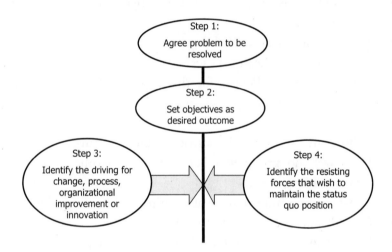

The forces for and against change can appear on both sides of the force field which typically can include forces such as:

- People, team or individuals
- Organizational structure
- The PESTLE elements
- The power of suppliers, customers or competitors
- Product or services delivery
- Technological changes
- Financial targets or constraints

FACILITATOR'S CHECKLIST

At each of the four stages, the following checklists will help the facilitator plan and run a workshop. In addition the consultant's checklist shown in Chapter 19 can also be used to gain a broader understanding of an organization.

Questions to ask to define clear purpose:
- Why is the workshop happening now?
- What else is going on?
- What else has 'worked' in this organization or for this group?
- What is the purpose of the event?
- Are there any other purposes?
- What are the challenges for this group right now (business issues, organizational issues, results issues, external environment issues)?
- Who is in the group (background, cross-cultures)?
- How well do group members know each other – how do they work together?
- What are the important relationships within the group?
- Can all purposes be met via this workshop?
- Is there any pre and post work to be done (coaching, informing, teaching, etc.)?
- How engaged are the group in this topic?

Questions to ask when designing the workshop:
- How many participants are there?
- What are their backgrounds/preferences/nationalities, etc.?
- How long have we got?
- What do people need to go away with?
- How familiar are people with this topic?
- Is there any updating to be done and how will this be done?

- What's the mix of management levels? Is this significant?
- How much small group/large group discussion should there be?
- How much time should be spent on getting to know each other?
- How much time should be spent on tackling tasks?
- How will you manage each section of the workshop – what tools and techniques will you use?
- What's the balance between reflection and activity – is this appropriate?
- Does the workshop flow make sense?
- Is there a theme for the whole workshop event?
- Have you devised a method for capturing thoughts, ideas and actions?
- Is there enough diversity of activity to retain interest?
- Have you considered the cultural mix?
- Is it a top team?

Questions to ask about the actual event:
- Have you got enough space, paper, flipcharts, wall space, bluetack, pens, break-out rooms, refreshments?
- Have you planned well to accommodate visitors from afar (e.g. check-in, jet lag, calling home)?
- Does everyone know where to come?
- Does everyone know the purpose and have access to pre-reading?
- Have you prepared a strong piece at the start to position the event?
- Are you the right facilitator? Are you seen as unbiased? Is this important?
- Do you have a plan of what you are doing and a timetable?
- Is your mind clear of distractions
- Is the seating right? Can you see everyone?

- Will you be able to manage the discussion alone? Do you need a co-facilitator?

Questions to ask afterwards:
- How memorable was the event?
- Did the event achieve its purpose?
- Did everyone get included?
- What should go in your workshop report? Will anyone read it?
- What is the best way of dealing with recorded information on flipcharts and notes?
- Do you recommend any next steps from your own perspective?
- How well did you do your bit?
- Have you arranged to unwind in an appropriate way? (Workshops are exhausting for the facilitator!)

From *Facilitation Made Easy*, Esther Cameron, 2005. Reproduced with permission of Kogan Page Press.

GUIDELINES FOR FACILITATING SMALL GROUPS: 4 TO 12 ATTENDEES

These next two pages provide some excellent guidelines for those involved in workshop facilitation with a clear distinction being made with respect to the size of the group and the different features and dynamics that each has.

1. Always have in mind the task of the group and if necessary periodically remind the group of it.
2. The leader is there to promote communication, not as the fount of all knowledge.
3. Avoid introducing too much material; encourage personal contributions above mere intellectual knowledge.

4. Encourage personal contributions by sharing views and feelings, especially group feelings.
5. Try to use silences creatively.
6. Be wary of the cosy 'united' group and encourage creative dissent.
7. Watch for openings for the silent members.
8. Be firm, but caring, with the dominant member(s).
9. Encourage group members generally to own feelings and opinions, rather than make one person appear unusual.
10. Try to balance the needs of the individuals and the needs of the group.
11. Make clear and definite arrangements about time, frequency and place.
12. Consider the right size of a group, and the balance of its membership.
13. Always consider the feelings engendered by changes of membership.
14. Bosses (and other authority figures): beware of your presence in the group.

Key features of small groups

- They are more intimate and personal. People have more time to get to know each other.
- Group dynamics can be more personal and intense.
- There is more time.
- There is more flexibility.
- This is more opportunity to tailor the experience and the learning to the group.
- They are more likely to participate and to take decisions by consensus.
- They tend to do less, but what they do is done well and there is stronger consensus.

Use of small groups

- Small groups are good for development purposes where you want people to feel comfortable to learn and experiment in a safe environment.
- Small groups are good for complex understanding.
- Small groups are good for situations where you need to be flexible and exploratory.

Reproduced with kind permission of Michael Jacobs, *Swift to Hear – facilitating skills in listening and responding*, SPCK Publishing.

GUIDELINES FOR FACILITATING LARGE GROUPS: MORE THAN 12 ATTENDEES

1. Balance the limitations on communication with the advantage of spread of opinion.
2. Try to arrange seating so that people can see and hear each other.
3. Do not be taken in by the passivity of many or the accomplished words of the few.
4. Encourage the expression of clear, simple views.
5. Do not become trapped in legislative procedures.
6. Discourage 'them' and 'us' slogans.
7. Be wary as a facilitator of accepting the 'messianic' role.
8. Reflect back accurately from one part of the group to another.
9. Demonstrate in your own contributions how you wish others to communicate to the large group.
10. Respond to individual contributions.
11. Clarify points of difference, summing up different aspects of discussion as the meeting proceeds.
12. Clarify the agenda under discussion and rules for voting or decision making.
13. Provide clear leadership without dictating the outcome of discussion.

14. Clarify what is reasonable for a large group to discuss and decide.
15. Use small groups in conjunction with the large group.
16. Facilitate large groups with at least one other leader.

Key features of large groups

- They are more impersonal. People have less time to get to know each other.
- There is less emphasis on relationship and a stronger emphasis on task.
- There is less time.
- There is less flexibility.
- They are more hierarchically planned and structured.
- It is easy for participants not to participate and to take decision making to be more structured, and it can be more difficult to achieve consensus.
- There is more likelihood of cliques and factions.
- They can do more, but it is harder to check understanding or agreement.

Use of large groups

- Large groups are good for cascading information and understanding in a short time frame.
- Large groups are good for generating broad information or feedback in a short time span.
- Large groups are good for projects where you are trying to clarify the overlaps or points of contact in a bigger framework.

Reproduced with kind permission of Michael Jacobs, *Swift to Hear – facilitating skills in listening and responding*, SPCK Publishing.

THE WORKSHOP LIFE CYCLE AND ITS FOUR CONTENT PHASES

The workshop life cycle follows the same principle as the quality management 'plan-do-review' steps as shown in this first model; however, the second model illustrates the four phases involved in running the workshop. As in all projects which have a start, middle and an end so too do workshops and in general there are four main content phases which are represented in the model here.

This second model suggests that different activities or exercises are appropriate at different times and for different functions. Here the middle is divided into two phases and comprises most of the workshop duration.

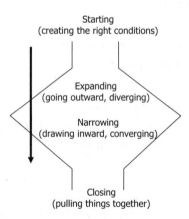

Workshop activities

- Starting – rounds, ice breaker and culture setting, rules of the day, etc.
- Expanding – brainstorming all forms of information gathering and energizers.
- Narrowing – fishbone diagrams and all forms of problem solving that narrow to conclusions.
- Closing – evaluation and celebration and action planning, rounds.

The model shows that the workshop group goes through a cycle in itself with an outward movement followed by an inward movement. These stages are normally unconscious if working individually but when facilitating groups, knowledge of this will increase the options of design and delivery. This is not a uniform process as sometimes a phase is quick while others may last a long time. If a phase is skipped completely the group will often come back later to deal with the issues involved in it. Indeed the group may even cycle through a phase several times before it is satisfied with the results from it.

Model reproduced with kind permission of Nick Eve, *The Facilitator's Development Programme Course Manual*, Elements, UK.

REFERENCES

Adair J. (1988) *Effective Leadership*, Pan Publishing

Afuah A. (2003) *Innovation Management*, Oxford University Press

Ahoy C. (1999) Process mapping, facilities planning and management, *Facilities News Bulletin*, Iowa State University. September

Ansoff H. I. (1968) *Corporate Strategy*, Penguin

Armstrong M. (ed.) (1994) *Strategies for Human Resource Management*, Kogan Page

Assael H. (1992) *Consumer Behaviour and Marketing Action*, PWS-Kent Publishing, Boston, USA

Barksdale H. C. and Harris C. E. (1982) Portfolio analysis and the product life cycle, *Journal of Long Range Planning*, pages 74–93, Number 15

Baxter M. R. (1995) *Product Design: a practical guide to systematic methods of new product development*, Nelson Thornes (Publishers) Ltd

Bernhard L. A. and Walsh M. (1995) *Leadership – The Key to Professionalization of Nursing*, 3rd edition, Mosby, St Louis

Blake R. R. and Mounton J. S. (1985) *New Management Grid: The Key to Leadership Excellence*, 2nd edition, pages 11–12, Elsevier

Blanchard K. (1994) *Leadership and the One Minute Manager*, Harper-Collins Publisher Ltd

Brindley C. S. (2004) (ed.) *Supply Chain Risk*, Ashgate Publishing

Burtonshaw-Gunn S. A. (2004) Examining risk and supply chain collaborative working in the UK construction industry, in *Supply Chain Risk*, C. S. Brindley (ed.), Ashgate Publishing

Burtonshaw-Gunn S. A. (2005) Extending the concept of 'added-value' to consultancy, *Professional Consulting*, Issue 14. Publication of the Institute of Management Consultants, UK

Burtonshaw-Gunn S. A. (2005) Considerations of pre-contract risks in international PFI projects, *2nd International SCRI Symposium*, University of Salford, April

Burtonshaw-Gunn S. A. (2006) Knowledge Management: a tool for gaining competitive advantage through intellectual capital development, *Professional Consultancy*, Issue 17. Publication of the Institute of Management Consultants, UK

Burtonshaw-Gunn S. A. (2008) The importance of pre-contract risk assessment and management in PFI international projects, in *Supply Chain Risk: A Handbook of Assessment, Management and Performance*, R. L. Ritchie and G. Zsidisin (eds). Springer International Publications, USA

Burtonshaw-Gunn S. A. (2007) Networking – a personal view, *Professional Consulting*, Issue 20, Institute of Business Consulting, UK.

Burtonshaw-Gunn S. A. and Ritchie R. L. (2007) Developments in construction supply chain management and the impact on people and cultural change, in *People and Culture in Construction*, A. Dainty (ed.). Taylor & Francis, Oxon

Burtonshaw-Gunn S. A. and Salameh M. G. (2007) Change management and organisational performance, in *Effective Executive*, June 2007. ICFAI University Press Hyderabad, India

Cameron E. (2005) *Facilitation Made Easy*, Kogan Page Press, London

Chadwick L. and Pike R. (1982) *Managing and Control of Capital in Industry*, The Chartered Institute of Management Accountants (CIMA), London

Chartered Management Institute UK, *Business Continuity and Supply Chain Risk*, 2002

Christiansen J. (2000) *Building the Innovative Organization*, Macmillan Business Books

Clawson J. (1983) *Systems Theory and Organizational Analysis*, The University of Virginia, Darden School Foundation, Charlottesville, Virginia, USA

Cole G. A. (1997) *Strategic Management*, 3rd edition, Continuum Publications, London

Cook S. (2000) *Customer Care*, Kogan Page Limited

Cooper C. L. (ed.) (1975) *Theories of Group Processes*, John Wiley & Sons

Cope M. (2003) *The Seven Cs of Consulting*, 2nd edition, FT Prentice Hall

Coulson-Thomas C. (1996) (ed.) *Business Process Re-engineering: myth and reality*, Kogan Page

Czinkota M. R. (1982) *Export Development Strategies: US Promotion Policy*, Praeger

Dawson T. (2000) *Principles and Practices of Modern Management*, Liverpool Academic Press

DeKluyer C. A. (2000) *Strategic Thinking*, Prentice Hall

Denscombe M. (1998) *The Good Research Guide*, Open University Press

Deming W. Edwards- (2000) *Out of Crisis*, pages 22–24. W. Edwards-Deming Institute, published by The MIT Press

Dixon R. (1993) *The Management Task*, Institute of Management/ Butterworth-Heinmann, Elsevier

Eve N. (2005) *The Facilitator's Development Programme – Course Manual*, Elements Ltd

Fomburn C., Tichy N. M. and Devanna M. A. (1984) *Strategic Human Resource Management*, John Wiley & Sons, New York

Fisher L. (1977) Industrial marketing, in E. P. Hibbert, *International Business – strategy and operations*, Macmillan Business

Greiner L. A. (1972) *Harvard Business Review*, July/August

Handy C. (1976) *Understanding Organizations*, Penguin

Hannagan T. (2005) *Management Concepts and Practices*, 4th edition, Pearson Education

Harris J. (1997) *Sharpen your Project Management Team Skills*, McGraw-Hill

Hay J. (2002) *Effective Consulting Magazine*, August 2002, Pentre Publications

Heron J. (1999) *The Complete Facilitator's Handbook*, Kogan Page

Hibbert E. P. (1997) *International Business – strategy and operations*, Macmillan Business

Honey P. and Mumford A. (2006) *The Learning Styles Questionnaire*, 80-item version, Peter Honey Associates

ISPL (2001) *101 Ways to Approach Value Review, Institute of Leisure and Amenity Management, Best Value Working Group*, 1st edition, Institute for Sport, Parks and Leisure

Jacob M. (1985) *Swift to Hear – facilitating skills in listening and responding*, SPCK, London

Johnson G. and Scholes K. (2002) *Exploring Corporate Strategy*, 6th edition, Pearson Education

Keegan W. J. (1969) Multinational product planning: strategic alternatives, *Journal of Marketing*, No. 33. American Association of Marketing

Kolb D. A. and Fry R. (1975) Towards an applied theory of experimental learning, in C. L. Cooper, *Theories of Group Processes*, John Wiley & Sons

Kipling R. (1903) The Elephant's Child from the *Just So Stories*

Kübler-Ross E. (1969) *On Death and Dying*, Macmillan, New York

Kubr M. (ed.) (1994) *Management Consulting – a guide to the profession*, The International Labour Organization, Geneva

Lancaster G. and Reynolds P. (2002) *Marketing Made Simple*, Butterworth-Heinmann

Lengnick-Hall C. A. and M. L. (1988) A perspective on business strategy and human resource strategy interdependence, *Academy of Management Review*, Volume 13, Number 3, pages 454–470

Lock D. (ed.) (1992) *The Handbook of Management*, 3rd edition, Gower Publishing Limited

Lock D. (1995) *Project Management*, 6th edition, Gower Publishing Limited

Lock D. (2003) *Project Management*, 8th edition, Gower Publishing Limited

Majaro S. (1988) *Managing Ideas for Profit: the creative gap*, McGraw-Hill

Margerison C. J. (2000) *Managerial Consulting – a practical guide*, 2nd edition, Gower Publications

McGregor D. (1990) The human side of enterprise, reproduced in D. S. Pugh (ed.), *Organization Theory*, Penguin

McNeil P. (1990) *Society Now: research methods*, Routledge

Mendlow A. (1992) *Proceedings of the Second International Conference on Information Systems*, Cambridge MA Springer Science and Business Media

Morris S. and Wilcox G. (1996) *Connecting with your Customers*, Institute of Management/Pitman Publishing

Ness D. B. and Greiner L. E. (1985) 'Seeing Behind the Look Alike Management Consultants' *Organizational Dynamics*, Volume 13, pages 68–79, Winter. Elsevier

Ohno T. and Mito S. (1998) *Just in Time for Today and Tomorrow*, New York Productivity Press

Poirier C. C. (1999) *Advanced Supply Chain Management*, Berret-Koehler Publishers Inc.

Porter M. E. (1985) *Competitive Advantage: creating and sustaining superior performance*, Free Press, Simon & Schuster Inc., New York

Porter M. E. (1990) *The Competitive Advantage of Nations*, Simon & Schuster Inc., New York

PRINCE Information from the Association of Project Management Group Ltd, Sword House, Totteridge Road, High Wycombe, Buckinghamshire HP13 6DG

Pugh D. S. (ed.) (1990) *Organization Theory*, Penguin

Reading C. (2002) *Strategic Business Planning*, 2nd edition, Kogan Page Limited

Robbins H. and Finley M. (2000) *Why Teams don't Work, What Went Wrong and How to Make it Right*, Berrett-Koehler Publishers, Inc., San Francisco, CA

Robson C. (1993) *Real World Research*, Blackwell Publishing

Ruble T. L. and Thomas K. W. (1976) Support for a two-dimensional model of conflict behaviour, published in *Organizational Behaviour and Human Performance* (now known as *Organizational Behaviour and Human Decision Processes*), Volume 16, pages 143–155. Elsevier

Sadgrove K. (1993) *The Green Guide to Profitable Management*, Gower Publications, 1994

Saunders M. (1994) *Strategy Purchasing and Supply Chain Management*, Pitman Publishing

Schein E. H. (1969) *Process Consultation: its role in organization development*, Addison-Wesley Publishing Company, Reading, MA, USA

Slack N., Chambers S. and Johnston R. (1995) *Operations Management*, Pitman Publishing

Slater S. (1999) *Corporate Recovery*, Penguin Books

Talwar R. (1996) The wonder drug for the 1990s, in Coulson-Thomas (ed.), *Business Process Re-engineering: myth and reality*, Kogan Page

Tidd J., Bessant J. and Pavitt K. (2005) *Managing Innovation*, 3rd edition, John Wiley & Sons

Trannenbaum R. and Schmidt W. H. (1973) How to choose a leadership pattern, *Harvard Business Review*, May–June

Tuckman B. W. and Jensen M. A. C. (1977) Development sequences in small groups, *Psychological Bulletin*, Volume 63, Number 6. The American Psychological Association

Turton R. J. (1991) *Behavior in a Business Context*, Chapman and Hall now Springer Science and Business Media

Walters D. (2002) *Logistics: an introduction to supply chain management*, Palgrave Macmillan

Weiss D. (1999) *High Impact HR: transforming human resources for competitive advantage*, John Wiley & Sons Canada Limited

Wideman M. (1992) *Project and Program Risk Management*, Project Management Institute

Womack J. P. and Jones D. T. (1996) *Lean Thinking*, Prentice Hall

Worsley P. (1992) *The New Introducing Sociology*, Penguin, London. Contributors: F. Bechhofer, R. Brown, M. Jeffreys, M. Mcintosh, H. Newby, J. Rex, W. Sharrock, J. Young and M. Young

Yip G., Loewe P. M. and Yoshino M. E. (1988) How to take your company to the global market, *The Columbia Journal of World Business*, Volume 23, Number 2, Winter

INDEX